Growth Challenges and Government Policies in Armenia

The World Bank
Washington, D.C.

ISBN: 0-8213-5089-7
ISSN: 0253-2123

Library of Congress Cataloging-in-Publication Data has been applied for.

CONTENTS

Tables

Boxes

Charts

ABSTRACT

This study reviews growth trends in Armenia for the period 1994-2000, outlines major weaknesses of existing development patterns, and suggests a package of policy recommendations designed to accelerate enterprise restructuring, attract investment, and encourage the creation of new businesses in the medium term (three to five years). Such steps are needed to sustain the current growth rate, to stop emigration among the young and skilled, and to reduce poverty.

The study identifies three factors that represent critical constraints to sustainable economic growth in Armenia—a poor business and investment environment, weak managerial skills, and uncertainty about the country's economic and political prospects in an unstable region. These factors are mostly responsible for the main weaknesses of the existing growth pattern such as a narrow sectoral base for growth, insufficient new entry and job creation, and depressed export and investment levels.

To make growth broad-based, Armenia's government must create an environment that is supportive to accelerated development of the private sector. While preserving its recent macroeconomic gains, the government must focus its medium-term strategy on improving the business environment, promoting deregulation, removing administrative barriers to investment, and setting up mechanisms for public-private dialogue. Complementing this "top-down" agenda must be a set of selective, bottom-up interventions to promote new business entry, especially in skill-based and export-oriented sectors. The study argues that within the existing institutional framework, the provision of government support for private sector development should be concentrated in several specially established restructuring agencies. These agencies would become a primary instrument to facilitate expansion of new entry (both domestic and foreign) by expanding provision of business development services, opportunities for management and business training for existing managers and business owners, and supporting new linkages between Armenian firms and global markets.

ACKNOWLEDGEMENTS

The report was prepared by a core team that includes Lev Freinkman (team leader), Karen Grigorian, Gohar Gyulumyan, Yevgeny Kuznetsov, and Zakia Nekaien-Nowrouz. Usha Rani Khanna edited the report. Background papers for the report were prepared by Luis Alvaro-Sanchez, Vahram Avanessyan, Geeta Batra and Andrew Stone, David Grigorian, Artsvi Kahchtryan, Une Lee, Alexander Poghossian and Vahram Stepanyan, Evgeny Polyakov, and Ruslan Yemtsov and Armine Petrossian.

The team also greatly benefited from broad support and cooperation with Armenian authorities, especially the Ministry of Finance and Economy, the Central Bank, and National Statistical Service. In addition, a large group of individuals contributed their input and comments, including Gohar Abajan, Ataman Aksoy, Arusyak Alaverdyan, Konstantin Atanesyan, Yuri Boutayev, Peter Fallon, Lars Jeurling, Vladimir Kreacic, Mark Lundell, Robert Nooter, Christian Petersen, Gevorg Sargysyan, David Shahzadeyan, Jonathan Walters, and Salman Zaheer. Samuel Otoo is the Sector manager, and Pradeep Mitra is the Department Director. Judy M. O'Connor is the Country Director for Armenia.

ABBREVIATIONS AND ACRONYMS

ADA	Armenian Development Agency
AMD	Armenian Dram
ARIA	Moldovan Agency for Enterprise Restructuring
ASYCUDA	Automated System for Customs Data
BOP	Balance of Payment
CCC	Council of Court Chairmen
CEDECE	State Commission for Economic Development and External Commerce
CEE	Central and Eastern Europe
CIS	Commonwealth of Independent States
CPIA	Country Policy and Institutional Assessment
CPI	Consumer Price Index
EBRD	European Bank for Reconstruction and Development
EPZ	Export Processing Zone
EU	European Union
FDI	Foreign Direct Investment
FIAS	Foreign Investor Advisory Service
FSU	Former Soviet Union
GOA	Government of Armenia
GDP	Gross Domestic Product
IAC	Information and Advisory Center
IBRD	International Bank for Reconstruction and Development
ICRG	International Country Risk Guide
IFS	International Financial Statistics
ILO	International Labor Organization
IMF	International Monetary Fund
IP	Industrial Park
IT	Information and Telecommunication
JSCL	Joint Stock Company Law
MBRC	Macedonian Business Resource Center
MOFE	Ministry of Finance and Economy
MOTC	Ministry of Transport and Communication
NAFTA	North America Free Trade Agreement
NGO	Non-Government Organization
NIE	Newly Industrialized Economies
NK	Nagorno – Korabakh
NSS	National Statistical Service
OECD	Organization of Economic Cooperation and Development
OTE	Hellenic Telecommunication Organization
PIAL	Privatization Implementation Assistance Loan
PIU	Project Implementation Unit
PPP	Purchasing Power Parity
PSD	Private Sector Development
RA	Restructuring Agency
R&D	Research and Development
ROA	Republic of Armenia
RPC	Russian Privatization Center
SME	Small and Medium Enterprises
SOE	State-Owned Enterprise
TB	Treasury Bill

TI	Texas Instrument
TRACECA	Transport Corridor Europe Caucuses
TVE	Township–Village Enterprise
USAID	United States Agency for International Development
USSR	Union of Soviet Socialist Republic
VAT	Value Added Tax
WSJ	Wall Street Journal
WTO	World Trade Organization

CURRENCY EQUIVALENTS
(Exchange Rate Effective June 30, 2001)

Currency Unit	=	Dram
Dram	=	US$0.0018
US$1.0	=	554 Dram

WEIGHTS AND MEASURES
Metric System

EXECUTIVE SUMMARY

Since the mid-90s, the Armenian Government has been among the most advanced reformists in the former USSR, and Armenia has been among the highest growing economies in the region. Nevertheless, Armenia still is a resource-poor, landlocked economy with underdeveloped institutions, low income levels (which is about two-thirds of the average for the CIS), and a high, although rapidly diminishing, stock of human capital. The country's future depends on the government's ability to expand investment in and export opportunities for Armenian firms by helping them to restructure and by facilitating their linkages with global markets.

This report reviews growth trends in Armenia for the period 1994-2000, outlines major weaknesses of existing development patterns, and suggests a package of policy recommendations designed to accelerate enterprise restructuring, attract investment, and encourage the creation of new businesses in the medium term (three to five years). Such steps are needed to sustain (and preferably to increase) the current growth rates, to stop emigration among the young and skilled, and to reduce poverty.

The government needs to focus much more clearly on generating the environment for private sector led growth by removing bottlenecks in policies, infrastructure and institutions that prevent new private businesses from flourishing. International aid donors can help by supporting the removal of administrative barriers for investments, the rehabilitation of infrastructure, and the creation of "restructuring agencies" that will enable firms in key sectors to overcome or avoid common constraints to business growth in Armenia. Successful restructuring by such firms should have a demonstration effect on the country's economy and help consolidate public support for moving forward the program of reform begun a decade ago.

Armenia's Economy Has Been Growing Since Mid-90s but it Currently Faces the Risk of Slowdown

Over the last several years, Armenia has made impressive progress in establishing a suitable framework for structural reforms. Despite external shocks, macroeconomic conditions have remained quite stable, with low inflation, a relatively stable exchange rate, a sufficient level of international reserves, and considerably reduced budget and quasi-budget deficits.

Armenia's growth performance has been strong compared to the rest of the Commonwealth of Independent States (CIS). After an estimated 60 percent decline between 1991 and 1993, real GDP grew 5.4 percent in 1994. Since then, annual growth has averaged about 5 percent—a remarkably resilient performance in the face of the Russian financial crisis of 1998 and political assassinations in October 1999. In the second half of 2000, the economy has shown an additional improvement in performance, supported by export expansion.

The country's economic expansion in 1995–2000 was fueled by a recovery from the severe contraction of the early 1990s. Factors that contributed to growth included recovery in electricity supply, expansion of external private transfers that pushed domestic demand, and a major program of international assistance that made Armenia a leading regional recipient of donor funding in per capita terms. On average in 1995–99, donors provided about 7 percent of Armenia's GDP in annual budget support mostly through a combination of grants and low-interest credits.

Economic growth was also supported by a relatively strong recovery in agriculture backed by a privatization of rural land very early in transition and considerable import substitution in food consumption.

These factors are not long-term engines of economy-wide growth, however, and current growth rates will not be sustained unless major constraints are removed.

Patterns of Growth

Forty-three percent of the increase in real GDP in 1994–99 came from expansion in the service sector. Agriculture contributed an additional 30 percent. The contribution of the industrial sector, where Armenia's skilled labor represents a strong potential comparative advantage, was just 13 percent.

The output of the country's traditional industrial companies grew more slowly than did the economy as a whole, and their productivity and rates of capacity use slipped. The largest enterprises seriously underperformed the rest of the industrial sector. The share of the country's total industrial output produced by the 100 largest enterprises dropped from 28 percent in 1997 to below 20 percent in 1999, while the share of registered firms reporting profits declined from 64 percent in 1997 to 33 percent in 1999.

The largest Armenian enterprises are much less productive than their counterparts in Lithuania and Kazakhstan. Lithuania's enterprises were about eight times more productive than Armenia's in 1997, in terms of sales per employee, and the gap appears to have widened in 1998–99.

Cross-country analysis of large enterprises also suggests a rather low level of capacity utilization in Armenian firms. Improving capacity utilization for Armenian industry is becoming increasingly difficult, however, as old markets in Central and Eastern Europe continue to shrink. Unless and until new product markets are discovered (or old markets recovered), the financial viability of most of Armenia's large companies is highly questionable. Moreover, in a number of cases traditional markets and value chains for these companies entirely disappeared. And, even in more favorable cases capturing new markets will take time, and serious investment in technology and training and major policy efforts will be needed.

The birth rate of new companies remains depressed, as does their rate of survival. One of the broad lessons of transition in Central and Eastern Europe is that large firms formerly owned by the state support growth largely to the extent that they provide assets and human capital for new entries driven by dynamic local and foreign managers. The same experience suggests that so-called first movers, firms that have been making successful but risky investments in developing new products, approaching new markets, and building new partnerships, are more likely to be new entries than traditional firms. In the transition economies of Central and Eastern Europe, as in other parts of the world (notably Latin America), successful restructuring at the micro level has hinged on management turnovers and changes in management culture.

Company registration data show that the number of small new firms in Armenia is low by international standards. By late 2000, as estimated, Armenia had about more than 30,000 operational businesses, which amounts to less than 10 entities per 1,000 inhabitants. Modern market economies have much higher incidence of SMEs, e.g. Germany has 37 registered SMEs per 1,000 inhabitants, Slovenia 45, and the United States 74. Moreover, there is concern that the growth in the number of firms in Armenia has been rather slow recently, which reflects high costs of entry.

About 60 percent of Armenia's GDP is produced not by traditional enterprises that were established in the Soviet times, but by the new private sector (Table 1), a high level that is similar to many leading economies in transition. However, the structure of the new private sector in Armenia differs from that found in more successful economies. Registered companies account for less than a quarter of the business activity of the *de novo* sector. The rest derives from predominantly low-productivity informal activities in agriculture, commerce, and urban services.

Table 1. New Private Sector Activity as Share of GDP (percent)

Type of activity	Share of GDP
GDP produced by new private sector	60
New firms in industry	4
New firms in other sectors	9
Individual entrepreneurs	6
Informal (non-registered) business activity of households	16
Family farms	25
Other (including traditional companies)	40
Total	100

Source: World Bank estimates based on data from Armenian National Statistical Service.

The private sector in Armenia can be visualized as a pyramid consisting of three types of economic activities (Table 2). At the base of the pyramid are the formal subsistence-type activities in which virtually the entire economically active population is engaged. Productivity is very low and self-employment high. The subsistence economy has absorbed the shocks produced by contraction of the inherited economy of state-owned and privatized organizations that constitute the second layer of the pyramid. The third layer—quite small in terms of employment and output but high in productivity—consists of new SMEs. With approximately 7,000 employees, new industrial SMEs produce about US$230 million in output. In the inherited economy, by contrast, 80,000 employees produce US$340 million in industrial output. The seven-fold gap in labor productivity between start-up firms and inherited enterprises shows the great growth potential of breaking up inherited assets into spin-offs and transforming informal economic activity of population into more traditional SMEs.

Table 2. Three Spheres of Economic Activity in Armenia

Segment of the economy	Employment and output	Objectives for public interventions
Entrepreneurial/SME Start-ups and spin-offs with 5–50 employees	7,000 employees US$230 million	Facilitating entry and expansion based on productivity growth
Inherited Large privatized and state-owned firms and R&D organizations	80,000 employees US$340 million	Liquidation, bankruptcy, improvement of corporate governance Recombination of assets, restructuring through spin-offs
Self-employed/informal Family production and informal urban microenterprise, including activities for home consumption and informal operations	Nearly the entire population US$21 million (industry only) (1.1 percent of GDP)	Increasing productivity of family economy through microcredit and business development services

Note: Industrial sector includes manufacturing, energy, and mining.
Source: Armenian National Statistical Service, based on household surveys (for self-employment), enterprise surveys, and other data.

Areas of Concern

The incidence of poverty in Armenia between 1996 and 1999 (using the comparable poverty line based on the minimum food basket and allowances for essential nonfood spending) has remained at around 55 percent of the population. One in three workers is either unemployed or has been on prolonged administrative leave, according to the government's 1999 labor survey, and many have dropped out of the labor force. Almost half of the country's adults of prime working age (25–49 years old) lack gainful employment. At least 20 percent of the population has left the country since the late 1980s.

Growth has not yet made up for jobs lost to downsizing, and the sector and enterprise bases of growth have been narrow—a fact that explains the "mystery of growth without poverty reduction." Traditional enterprises had a stronger impact on employment and income levels than did new companies characterized by relatively high productivity but low demand for labor. Soviet-era firms have continued to shed their labor, forced by further compression of traditional markets in the former Soviet Union and by tighter budget constraints, while entry of new, labor-intensive SMEs has been insufficient to soak up surplus labor. Potential income gains from growth in the agriculture and budget sectors were largely wiped out by unfavorable changes in relative prices and wage arrears.

Overall, despite a relatively strong recent performance, economic growth in Armenia has not been supported by strong enterprise restructuring or by massive entry of new private business. As a result, the country faces a noticeable imbalance between its relatively strong macroeconomic fundamentals (and substantial structural reforms), and a weak supply and investment response. Unless this issue is addressed, the growth rates of the last 5–6 years will be unsustainable. That is, while Armenia needs and has a potential to generate a high growth episode over the next decade, without additional reforms at the microeconomic level, the economy is likely to slow down relative to the current growth rates.

The winners from economic growth in Armenia are excessively concentrated. About a thousand employees in the country's diamond industry were responsible for $70 million in exports in 1999—30 percent of the country's manufacturing exports. Another thousand employees produce $15–20 million in exported software. While the economic impact of these sectors on national living standards is rather modest at the moment, they could form the nucleus for faster and more broad-based economic growth if they can be consolidated into export-oriented clusters offering high value added—and if their performance can be replicated elsewhere in the economy.

Privatization in Armenia has generally led to a consolidation of control by incumbent managers. Mass privatization in the CIS generally has not yet brought significant improvements in enterprise performance. However, statistical analysis has shown that performance varies considerably with ownership structure. Foreigners, banks, small groups of individual owners, and managers (to a smaller extent) tend to be the most effective owners, while diffused ownership (either by workers or by large numbers of citizens) and ownership by insiders are associated with poorer performance.

Two of the most effective ownership classes (banks and foreign investors) have played a very limited role in Armenia, which may partially explain the relative weakness of enterprise restructuring in the country. At the same time, the cross-country comparison presents a puzzle with respect to ownership by management. On average in the CIS, management ownership tends to support restructuring, but not in Armenia—at least not yet. In a surprising number of cases, the strategy of incumbent managers who became owners appears to have been focused on asset stripping.

In 2000, merchandise exports were only 14 percent higher than they were in 1995, amounting to just 16 percent of GDP. Low export levels currently represent a major source of macroeconomic risks in Armenia. As in other small economies, Armenia's longer-term growth prospects to a large extent depend upon developing much stronger export capabilities.

Armenia still exports quite a limited number of products—a weakness in the country's export structure. Only about 60 types of products (according to the four-digit commodity classification) were regularly exported in 1995–99. Fourteen top products accounted for 87 percent of total merchandise exports in 1999 (compared to about 80 percent in 1995). Except for diamonds and gems, Armenia's leading exports are concentrated in sectors (energy, metallurgy, and mining), where the country does not have strong comparative advantages in the long term. Metal scrap remains a significant part of overall exports, and the market share of agricultural and food products has increased as well. At the same time, except for software, no significant new export sector has emerged.

Countries outside the FSU accounted for 75 percent of Armenia's new export markets in 1999, up from 37 percent in 1995. When diamond exports are measured on a net basis, however, the overall share of non-CIS countries is considerably lower and does not exceed 40 percent. Therefore, while some diversification of exports has taken place, it is still less advanced than the data on gross exports suggest. Overall, a considerable share of traditional Armenian exports (food, footwear, equipment), especially from SMEs, continues to go to CIS countries. Many enterprises, especially those with no foreign ownership, are unable to find strategic partners and new markets outside the former Soviet Union (FSU).

Investment in Armenia is low. Based on an alternative interpretation of the data, the report estimates that the current level is about 15 percent of GDP, 4–5 percentage points below the level reported in official data[1] and well below the investment needs of the country. By contrast, gross domestic investment in the leading transition economies of Central Europe and the Baltics was more than 20 percent of GDP in the latter half of the 1990s.

The development impact of current investment is even lower than investment volumes would suggest. Investments are heavily concentrated in the public and household sectors (including housing, utilities, and infrastructure), and much less so in sectors that reflect and contribute to enterprise restructuring and productivity growth. Such an imbalanced investment structure derives from both supply (availability of donor financing) and demand (weakness of the private sector, needs of the earthquake zone) sides.

Armenia's public external debt stood at $862 million (45 percent of GDP) at the end of 2000. The large share of concessional credits and the small share of commercial debt protect the country reasonably well against hikes in international interest rates and significant shifts in value of the major international currencies. Still, in terms of net present value, external debt at end-1999 was about 153 percent of exports of goods and services and 167 percent of fiscal revenues, so although the current overall debt burden is moderate in terms of the size of the economy, it is high relative to expected earnings. The debt ratios improved somewhat in 2000, after a 15 percent expansion in exports in the second part of the year. However, given the debt burden relative to current export and fiscal revenue levels, it is important that foreign financing in the next several years be provided as grants or on a highly concessional basis.

Stubborn Problems Constrain Armenia's Ability to Restructure its Economy and Achieve Sustainable Growth

Three factors represent critical constraints on sustainable economic growth—a poor business and investment environment, weak managerial skills, and uncertainty about the country's economic and political prospects in an unstable region.

Government has not yet Provided for Sufficient Improvements in the Country's "Challenging" Business Environment

Despite considerable progress with structural and institutional reforms, including in such important sectors as power generation and distribution, banking supervision, social protection, and land reform, Armenia's basic institutions in support of the market environment remain weak. This is not

---

[1] The main report provides an explanation of this discrepancy in estimates for investment rate.

surprising given the scale of the task and the severe resource limitations the country faces. However, Armenia has tried to build too many new institutions simultaneously without proper prioritization and sequencing, for instance in the area of capital markets development. This excessively broad institutional agenda, which is at least partly donor-driven, has weakened several core functions of economic management and created problems of inter-agency coordination.

Presently the state lacks the capability and in some cases incentives to create an effective business environment by enforcing the country's favorable legal framework. In the early 1990s, the Armenian government was very decisive in advancing its broad liberalization agenda, removing various restrictions on trade, prices, exchange rates, and interest rates. Since 1996, the country's macroeconomic environment has contained few distortions related to formal government regulations, the nominal tax regime, and budget subsidies. The notional business environment reflected in laws and regulations is relatively good.

At the microeconomic level, however, the situation is different. The state was not capable yet of enforcing the favorable legal framework so as to create an effective business environment. Liberalization and deregulation bring tangible benefits only if they are supported by sufficient government capacity to protect the liberal economic regime. If this capacity is lacking, as Armenia's experience confirms, one may expect that central regulations have a tendency to be replaced by decentralized regulations imposed by local governments, special interest groups, and sectoral agencies—unpredictable practices that are profoundly discouraging to business and investment. In the absence of a well-established government policy in this area and given Armenia's frequent changes in government, numerous controlling agencies, and weak central oversight, a "decentralized model" of excessive and unpredictable regulation has emerged.

The Armenian government is large and exerts substantial pressure on the relatively weak and small private sector. According to World Bank estimates, Armenia's budgetary sector in 1998–99 employed almost 10 percent of the country's population. In the OECD states, by contrast, the average share is 7.7 percent and in the FSU states about 8 percent. The regulatory functions of government are fragmented, and individual agencies receive little central oversight. A 1994 presidential decree granted 17 separate state agencies the right to conduct business inspections. In summer 2000, a new law on inspections somewhat reduced the number of inspecting agencies and introduced a more transparent framework for state inspections of businesses.

Business surveys conducted in Armenia in 1996–2000 identify taxation, policy instability, and lack of financing as leading constraints to effective operation and expansion of firms. A 1999 enterprise survey conducted in 22 economies in transition under supervision of the World Bank and the European Bank for Reconstruction and Development produced similar findings:

- As in other countries in Central and Eastern Europe, tax rates and regulations are the leading regulatory problem for Armenian businesses.[2] Tax administration problems derive not only from government policies, but also from the accounting practices and financial capacity of firms.

- Political and policy uncertainty arise not only from recent events and decisions but also from the fact that businessmen find it difficult to get timely information on changes in laws, regulations, and policies affecting them, and the government rarely consults affected businesses before making critical decisions.

---

[2] Tax rates were considerably reduced, while the tax structure was simplified, by the decisions adopted in the second part of 2000 and in 2001.

- High interest rates are perceived as a serious financial constraint on Armenian businesses. Firms, especially small firms, rely heavily on family and friends for finance.

- Roads are the leading infrastructure constraint. Customs processing in Armenia delays imports more than in other countries of the region.

- Businesses give the Armenian government poor ratings for helpfulness, efficiency, and the quality and integrity of public services.

Even when compared to other CIS economies, Armenia's business environment must be considered very challenging. Armenian firms report being solicited for bribes more often than in most economies in transition, especially in dealings related to taxes, licenses, and courts. Armenian firms also face much less predictability in the unofficial payments they have to make (Table 3).

Table 3. Firms Reporting Frequent Solicitations of Informal Payments from Government Employees

(Share of firms that gave answers 1 (always), 2 (mostly) or 3 (frequently) to questions on informal payments; respondents have six options to select from.)

	Irregular payments made to government	Advance knowledge of amount of payment	Service delivered as agreed once payment is made	If payment is made to one official, another will request payment for the same service	If official breaks rules, business can appeal to superior and receive correct treatment without recourse to irregular payment
OECD	0.12	0.26	0.62	0.17	0.45
CIS	0.29	0.46	0.75	0.35	0.38
CEE	0.33	0.48	0.73	0.28	0.36
Armenia	0.40	0.51	0.73	0.36	0.37

Note: OECD=Organization for Economic Co-operation and Development, CIS=Commonwealth of Independent States, CEE=Central and Eastern Europe.
Source: 1999 enterprise survey undertaken for the World Bank and European Bank for Reconstruction and Development.

Insufficient Demand for Change Raises the Risk of a Stagnation Trap

The report identifies simultaneous market and government failures that together set a stage for a potential stagnation trap. These include:

- Slow pace of deregulation reform and insufficient support an investment-friendly business environment.

- Mismatches in resource allocation: new entrepreneurs have restricted access to available assets, including equipment, industrial space, and land, which remain largely underutilized.

- Insufficient supply of new managerial skills. Business training programs have been established, but they remain largely isolated from the business needs of existing managers and business owners.

Coordination Problem and First Movers. The profitability of an individual investment is dependent on what happens elsewhere in the economy. But, if all investors wait for an auspicious environment and nobody moves first, nothing happens. The resulting "coordination problem" is a reflection of economic and political uncertainty that depresses demand for assets and business expectations. This is why "first movers" are critical for changing economic perceptions about the quality of the investment climate and triggering a supply response.

Notional and Effective Incentives. Even if the business environment is reasonably friendly, firms must have minimum skills to benefit from it. Enterprise restructuring is a challenge for a post-socialist manager who needs new skills to deal with new markets, partners, and ways of doing business. Knowledge- and skill-based constraints are especially severe in small, isolated economies such as Armenia, which have thin internal markets for information, weak traditions of interfirm cooperation and external partnership, and, therefore, generally high costs of entering new export markets.

Under such circumstances, even the right incentives for restructuring might not be sufficient to start the restructuring process. Capabilities and opportunities for restructuring are at least as important. A firm that has correct incentives but no capacity to act on them has no effective incentive at all.

Stagnation Trap. The unfriendly business environment, the coordination problem, and skilled-based constraints for restructuring combined pose a risk of the stagnation trap, which sets in when low levels of investment and entrepreneurial activity support pessimistic investment expectation and vice versa. The poor business environment discourages first movers, which in turn aggravates the coordination problem, resulting in even lower investments and even fewer new entries. In addition, low entrepreneurship in such an economy produces too little pressure to reform the business environment and therefore further supports stagnation.

Thus, Armenia faces a serious risk of being caught in the stagnation trap, which, if it happens, has the potential to become quite stable because existing demand for change is neutralized by powerful factors.

- The country's relatively strong but unsustainable economic recovery allows for complacent delays of unpopular reforms.

- The most able and vocal proponents of reform tend to emigrate.

- Aid provided by international donors acts as a balance-of-payment shock absorber. Because nominal growth rates are high and the Armenian government has a record of reform, donors have been less insistent about the need for improvements in the investment climate.

- Powerful interest groups represent those who benefit from the status quo.

- Because of its small internal market, Armenia attracts little external investment interest, while members of the Armenian Diaspora tend to limit their criticism out of concern for the government's reputation.

Other Constraints to Growth are Serious but Surmountable

Other constraints are important but need not prevent further restructuring and growth.

The *blockade* resulting from the unresolved Nagorno-Karabakh conflict has raised transportation costs, closed export markets in Turkey and Azerbaijan, provoked excessive defense spending, and raised investment risks. However, its direct costs declined significantly after 1995 for private operators who found ways to handle the transportation obstacles. Expansion of Armenia's exports is possible with improved marketing capabilities and expanded international partnerships. The blockade also has its "positive" side, at least short term: it has been serving as an effective protection against import competition in two major sectors of the economy—agriculture and food processing.

Short-term gains from lifting the blockade could be significant, although they would not alone solve the country's development problems. It is estimated that without the blockade annual merchandise exports could quickly increase by $300 million, compared to the level of late the 90s.

The high *cost of borrowing* is a drag on private sector development. The Armenian economy remains highly undermonetized, and the banking sector is small and segmented, making the costs of bank credit prohibitively high. But expensive borrowing is to a large degree a result, not a source, of more fundamental economic weaknesses. The unfriendly business environment creates strong incentives for firms to remain in the informal economy and to operate outside the banking system, keeping monetary depth low while greatly increasing the risks and costs of bank lending. In addition, the existence of numerous under-utilized donor-sponsored credit lines in Armenia provides ample evidence that further expansion in private credit is constrained by the lack of bankable projects, not by insufficient funding. Experience from other developing economies suggests that the early stages of enterprise restructuring are often financed not by banks but by other sources, such as commercial credit from suppliers and other partners.

The possibility that a low equilibrium trap may form in the financial sector cannot be dismissed, however. In such a trap, adverse factors exert a mutually reinforcing negative impact on longer-term development prospects:

- Demand constraints—quality of business plans, low transparency of borrowers, improperly registered property rights—mean that much more funding is potentially available (from credit lines) than is actually used.

- The funds that are used are too expensive because the costs of intermediation have been raised by the small size of banks, weak judicial protection of lenders' rights, and unresolved property rights issues (e.g., for urban land) that limit the value of potential collateral.

- Too low a share of the funds that banks channel to the real sector return as private sector deposits. The low rate of "recycling" can be traced to informality and the confidence crisis.

Budget constraints on Armenian enterprises are not firm, and subsidies are still too high. Experience with transition elsewhere since 1990 suggests that hard budget constraints are not just a critical element of macroeconomic stabilization; they are also needed for enterprise restructuring and the credibility of reforms. When compared to several of the largest CIS economies, budget constraints in most of Armenia's enterprise sector in the late 1990s appear relatively firm.[3] Still, total annual subsidies—including accumulated debts to utilities and tax arrears—are estimated to have been 6–7.5 percent of GDP in 1996–99. At least two-thirds of these subsidies in all years except 1999 were provided through quasi-fiscal channels such as non-paid services of utility providers, mostly in power, gas, and heating.

---

[3] In Russia heavy hidden and untargeted subsidies, provided through systematic nonpayment of taxes and energy costs, amounted to 7–10 percent of GDP annually in 1995–97. Adding explicit budgetary subsidies brings the total to more than 15 percent of GDP. Such soft budget constraints have stifled enterprise restructuring and growth and contributed significantly to the 1998 crisis through accumulation of public debts. See Brian Pinto, Vladimir Drebentsov, and Alexander Morozov (2000), "Give Macroeconomic Stability and Growth in Russia a Chance." Policy Research Working Paper 2324, World Bank, Washington, D.C.

The largest recipients of subsidies were households, which had been subsidized indirectly through infrastructure services such as energy, water, and irrigation. Commercial enterprises received a smaller share of total subsidies, and such subsidies have been heavily concentrated in a few of the largest companies—both state-owned and recently privatized. The liquidation or forced restructuring of these firms would have a beneficial impact on the entire enterprise sector, but there is no evidence that the soft budget constraints for a few large companies has slowed down the overall enterprise restructuring process. Arrears and implicit subsidies in Armenia are a fiscal problem rather than one of restructuring. Implicit subsidies also consume scarce public resources, which alternatively could be used more efficiently by providing a targeted social assistance for the most needy.

Despite considerable *fiscal adjustment* since the mid-1990s, the sustainability of fiscal performance remains a major concern. On the spending side, an additional reallocation of funds will be required to concentrate limited resources in the most critical areas, especially those related to support of primary social services and basic infrastructure. Without such a shift, the country's human capital base will continue to erode, raising the price of future broad-based growth. Revenue collection, although improved since 1996–97, is still far below expectations due in part to the size of the informal economy and persistent weaknesses in tax and customs administration.

The dram had appreciated considerably in 1998-99 against the currency of many of Armenia's regional trade partners, making the country's exports more costly. In contrast to most CIS countries, Armenia managed to avoid major macroeconomic disruptions from the 1998 Russia crisis, such as significant devaluation of the national currency and an inflation hike. A combination of tight monetary policy, relatively high hard currency reserves, and low levels of short-term debt accounts for the stability of the dram in 1998–99. In general, such stability is quite positive for economic management and for the credibility of the local currency. However, it came at the price of considerable appreciation against the currencies of many of Armenia's regional trading partners.

The real value of the dram in early 2001 was close to its level in January 1997. That value was a product of two opposing trends: appreciation against CIS currencies and depreciation against the currencies of the rest of the world. In early 2001, after the ruble had recovered somewhat, the dram was still 60 percent more expensive than the Russian currency and almost 50 percent higher than the Georgian lari.

Because many of Armenia's exporters do not yet have sufficient skills to penetrate new markets outside the FSU, they are unable to switch their exports quickly in response to exchange rate developments. Thus, the appreciation of the dram in the aftermath of the Russia crisis significantly affected the competitiveness of traditional exporters whose main markets are in the FSU. The appreciation exacerbated the impact of lower demand from Russia and other CIS states, both of which contributed to the deterioration of Armenian exports and industrial performance in 1998–99.

The dram's appreciation may have been excessive. Arguably, the government's policy response to the Russian crisis in late 1998 and early 1999 could have been less restrictive, allowing for more depreciation of the dram relative to the U.S. dollar. Now, however, the government's power to restore the pre-crisis exchange rate proportions is limited, and the overvalued dram may continue to affect the competitiveness of a specific segment of Armenian exporters. This finding reinforces the importance of correcting the fundamental weaknesses identified above—management capacity and distortions in the business environment that depress competitiveness.

The crisis in Russia, and more recently economic developments in Turkey, underline intrinsic macroeconomic vulnerabilities of the Armenian economy. Macroeconomic management in a small, open economy could become very challenging when its much larger neighbors and main partners have volatile exchange rates.

To Make Growth Broad-Based, Armenia's Government Must Create an Environment for Accelerated Development of the Private Sector

By establishing a stable macroeconomic environment and liberal trade regime, the government introduced a critical precondition for future export-driven growth. The binding constraint now relates to structural and micro-level fundamentals. While preserving its macroeconomic gains, the government must focus its medium-term strategy on improving the business environment, promoting deregulation, removing administrative barriers to investment, and setting up mechanisms for public-private dialogue—a "top-down" agenda that is traditional for economies in transition. Complementing that agenda must be a set of selective, bottom-up interventions to promote new business entry, especially in skill-based and export-oriented sectors (Table 4). Without additional effort to support private sector development and improve the business environment, it is likely that Armenia's overall growth rate would slow down in the coming years as the momentum provided by the recovery from the initial collapse dissipates.

Table 4. Summary of the Proposed Growth Strategy

Main pillars	Core polices	Immediate priorities
Maintaining a sustainable macroeconomic framework and liberal trade regime	Strengthening the quality of macroeconomic management	Reducing fiscal and quasi-fiscal risks Improving Armenia's debt profile Joining the World Trade Organization
Improving the quality of the business environment	Advancing the deregulation agenda Setting efficient mechanisms for public-private consultation Supporting financial deepening	Reforming tax administration and customs to lower the costs of compliance and provide equal treatment of taxpayers Reforming tax policy to promote simplification and equal treatment Further consolidating, downsizing, and rationalizing government inspections Liberalizing registration and licensing procedures Establishing a modern framework of company law Removing outdated laws and regulations from the regulatory framework
Facilitating economic restructuring and new private entry	Strengthening core government functions related to economic development and private sector growth Expanding opportunities for management and business training for existing managers and business owners	Establishing core restructuring agencies to facilitate expansion of new entry and support first movers in the private sector. Agencies include: • An investment promotion agency to support business linkages and inflows of foreign direct investment • An enterprise restructuring agency to restructure on a case by case basis large enterprises into start-ups and spin-offs • A business advisory center to provide business development and advisory services for new entry • An information technology business incubator to pilot new policies of public support for new entry in the skill-based sector

Effective Deregulation will Improve the Business Environment

The Government increasingly recognizes the need for more focused efforts to improve the business environment. Beginning in 2000, a program of measures has been adopted to this end, which is being supported by the Fourth Structural Adjustment Credit (SAC IV) from the World Bank. Key elements of the program include:

- Reforming tax administration to reduce compliance costs for taxpayers while raising collections.

- Developing a customs system that facilitates trade, generates revenues, and prevents the flow of illegal goods.

- Improving taxpayer services to build confidence, and establishing a forum for public-private dialogue in this major area of the reform program.

- Simplifying the tax system and making it more equitable.

- Further consolidating, downsizing, and rationalizing government inspections to reduce the number of agencies and agents with inspection powers.

- Liberalizing registration and licensing procedures with the objective of reducing the costs of interaction between the public and private sectors.

- Establishing a modern framework of company law and making other improvements to the legal framework.

- Repealing or rescinding outdated (mostly Soviet-era) laws and regulations that clash with market economy principles.

- Strengthening mechanisms of public-private consultation to improve the government's capacity to address problems faced by the private sector.

Other priorities of the strategy to improve the business environment include:

- Deepening the financial system through policies to reduce lending risks and the costs of borrowing, encourage consolidation in the banking system, and force banks to increase their capitalization.

- Accelerating development of land markets.

- Improving the quality of infrastructure services, such as telecommunications, transportation, and urban water supply.

- Strengthening regulatory capacity to support privately owned operators in energy and infrastructure.

- Improving the transparency and technical quality of privatization processes so as to attract strategic investors into the largest state-owned companies.

These initiatives are very timely and it is important that the Government carry through expeditiously with implementation.

Selective Interventions are needed in the Short Term to Promote New Entry and Restructuring, Especially in Skill-based and Export-oriented Sectors

The traditional top-down approach to restructuring has limitations in Armenia's circumstances. Outright liquidation of loss-making companies, for example, is not an attractive option, because pervasive uncertainty depresses demand even for viable assets. Establishing an efficient national system for bankruptcy and liquidation, another common top-down strategy, may be too institutionally demanding for immediate imposition in Armenia. Such a system will be achieved only gradually, as the capacity of various institutions is raised.

Because Armenia has neither the time, nor the capability, nor the budgetary resources for full-scale institutional reform, credible reforms that create incentives and opportunities for restructuring are critical. Institutional short-cuts—in the form of restructuring agencies—can help Armenia economize on institution-building by ensuring a functional fit between country conditions and the demands of restructuring.

Short-cuts are also required because improvements in the business environment do not always bring an immediate investment response. The massive brain drain that Armenia is experiencing indicates that the window of opportunity for embarking on a high-growth trajectory may not remain open much longer. If the country's stock of skilled personnel drops below some critical threshold level (widely recognized though difficult to quantify), skill-based industries will be much slower to develop. Hence, the need for "bottom-up" changes in industrial policy that will build on positive (but slow) changes in firms' behavior and thus generate momentum for broader improvements.

Active government policies to support private sector development should aim to ensure that private sector agents will be able to capitalize on gains associated with an improving investment climate. Although public interventions can rarely jump-start positive trends in the private sector, they *can* accelerate and mainstream positive trends already underway. The same principle applies to restructuring and institutional change.

The strategy of private-sector-led growth includes policies to facilitate:

- Increasing private sector employment in SMEs by reducing the costs of new entry and, even more important in the Armenia context, of staying in business and growing.

- Restructuring the assets of large enterprises that were parts of value chains that no longer exist.

- Selecting, as a pilot for new policy initiatives, one or two skilled-based sectors in which to develop and exploit core competencies as engines for economy-wide growth.

- Designing mechanisms to ensure that the benefits of those engines spill over into the rest of the economy.

- Expanding business development services to support the expansion of companies that survive the transition and contribute to local value chains.

- Upgrading sectoral policies to maintain local competencies to produce needed services efficiently in sectors such as agriculture, housing, utilities, and transportation.

Nascent export-oriented clusters such as software and diamond-polishing are likely to benefit most quickly from the proposed selective interventions, creating the conditions for a broader export push that will leverage Armenian skills and assets in other sectors that have been doing relatively well over the last 4–5 years—mining, tobacco, wines, food processing, and some apparel-related activities.

The core of the proposed strategy of selective restructuring is support for first movers and the development clusters that emerge around them. The Armenian economy has its first movers—companies that actually take a lead in the restructuring process. Their number is small, and as a rule they remain unsophisticated, with limited potential for expansion, especially into non-CIS markets. Their very existence, however, especially in high-skill industries such as software, provides a window of economic opportunity. The government's major objective should be to design policy interventions and supporting institutions to help existing first movers to expand—and new ones to emerge—and to create linkages between first movers and the rest of the economy.

Sectoral studies prepared by the World Bank staff in 1999–2000 and summarized in the main report recommend specific policy reforms for individual sectors—such as energy, agriculture, telecommunication, transport, and housing—that complement the strategy presented above. The recommended sectoral interventions would support expanding opportunities for business linkages (in transport and telecommunications), reduce critical constraints for skill-based development (in telecommunications), support new labor-intensive entry (in food distribution and housing), and have a significant impact on macroeconomic and fiscal sustainability (reduced energy losses).

International Aid Donors Can Advance the Growth Strategy by Supporting the Creation of "Restructuring Agencies"

Donors could help accelerate the restructuring process by supporting the establishment of critical restructuring organizations and encouraging government ownership of restructuring activities. Current volumes of assistance available for Armenia, appropriately reallocated, are adequate for the task.

With donor assistance, the government should establish several public-private organizations ("restructuring agencies") to provide public assistance to the private sector related to restructuring, export promotion, acquisition of new skills, and international networking. As a first step, three such organizations should be created:

- An enterprise restructuring agency to address the restructuring problems of the largest existing companies. A similar agency in Moldova is described below.

- An advisory center to provide basic technical assistance, including export promotion and training, to start-ups and to support development of local business associations and other business organizations.

- An investment promotion agency to represent Armenia to international investors and support expansion of emerging clusters that have proved their international competitiveness. Such an agency already has been established in Armenia, but it is still at an early stage of development.

The major advantage of restructuring agencies lies in the consolidation of institutional support and various public services under one roof, reducing the cost to business of institutional segmentation. Given the weaknesses of traditional market institutions in Armenia, restructuring agencies help fill the gap by packaging assistance and protecting clients from the unfriendly business environment.

In what appears to be a global trend, various countries have piloted hybrid organizations that specialize in supporting private sector development. The new hybrids combine to various degrees the functions of traditional consulting companies, investment promotion agencies, nongovernmental organizations, and investment banks. They may take the form of a foundation (Chile), equity seed fund (Denmark and other countries in Western Europe), business advisory center (FYR Macedonia), or restructuring agency (Moldova). Services include traditional restructuring instruments such as management training, business incubators, seed financing, advisory and information services, matching grant schemes, and facilitation of private-to-private collaboration through business associations. Packaging such services in response to specific local needs appears to generate considerable value added. The main performance indicator for these agencies has to be linked to the number and performance of first movers in the economy.

By protecting first movers, these agencies may be able to trigger a more intensive restructuring process. Successfully restructured first movers become role models for the rest of the enterprise sector, and they often work with other enterprises to help mainstream their initial successes.

International experience shows that the activity of restructuring agencies can strengthen reform coalitions in a difficult political environment. Agencies develop new, influential networks of managers and consultants who have been involved in their programs and have a stake in reform. They raise demand for restructuring by creating a shared understanding among managers and government officials of the needs for restructuring and the value of intensive use of external consultants.

The experience of Moldova's Enterprise Restructuring Agency (ARIA) may be especially relevant for Armenia (Box 1). ARIA has successfully promoted enterprise restructuring by liquidating large, traditional industrial enterprises and creating a new institutional structure—the industrial park—that has stimulated spin-offs and start-ups using existing assets. The industrial park assists new entrants by providing a package of three critical services:

- Access to productive assets.

- Advice on using the assets to take advantage of market opportunities and managerial capabilities.

- Protection from administrative harassment.

The main report provides further recommendations for institutional design of restructuring agencies, including:

- Criteria for selection of assets for restructuring. Low rents from the assets are a major criterion.

- Performance-based incentives for agency staff. Compensation of project teams should be linked to restructuring outcomes and not to production of reports.

- Continuous learning. Young and energetic staff are motivated by more than pay; opportunities to learn new skills and master new challenges are just as important.

- Multisectoral mandate. Cross-cutting functions help an autonomous agency maximize its interaction with the rest of the government. A good example is investment promotion. Efficient investment promotion agencies deal daily with issues that overlap with the responsibilities of many other agencies, which must be convinced to change their policies and be broadly cooperative. Investment promotion agencies have two clients: potential private investors and the government at large.

Box 1. Moldova's Enterprise Restructuring Agency

Moldova's Agency for Restructuring and Enterprise Assistance (ARIA) was created in 1995 to accelerate the adjustment of newly privatized enterprises to market conditions. It was supported by two private sector development loans from the World Bank. ARIA supports the private sector through training, policy advocacy, business support, and other services.

ARIA has created industrial parks on the premises of large, nonviable, state-owned enterprises. The physical plant of the original enterprises has been reconfigured into premises that provide security, physical infrastructure, and business services for small and medium-size enterprises and other businesses emerging from the liquidation of the original enterprise.

ARIA has succeeded by working with existing capital and human resources in developing an efficient solution to politically-charged issues of liquidation and restructuring. It has empowered managers, but if they did not cooperate, it has replaced them. Another important feature of the ARIA model is intensive use of domestic consultants, a practice that not only saves money but also promotes growth of the local consulting industry, which then replicates the project strategy with other enterprises. Foreign consultants are used for training and only where absolutely necessary.

Data collected from firms indicate that ARIA's projects have had a substantial impact on restructuring. In 1995, the firms that later found their way to ARIA were on average worse off than other firms, both in terms of productivity and profitability. By the end of 1999, despite worsening economic conditions in Moldova, ARIA-assisted firms were more productive than their unassisted counterparts. They exported more and paid more in taxes per worker. ARIA's assistance is positively, significantly, and consistently correlated with growth in sales, exports, and productivity.

Source: World Bank (2001b).

Other steps could increase the efficiency of donor assistance for restructuring:

- Consolidate and package delivery of technical assistance. Although Armenia has recently become one of the leading recipients of donor-funded technical assistance in the region, the results of numerous programs dedicated to private sector development have been much less visible than one might expect.

- Introduce high-intensity assistance programs and focus them on a limited number of potential leaders (first movers) with established track records. Such programs should provide a broad package of longer-term assistance.

- Widen the participation of local counterparts and strengthen incentives to support transfers of knowledge and skills to recipients.

- Expand support for development of local private business organizations as instruments of collective learning and private cooperation, and as major proponents of further reforms.

Success in Nascent Export-oriented Clusters will help Attract Foreign Direct Investment to These and Other Sectors

Sustainable levels of job creation and economic growth in Armenia—prerequisites for social and political stability in the country—will depend to a large extent on foreign direct investment. Most of Armenia's industrial assets were created as a part of technological chains that by now have largely disappeared. The country faces a challenge of reindustrialization: Existing assets (both capital and labor) need to be restructured and upgraded so as to fit into new global and regional value chains. The necessary changes will require considerable investments, far beyond those possible from Armenia's domestic savings. Foreign investment is also a major source of new management culture, market knowledge, and technology transfer, and so can contribute to meeting Armenia's need for managerial skills. The Armenian Diaspora could partially be more important as a source of managerial expertise and an entry point to the outside world rather than a source of investment financing.

Armenian institutions responsible for investment promotion and investment support are still weak, even compared to other FSU states. Little effort has been made to build the infrastructure needed to attract investments and support investors in the early stages of their ventures. In particular, the government has not been able to tap into the investment potential of the Armenian Diaspora and to channel the ongoing flow of Diaspora-funded humanitarian assistance into real sector investments.

It would be unrealistic to expect a surge in conventional foreign direct investment in the short term. With respect to investment promotion, Armenia must pass through a "preinvestment stage" of investment promotion, during which the government needs to make progress in improving the business environment and training more managers, which together would make local assets more attractive to foreign investment. Management training is critical because it would set the scene for successful cooperation between local and foreign managers—a prerequisite for conventional foreign direct investment. To be successful, management training should be closely linked with implementation of specific restructuring projects and with promotion of business linkages between local firms and the outside world.

The Software Industry is a Logical Place for Private Investment to Begin

The strong expansion of the software sector in 1997–2000 represents one of the brightest spots in Armenia's recent industrial development. Output and exports of the country's software companies doubled each year from 1997 to 1999, to reach $15–20 million. Under favorable circumstances, the sector could produce a major spillover effect on the rest of the economy in terms of productivity and global linkages. Western companies—often owned or managed by overseas Armenians—have shown strong interest in the sector as a response to the global shortage of programmers.

At the moment the software sector remains small—its 1,000 employees produce about 7–8 percent of the country's merchandise exports (as officially reported). Its current pace of expansion could be undermined by inadequate telecommunication services, shortages of management skills and business development services, insufficient protection of property rights in software products, outdated software training in local universities, and the limited pool of available programmers, in addition to the general constraints that hamper private sector expansion.

Given the successful growth of the sector—an entirely spontaneous, market-driven process—it is logical for the government to explore ways of supporting and accelerating that expansion. The sector's potential, as well as its current constraints, make it an ideal pilot case for a strategy of private sector driven, skill-based growth aided by government interventions that are relatively short-term, nondistortionary, and replicable to other sectors of the economy. The need for a tangible demonstration effect is particularly acute in Armenia, where the most talented individuals leave the country because they have lost faith in the ability of the economy to turn around.

Key elements of the government's strategy in the software sector might include:

- Implementing the policy reforms called for by the recently adopted sector master plan.

- Setting up institutions such as incubators or other forms of managed industrial space for new software and e-business firms.

- Improving the communications infrastructure and reducing the cost of internet communications.

- Strengthening key supporting institutions and systems, including those that protect intellectual property rights and ensure contract enforcement.

- Promoting spillovers from software development and demand for software products in related sectors such as publishing, engineering, and other skill- and knowledge-based services.

- Facilitating intrasectoral links and private cooperation in the sector to accelerate business learning, reduce risks and costs of external expansion, and support stronger international linkages.

A new incubator for information technology businesses—a joint project of the government and the World Bank—will address some of the foregoing objectives using new forms of cooperation among the government, donors, the Armenian Diaspora, and the local private sector. Its main objective is to produce a demonstration of business success powerful enough to act as a catalyst and help break the vicious cycle of low expectations, low demand for institutional change, and low investment and outcomes. If successful, the main features of the project could be scaled up and replicated in other sectors.

The project is expected to have the following components:

- Managed work space (with satellite dish) for small and medium-size companies will provide a productive business environment and infrastructure.

- A business development facility will provide marketing, managerial, and other business linkages to connect Armenian firms with the Western demand for software.

- A skill development fund will create programs to enhance joint industry-university skill and a continuing education process, beginning with student apprenticeships in local export-driven companies.

1. INTRODUCTION

The Armenian economy has been growing at an average rate of about 5% since 1994. But this growth has been driven primarily by a recovery from a major contraction in output that occurred in the early 1990s. The current growth is not based on any substantial changes in either enterprise behavior or investor attitude that could be considered longer-term sources of economic expansion, export growth and job creation. Despite Armenia's rather stable macroeconomic performance and reasonable structural reform track record, the last several years have not brought an adequate supply response or noticeable improvements in living standards for the majority of the population. Given the entrenched weaknesses of its existing growth patterns, it is doubtful that the current growth rates can be sustained in the medium term without more intensive enterprise restructuring and a stronger investment response.

Thus, the challenge Armenia faces is two-fold. First, it needs to sustain high growth rates and, if circumstances permit, reach a high growth rate episode for the next 6-8 years. Second, Armenia needs to change the quality of growth – migrating to a growth path, which would a have a stronger correlation between economic expansion and improvements in living standards, reduction in poverty, and recovery in employment.

Various attempts have been made over the last several years to summarize both the major constraints on Armenia's growth and its sources of comparative advantages. The results of these studies show a remarkable consensus. The Government of Armenia has also acknowledged its broad agreement with these findings. The Armenian economy's small size, current simplicity of structure, disadvantages of geographical location, and limited natural endowments are among the major reasons for such a strong public consensus on growth constraints as well as for the limited number of real strategic choices that Armenian policymakers have at the moment. At the same time, the educated and entrepreneurial labor force and potential support from the Diaspora are usually treated as the main comparative advantages for Armenia.

Given the broad consensus on a number of issues, the objective of this report is not to repeat the analysis, made several times before, but, first, to look at underlying factors that could solve the puzzle of the growth trends in the period of 1994-2000 (six years of growth without poverty reduction), and, second, to develop a set of policy recommendations which may accelerate the utilization of Armenia's available advantages within a realistic set of economic and political constraints. In this respect, the report is focused on the following key development challenge. How to promote growth in the improbable environment of rudimentary institutional development and income levels, both comparable to Sub-Saharan Africa, yet human capital comparable to the OECD countries? And how to accelerate enterprise restructuring and new private entry in a situation marked by pervasive uncertainty, massive brain drain and asset stripping?

Thus, the report focuses on two main questions:

- What are the broad structural weaknesses of the Armenian economy, in both the private and public sector, that have produced the current deformations in its growth path?

- What policy and institutional reforms should be at the core of the government strategy to address these weaknesses?

The report has the following structure. The analysis starts in Chapter 2 by identifying major problems in the current growth path, such as weak export and investment performance, low rates of new entry and employment generation, and, as a result, surprisingly weak impact of the growth on poverty reduction. Chapter 3 suggests two major inter-related factors that have supported such a deformed growth path – a poor business environment and weak private sector capabilities that prevent Armenian firms from integrating into the global economy. This chapter also briefly discuses several political and historical factors that have contributed to such weaknesses in both the business environment and private sector capabilities. At the same time, this chapter suggests that several other factors, e.g. costs associated with the blockade of Armenian borders and limited opportunities for financing of the private sector, while important, do not currently constitute a binding constraint for future economic growth.

Chapter 4 presents a main set of policy recommendations aimed at removing the above-mentioned constraints for growth. It also argues that the immediate policy priority for the Government relates to a removal of administrative barriers for investments. The Chapters then presents a policy package to promote a deregulation agenda and advance broader improvements in the business environment, which to a large extent follows the respective elements of the Government program supported by the Fourth Structural Adjustment Credit of the World Bank.

Chapters 5 and 6 are focused on another strategic priority – acceleration of enterprise restructuring and new entry. Chapter 5 provides an analytical framework for more specific policy and institutional recommendations that are presented in Chapter 6. Chapter 5 argues that in Armenia's circumstances of simultaneous market and government failures, there is strong justification for active public sector involvement in enterprise restructuring by way of setting up specialized restructuring institutions (Restructuring Agencies).

These restructuring institutions are treated in the report as entry points for Government growth strategy – initially, they will deal with a limited group of managers and investors, who are better prepared to take risks and do things differently, but these institutions would be designed for gradual expansion of their outreach. Chapter 5 argues that in Armenia's conditions this approach could make a difference on both sides. First, it would improve supply of good assets -- help to develop local assets, mostly local managers, and make them "FDI ready". Second, it would strengthen demand for further reforms – support local reform coalitions and establish new models of entrepreneurial behavior to be mimicked by the second layer of Armenian companies.

Chapter 6 suggests three specific types of restructuring agencies to be established in Armenia. These would deal with (i) investment promotion, (ii) forced restructuring of large traditional industrial companies, and (iii) supplying SMEs with consulting and advisory services. This chapter also suggests how donors could contribute to the enterprise restructuring process.

Chapter 7 describes the major elements of necessary policy reforms in several core sectors, such as energy, agriculture and housing, and suggests how these sectoral reforms would contribute to the overall growth strategy.

The Appendix provides some relevant lessons from the modern economic theory for Armenia's growth prospects. Specifically, it argues that, based on the cross-country statistical evidence, Armenia's medium-term growth rates are unlikely to exceed 3.5-4 percent per year if there are no significant improvements in investment performance and advances in structural reforms.

2. MAIN CHARACTERISTICS OF THE RECENT GROWTH PERFORMANCE

2.1. Macroeconomic Overview of Recent Growth Trends

The Government of Armenia launched a major structural reform program shortly after its independence in 1991. It called for the liberalization of prices of most goods and services, setting up a liberal trade and foreign exchange regime and support for private sector development. Enterprise privatization was initiated, starting with small enterprises. The collective farm system was quickly broken up and land was privatized to small holders. Confronted with rampant inflation (and deep drops in GDP) during the early 1990s, Armenia implemented stabilization policies in the spring of 1994. Public expenditures were limited to priority items with a sharp reduction in fiscal transfers to enterprises, and Central Bank financing of the fiscal deficit was curtailed. In addition, since late 1994, the government's anti-inflationary efforts were aided by inflows of external financing from the IMF and the World Bank.

Armenia has made major progress in macroeconomic stabilization and in establishing a suitable framework for structural reforms since the mid 90s. Despite the strong negative impact of the recent Russia crisis, macroeconomic performance remains quite stable with low inflation, a relatively stable exchange rate, a sufficient level of international reserves, and a manageable level of fiscal deficit.

Inflation has fallen sharply. The annual inflation rate fell from 1820 percent in 1993 to 26 percent in late 1995 and to under 6 percent by the end of 1996. Annual inflation rose to 14 percent in 1997, following some increases in VAT rates, but in 1998-2000, inflation was fully under control.

On the structural reform side, the Armenian Government made substantial progress in reforming budget management, tax administration, CBA regulation, privatization, and various sectoral reforms, including in energy, education, health, and social protection. The Government maintains a liberal trade regime and remains active in upgrading the country's legal framework. A new company law and laws on real property, banks and banking, collateral, bank insolvency and commercial bankruptcy have also been adopted. By the end of 1997, over 80 percent of small enterprises and about 65 percent of medium and large enterprises had been privatized. The share of the private sector in GDP production increased from 11.7% in 1990 to 74.5% in 1998.

Compared to the rest of the CIS, Armenia's growth performance was rather strong. After more than 50 percent decline in GDP between 1991 and 1993, GDP recorded a growth of 5.4 percent in 1994. GDP growth rates have remained positive since that time (Table 2.1).

Armenia's economic growth also showed a remarkable degree of resilience in the face of two major shocks of the late 1990's. First, in the face of the Russia crisis, Armenia avoided both an exchange rate crisis and an acceleration of inflation, and after a brief slow-down the economy continued to expand. Then in October 1999, several leading Armenian politicians, including both the Prime Minister and the Speaker of Parliament, were assassinated. The political aftermath of the assassinations led to a considerable deterioration in fiscal and investment performance. Nonetheless, economic growth resumed by mid-2000. For 2000 as a whole, GDP growth reached 6% despite a severe drought.

These positive developments were supported by recent improvements in the external situation of the country. By the early 1990s, a conflict over Nagorno-Karabakh had led to a trade and transport blockade by Azerbaijan - traditionally Armenia's principal transit route for oil, gas and other products - and the closure of the Turkish border. The effects of this were compounded by civil strife in Georgia. Armenia's isolation from international markets has been significantly eased since a cease-fire was signed in 1994. Armenia has benefited from greater stability and economic recovery in Georgia, expanded trade with Iran and greatly increased informal trade with Turkey.

Table 2.1. Armenia: Selected Macroeconomic Indicators

	1990	1991	1992	1993	1994	1995	1996	1997	1998	1999	2000
								1.47090666	1.4797321		
Real GDP growth (%)		-11.7	-41.8	-8.8	5.4	6.9	5.9	3.3	7.3	3.3	6.0
GDP level (1990=100)	100	88.3	51.4	46.9	49.4	52.8	55.9	57.8	62.0	64.0	67.9
Value added in industry, growth (%)		-4.0	-59.7	8.9	9.6	2.6	1.1	1.3	-2.2	5.2	6.4
Level (1990=100)	100	96.0	38.7	42.1	46.2	47.4	47.9	48.5	47.5	49.9	53.1
Annual inflation, CPI		174.1	728.7	1822.9	4962.3	176	18.7	14	8.7	0.6	-0.8
Cumulative inflation, CPI (1990=100)	100	274.1	2,271	43,678	2,211,113	6,102,672	7,243,872	8,258,014	8,976,461	9,030,320	8,958,077
Real exchange rate, (1994=100)					100	159.0	180.0	169.2	176.0	163.6	157.2
Average Wage, US$					6	19	23	28	36	38	42
Treasury Bills: av. Real yields, %						-48.6	18.6	38.5	33.9	54.5	27.7
Exports, goods and services, mn $			230	174	242	300	368	330	360	383	441
- Annual growth (%)				-24.4	39.6	23.7	22.9	-10.3	8.9	6.5	15.1
Reserves (months of imports) (a)					4.2	3.1	3.0	3.5	3.9	3.8	3.6
As percent of GDP											
State budget revenue						14.4	17.6	19.7	17.1	19.3	16.5
State budget expenditure						24.0	26.3	25.7	21.9	26.5	22.8
Fiscal balance, accrual basis						-9.9	-8.7	-6.0	-4.8	-7.2	-6.4
Broad money, M2X							8.3	8.7	10.0	11.0	14.6
Credit to the economy, stock									8.4	8.6	10.1
Current account bal., excl. transfers							-29.8	-31.9	-30.6	-26.0	-24.0
Current account balance, overall							-18.2	-18.7	-21.2	-16.6	-24.4
Public debt, stock							32.6	39.0	41.4	46.3	45.0
Foreign direct investment							1.1	3.2	11.6	6.6	5.4
Growth of broad money, M2X (%)							35.6	28.7	36.0	13.6	38.7
Total credit growth (%)							36.8	-11.6	51.1	-0.8	9.0

(a) - next year import

Source: NSS, IMF

Despite this progress, Armenia's economic recovery remains fragile. Since 1991, poverty in Armenia has become widespread, with about 55 percent of the population being classified as poor or very poor back in 1996. Furthermore, the fallout from the 1998 Russia financial crisis and severe droughts in 1999-2000 were additional factors responsible for a decline in poverty despite economic expansion. Slow recovery in household incomes is a major source of remaining populist pressures on the Government's policies of market-oriented reforms and constitutes a substantial policy risk. The reason for the dissatisfaction of voters also relates to the high inequality in distribution of benefits associated with recent growth and stabilization.

Unemployment totals about 26 percent of the labor force in 1999[4] and remained practically unchanged since 1996. Most unemployed remained unregistered and therefore not eligible for public assistance. Poor job opportunities and low confidence in the Government's policies help to keep emigration at high levels. Emigration is especially high among the young and best educated people, which will further limit prospects for strong and sustainable growth.

The overall recent investment and supply response has also been much weaker than what may be expected from reviewing Armenia's macroeconomic progress. This reflects three main groups of factors which are discussed in detail in the following chapter: (i) major problems in the business environment, which greatly reduced opportunities for new entries and new investments; (ii) weak capacity of the private sector to enter new markets and build new partnerships; and (iii) high political risks that reflect both internal political tensions in Armenia and the unresolved Karabagh conflict.

Currency Appreciation

In contrast to most CIS countries, Armenia managed to avoid major negative macroeconomic consequences of the 1998 Russia crisis such as significant devaluation of the national currency and an inflation hike. A combination of tight monetary policy, relatively high hard currency reserves, and low levels of short term debts represent major factors responsible for stability of the dram in 1998-99. By the end of 1999, the dram lost less than 5% of real value relative to the US dollar, and appreciated relative to main European currencies. In general, such stability is quite positive for economic management and more specifically for credibility of the local currency. However, this came at a price of considerable appreciation of the dram versus currencies of its many regional trade partners. How significant was this effect and to what extent may it constitute a constraint for export growth?

Chart 2.1 provides two important insights regarding real exchange (RE) developments in the late 90s[5]. The chart depicts average dynamics of RE with weights that reflect the structure of Armenian foreign trade. It suggests:

- While the real value of the dram in early 2001 was close to its level in January 1997, for most of 1999 and early 2000 the dram value was 10-12% above this level. However, it seems unlikely that this magnitude of appreciation on its own could become a source of systemic export problems. At least partially it was compensated by the ongoing decline in average transportation costs. Also, average dollar wages in Armenia, while increased by 25% in 1997-1999, remained rather low, even within the CIS (Chart 2.2).

- However, Chart 2.1 suggests that rather modest average RE appreciation hides two different trends: major appreciation relative to the CIS, which at its peak exceeded 50%, and depreciation relative to the rest of the world. Such duality in the RE development should be

---

[4] Based on the household survey and using the ILO definition.
[5] Both charts 2.1 and 2.2 are based on the IMF reported data.

considered as a serious obstacle for Armenian exports. As it is argued below in the report, many Armenian exporters do not have sufficient skills yet to penetrate new markets outside of the FSU and thus can not switch easily their exports in response to exchange rate developments. Therefore, while affected by appreciation of the dram vs. CIS currencies, they can not seriously benefit from the dram depreciation at other markets.[6]

Chart 2.1. Real Exchange Rate Developments, 1997-2000, (Dec 96=100)

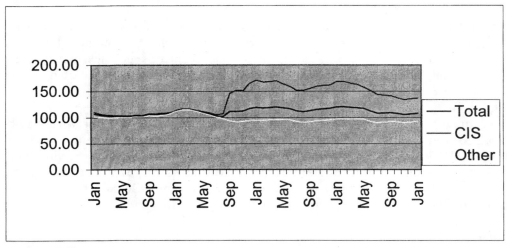

Source: IMF.

Chart 2.2. Dollar Wages in Selected CIS Economies, 1995-2000

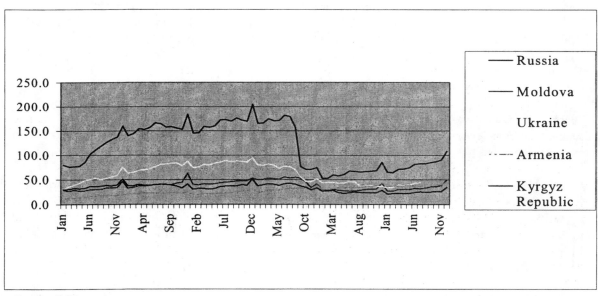

Source: IMF.

---

[6] One also should add that the average exchange rate in the Chart seems to overestimate the weight for non-CIS partners. This derives, as shown below in the export section, from the fact that the official Armenia trade data somewhat overestimate the share of non-CIS trade.

Overall, it sounds that the dram appreciation in the aftermath of the Russia crisis significantly affected competitiveness for many traditional exporters that have their main markets in the FSU. This further contributed to deterioration in both export and industrial performance in 1998-99, initially associated with a drop in demand from Russia and other CIS states. The scale of the appreciation impact diminished somewhat in 2000, due to a partial recovery of the Russian ruble. Still, in early 2001, the real value of the dram was 25-30% higher relative to a basket of CIS currencies than in early 1997. Specifically, the dram was 60% more expensive than the Russian ruble and almost 50% more than the Georgian lari (Chart 2.3).

Chart 2.3. Real Exchange Rate of Dram Vs. other Regional Currencies, 1996=100

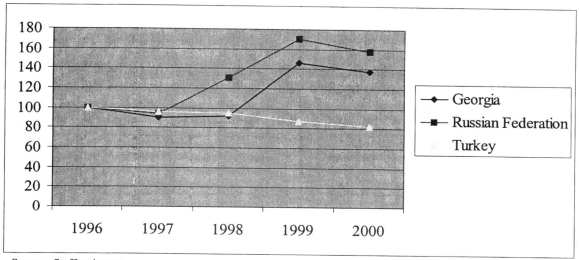

Source: Staff estimates.

Some recovery in exports to CIS in 2000 (Chart 2.4), which followed real depreciation of dram, seems to confirm sensitivity of Armenia's exports to FSU states to changes in real exchange rates.

Chart 2.4. Merchandise Trade with CIS, 1995-2000, million US dollar

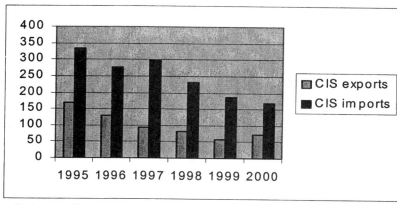

Source: Staff estimates.

At the moment, the Armenian Government does not have tools to resolve this problem and restore the pre-crisis proportions in exchange rates. This limitation for Armenian exports would remain in place for some time[7]. In terms of policy recommendations, this finding supports several core conclusions of this report that emphasize a need to address fundamental

---

[7] Much would depend on future rates of Russian ruble appreciation.

weaknesses of the Armenian economy to generate sufficient amounts of exports – insufficient management skills to penetrate new markets and excessive business costs associated with deficiencies in the local business environment.

The Russia crisis and more recently economic developments in Turkey underline intrinsic macroeconomic vulnerabilities of the Armenian economy. Macroeconomic management in a small open economy becomes unavoidably very difficult when your much larger neighbors and main partners have an unstable macro environment, including volatile exchange rate developments.

Financial Depth

The Armenian economy remains severely undermonetized even when compared to CIS countries that have shown weaker macroeconomic performance in the second half of the 90s (Table 2.2). There are several factors responsible for this; some of them are discussed in the next chapter. This section looks specifically at possible links between the recent monetary trends and Government macroeconomic policies of the late 90s.

Table 2.2. Indicators of Monetary Depth in Selected Economies in Transition, as Percent of GDP

	Reserve Money		Banking Credit to the Economy	
	1997	1999	1997	1999
Armenia	6.4	5.5	6.0	9.2
Azerbaijan	n.a.	7.8	n.a.	13.1
Kyrgyz Republic	10.0	8.9	n.a.	n.a.
Lithuania	8.6	9.6	11.1	13.6
Moldova	12.8	12.2	19.5	13.0
Ukraine	7.9	9.6	8.4	10.1
Memo: Poland	9.7	8.6	23.1	28.8

Source: IFS.

The analysis of the Government macro-economic policy targets in the late 90s seems to suggest some degree of inconsistency between fiscal and monetary objectives. The policy aimed at a combination of substantial budget deficits with low inflation targets and a stable exchange rate (Table 2.3). As in many other countries in such a situation, this led to a tight monetary policy. During 1997-2000, the target for budget deficit on average exceeded 5% of GDP, while inflation targets were really ambitious. Moreover, actual inflation was even lower than projected. Since late 1998, the Armenian economy has been facing deflationary pressures: the overall inflation rate was just above zero despite continuing considerable increases in utility tariffs (power, telecom, irrigation).

While a significant portion of Armenia's budget deficit financing was traditionally coming from external sources, it was critical for the monetary sector that in 1998-99 the Government did raise a significant part of the financing (and later re-financing) at the domestic market by placing Treasury Bills (TBs). In retrospect, it seems that the size of domestic borrowing was excessive (relative to the capacity of the domestic financial system) and the timing for it was rather unfortunate.

In 1998, as part of the global crisis of emerging markets, the Armenia TB market came under serious pressures due to a massive withdrawal of foreign investors, including Russian banks. The share of non-residents among TB holders fell from about 50 to 8 percent. Despite such a drastic decline in total demand, the Government decided to keep the overall amount of outstanding TBs intact and managed to attract additional local investors to the market. As a result, local holdings of TBs increased by 9 billion drams[8] or by more than 80%. This increase equaled about 1% of GDP. Such an expansion of local TB

---

[8] Note that the total dram money increase in 1998 amounted to only 11 billion drams.

holdings, given the existing level of monetary depth, was possible only at continuously high interest rates: average real TB yields amounted to 34% in 1998 and to more than 50% in 1999[9]. Moreover, high TB yields pushed up all other interest rates in the economy[10] and affected private sector borrowing.

Table 2.3. Selected Macroeconomic Targets and Outcomes

	1998*	1999*	2000**
Inflation target, annual average rate	9.4	2.7	2.6
Actual inflation, annual average rate	8.7	0.7	-0.8
Budget deficit projection, % of GDP	-5.6	-6.1	-4.8
Dram broad money, growth rate target	15.2	-0.7	13.7
Actual growth of dram broad money, annual growth	23.3	-2.1	34.4

* IMF, EBS/99/181, Sept 1999 (revised program for 1999).
** IMF briefing paper, Feb 22, 2000.
Source: IMF.

Some improvements in the institutional arrangements, relaxed monetary supply in 2000, and reduced Government net borrowing helped to reduce TB interest rates substantially in the course of 2000. This did result in significant reductions in interest rates and much faster growth in money aggregates. Still the real interest rates remain very high. As seems, there is considerable inertia in the system (path dependency) which is fueled by enrooted expectations of high interest rates and political uncertainty.

Combining the analysis of recent exchange rate and monetary developments, one may argue that the Government's response to the Russia crisis in 1998-99 was excessively restrictive. The Government would have been better off if it would have reduced the volume of TBs placements in the environment of massive withdrawals of non-residents. An alternative response in such circumstances would have been based on a less restrictive monetary policy and would allow for more domestic inflation, more nominal dram depreciation relative to the US dollar, and probably for lower real interest rates. Overall, the Government could have tried to avoid deflationary pressures and costs of excessive dram appreciation relative to currencies of its CIS partners.

Fiscal vulnerabilities. Despite considerable fiscal adjustment since the mid 90s, sustainability of fiscal performance remains a major concern. Revenue collection, while improved compared to 1996-97, is still much below expectations due in part to the high share of the informal economy and remaining weaknesses in tax and customs administration. On the expenditure side, there is a need for a considerable reallocation of funds in order to concentrate limited resources in the most critical areas, especially those related to support of primary social services and basic infrastructure. Without such a shift, erosion of human capital will continue, which would increase potential costs for future broad-based growth.

Political uncertainties that followed the tragic events of October 1999 resulted in considerable deterioration in tax performance and collection of public utilities. This led to a significant expenditure squeeze and further accumulation of budget arrears, including in core sectors (wages, social benefits, etc.). Total budget and pension arrears increased from less than 1% of GDP in September 1999 to about 5% of GDP at the end of 2000.

In addition, the Government faces considerable challenges in the quasi-fiscal area. While financing gaps in public utilities were reduced considerably since the mid 90s, especially in the power

---

[9] In addition, as suggested in the Armenia Targeted Financial Sector Review, several institutional weaknesses of the TB market reduced market competition and favored higher interest rates.
[10] World Bank (2000a).

sector, they are still excessive. Residual losses from non-payment and theft in the power sector amount to about 2.5% of GDP.

External debt. Armenia's stock of public external debt stood at $862 million or 45% of GDP by the end of 2000. The debt's relatively large grant element (36%) reflects the large share of highly concessional IDA credits and the small share of non-concessional commercial debt. Less than one-fourth of total nominal debts carry variable interest rates. This composition of debt protects Armenia reasonably well against higher international interest rates or significant shifts in value of the major international currencies. Total debt service amounted to 16% of exports of goods and services in 1999 and it is projected to stay below 15% starting from 2001. Armenia has a good record of servicing its external debt.

Overall, in terms of net present value, external debt was estimated at end-1999 at 153% of export of goods and services and at 167% of fiscal revenues, meaning that while the current overall debt burden is moderate in terms of the size of the economy, it is high relative to expected export earnings. The debt ratios improved somewhat in 2000, after a 15% expansion in exports in the course of the second part of the year. The medium-term forecast suggests further gradual improvements in the debt profile over the next several years, based on a stronger export performance and a continued moratorium on non-concessional borrowing. In addition, the authorities have been negotiating a restructuring of Armenia's large non-concessional debts with several creditors (Russia, Turkmenistan, and EU), which could result in further improvement of the debt profile. Overall, Armenia's debt should remain manageable as export performance continues to improve, but the World Bank does not envisage that Armenia will become creditworthy for IBRD lending during the next three years.

Overall, Armenia remains highly vulnerable to external shocks. Its major vulnerability derives from its very limited export volume. With annual merchandise exports of about US$250 million (less than 30 percent of the external debt stock), the country just does not have enough export proceeds yet for borrowing at market terms. Armenia's trade deficit is large and amounted to 29% of GDP in 1999. While Armenia continues to benefit from the considerable inflow of remittances and private transfers (7-8% of GDP a year) and official transfers (on average 6% of GDP a year in 1998-2000), it still has considerable residual requirements for external financing. The current account deficit after official transfers is projected to average 12% of GDP over the next three years.

Another vulnerability derives from the fact that, due to its economic structure, Armenia is still highly dependent on trade with the rest of the FSU. Also, in the absence of raw materials and primary processing facilities, Armenia relied heavily on imports of semi-finished and critical inputs, particularly of primary energy resources.

Armenia is a land-locked country within an unstable region. While both the conflict over Nagorno-Karabakh and the internal conflicts in Georgia have eased, there is still the risk of the resumption of hostilities, which is an important issue for potential investors. High transportation costs and unreliable communication, in part related to blockades, are a major tax on business activities, and more generally prevent Armenia from more efficient international integration. Moreover, progress towards a final resolution of conflicts could be slow, and Armenia will continue to pay for this through *inter alia* higher indices of country risks and higher transportation costs.

Other major macroeconomic issues that in the longer term could limit Armenia's economic prospects include:

- The high share of the informal sector[11] in the economy introduces additional uncertainties in economic development. It reduces the efficiency of government interventions, with especially adverse effects on taxation, the financial sector, and social protection.

- Due to low household incomes and small country size, domestic markets for most goods and services are thin, which in turn constitutes additional constraints for investments.

- The financial system remains highly underdeveloped with low financial depth and a severe dollar-based economy[12].

2.2. Armenia's Record of Growth Compared to CEE and Baltic Countries

Armenia has enjoyed 6 consecutive years of positive growth, a record that is more comparable to the countries in Central and Eastern Europe and the Baltics than to the other countries within the CIS as shown in Table 2.4. In a sample of 26 transition economies[13], almost all of the 15 economies that had experienced positive growth rates by 1994 were from Central and Eastern Europe and the Baltics with the exception of Armenia, the Kyrgyz Republic and Mongolia. The average transitional recession period for these 15 economies lasted 3.6 years with an average cumulative reported output decline of 33.6 percent. Relative to these 15 economies, Armenia is on the high end in terms of both the recessionary period and output drop.

Table 2.4. GDP Growth in Transition Economies
(percentage change from previous year), 1990-98

	1990	1991	1992	1993	1994	1995	1996	1997	1998	1999	Year Growth Started
Central & Eastern Europe	-7.0	-14.7	-5.9	-0.4	4.1	5.2	3.3	1.0	3.7	3.4	1994
Baltics	-3.4	-10.6	-26.0	-13.3	-3.4	2.8	4.0	7.9	4.5	-1.2	1995
CIS	-3.3	-8.1	-21.2	-11.4	-15.4	-5.8	-0.4	1.3	2.3	3.7	1997
Armenia	-5.5	-11.7	-41.8	-8.8	5.4	6.9	5.9	3.3	7.3	3.3	1994

Sources: National authorities; IMF estimates.

Armenia's growth is strongly correlated with its macroeconomic stabilization efforts, as it is for the other transition economies that experienced a restoration of economic growth. However, macroeconomic stabilization, while a necessary condition for growth, is not sufficient to sustain growth. Cross-country studies of transition have pointed to the role of systemic/structural reforms (i.e. institutional, legal, ownership and political changes within the economy) to promote growth. One measure of the overall reform effort is the Liberalization Index introduced by de Melo, Denizer and Gelb[14]. The Liberalization Index is a composite of various sub-indices and is available up to 1995. These sub-indices measure: 1) internal price liberalization; 2) privatization and new entry regulations; and 3) trade and exchange reform. The EBRD prepares a similar reform index, which also includes banking

---

[11] Based on the data from the National Statistical Service, this share maybe as high as 25-30% of GDP.

[12] It is estimated that Armenian residents hold up more than US$150 million in cash, which amounts to 7.5% of GDP and exceeds the amount of dram cash in circulation.

[13] This is taken from a sample of 26 transition economies including 10 economies in Central and Eastern Europe, the Baltic countries, 12 countries in the FSU and Mongolia. See Fischer, Sahay and Begh (1996) "Economies in Transition: The Beginnings of Growth."

[14] De Melo, Denizer and Gelb (1996).

reform in addition to those reforms measured in the Liberalization Index by de Melo, Denizer and Gelb. A composite of the two indices is given in Table 2.5.

Table 2.5. Reform Index in Transition Economies

	1990	1991	1992	1993	1994	1995	1996	1997	1998	1999	Year Growth Started
Central & Eastern Europe and Baltics	0.33	0.55	0.71	0.77	0.76	0.69	0.71	0.73	0.78	0.79	1994
CIS	0.04	0.10	0.29	0.36	0.45	0.50	0.53	0.54	0.58	0.57	1997
Armenia	0.04	0.13	0.39	0.42	0.42	0.53	0.60	0.63	0.67	0.68	1994

Note: Index is measured within the interval of 0-1, with 0 = to centrally planned and 1 = market economies.
Sources: De Melo, Denizer and Gelb (1996); EBRD Transition Reports; Havrylyshyn, Izvorski and van Rooden (1998).

While Armenia's Reform Index is consistently higher than the CIS average compared to the CEE and the Baltic countries, the regions with the leading reformers as measured by the index, Armenia's Reform Index is lower.

Various studies of growth in transition economies have found that the reforms, reflected by the Reform Index, have a strong and positive overall impact on growth.[15] Reforms appear to have an initial cost in that growth was found to be negatively associated with contemporaneous reforms. However, when controlling for other factors, lagged values of the reform variable have shown a positive effect on growth. Based on the cross-country statistical models, the report argues that without considerable additional reform effort, which would result *inter alia* in improvements in the business environment, it is quite unlikely that Armenia' medium-term average growth rates would be able to exceed 3.5-4% a year (See Appendix for mode details on application of cross-country growth models to Armenia data).

2.3.   Structure and Sources of Growth

Table 2.6 suggests that, based on the official data on national accounts, the largest part (43%) of the real GDP increase in 1994-99 came from the expansion in the service sector. Agriculture contributed an additional 30%. The contribution of the industrial sector, where Armenia has the strongest potential comparative advantage –skilled labor, was the smallest (13.3%).

Table 2.6. Structure of GDP Growth in 1994-99, 1994 Constant Prices, percent

	Real growth rates	Contribution to growth of GDP at factor costs
GDP at market prices	29.4	
Net indirect taxes	228.1	
GDP at factor cost	23.0	100.0
lture	15.5	30.3
Industry	10.1	13.3
Construction	46.5	20.0
Services	53.9	42.5

Source: Staff estimates based on the data from the NSS.

Main factors responsible for Armenia's rather strong growth performance in the second half of the 90s include:

---

[15] For example, see Selowsky and Martin (1997) and Havrylyshyn, Izvorski and van Rooden (1998).

- Energy. Successful rehabilitation of the energy sector removed one of the major constraints for economic development. Electricity supply has become much more reliable and is available on a 24 hour-a-day basis around the country (compared to several hours a day in 1993). This happened due to: (a) re-starting of the Nuclear power plant (one-third of power generation); (b) financial rehabilitation of the sector through improved payment discipline and increased electricity tariffs; and (c) continued access to somewhat subsidized imported energy inputs, including nuclear fuel.

- Agriculture. Radical privatization of rural land in 1991 and elimination of state farming set the scene for a stable recovery in the sector, based on an adequate incentive framework. The sector also benefited from the blockade, which made food imports more expensive and expanded the room for efficient import substitution. As a result, by 1999, agricultural output has almost fully recovered its pre-transition outputs.

- Services. As for all other economies in transition, business services (banking, telecommunication, insurance) experienced the strongest growth (but from a low base). Also, closer to the end of the period, growth in more traditional services (retail, catering, tourism, personal services) has improved (but remained limited mostly to Yerevan), fueled by recovery in personal incomes.

- External assistance. Over the last decade, Armenia became the major recipient of international assistance[16]: and in 2000 it expects to receive about US$240 million (11% of GDP) in total through a combination of official transfers and concessional loans or about US$70 per capita.[17] Armenia also benefits from considerable amounts of humanitarian and technical assistance that are not reflected in the budget. While international assistance has been substantial in all years since the 1988 Earthquake, it largely expanded since 1994, after the first successful IMF agreement. Table 2.7 describes the major macroeconomic impact of the official development assistance, among which its contribution to public investments is the most noticeable.[18]

- Private transfers. Armenia continues to benefit from the considerable inflow of remittances and private transfers (currently at 8-9% of GDP a year), which are mostly coming from relatives who either recently emigrated or who are temporarily working abroad (Box 2.1). According to household surveys, not less than 15% of families were recipients of regular private transfers. And for about 8% of households such transfers represented a major element of income support in 1999. This inflow was also lower in the early 90s, before explosion in emigration and before macroeconomic stabilization in Russia – a country where a large portion of recent Armenian emigrants live.

---

[16] Total wage fund of local labor, employed either by external development organizations or by expatriates, is estimated to exceed 1% of the official GDP.

[17] Assuming a population of 3.1 million.

[18] Note that the actual contribution was even higher due to a considerable overestimation, as shown below in the Investment section, of total investments by national statistics.

Table 2.7. Donor Budget Support in Armenia, 1995-99, as percent of GDP

	1995	1996	1997	1998	1999
Total budget support from donors	8.7	7.3	7.5	4.6	7.3
of which :					
Grants	3.7	1.5	1.8	1.5	1.5
Investment type of financing	N/A	2.2	2.2	2.3	3.4
Other external financing	5.1	3.7	3.6	0.8	2.4
Memo: Donor-funded investment as % of total investments in the economy	N/A	12.1	12.5	12.3	16.0

Source: Staff estimates based on the data from the MOFE.

Box 2.1. Migration in Armenia

In the course of the last 10 years, several migration streams appeared in Armenia. The *first flow* of migration was caused by the devastating 1988 earthquake, as a result of which around 200,000 people had left the country and resettled mostly in other FSU republics. The origin of the *second flow* in 1988-1990 was the Nagorno-Karabakh (NK) conflict. Combined, Armenia received around 500,000 refugees from NK and Azerbaijan proper. At the same time, about 170,000 Azeris had fled Armenia.

And, finally, the *third and the largest flow* of migration from Armenia was triggered by harsh living conditions during the cold winters of 1992-1994, when the country experienced severe energy outages due to a general economic crisis and territorial blockade.

According to some sources, approximately 700,000 Armenians had emigrated during that period, reaching the peak of 250,000 in 1993. Out of this number, the majority had resettled in Russia and few other FSU countries, and only 15% in Western Europe and USA. These numbers do not include seasonal labor migration, which also has expanded in the 90s. Population outflow somehow stabilized in 1996-1997. However, subsequent economic stagnation, turbulent political developments, and especially the infamous terrorist act in the Armenian parliament in October 1999 provided another impetus to further increase emigration.

Despite the widely-discussed effects of Armenia's obvious "brain drain", no serious study has been conducted on this issue to date. Nevertheless, some conclusions could be drawn based on scarce available data: around 30% of emigrants had college degrees, while 50% had at least high school-level education. While theoretically depriving the country of a professionally-qualified and economically-stable population, emigration is a substantial source of income support – according to some estimates, USD450 million is privately transferred annually to Armenia, and about 60-65% comes from recently emigrated Armenians.

Source: Poghossian (2000). Migration in Armenia. Background paper.

2.4.   Limited Income Benefits from Growth

Despite the fact that the average GDP growth rate in 1995-2000 amounted to about 5 percent per year, there is little evidence that growth resulted in any noticeable reduction in poverty, as follows from the recent poverty update, conducted by the World Bank.

The incidence of poverty (using the comparable poverty line based on the minimum food basket and allowances for essential non-food spending) in Armenia between 1996 and 1999 has remained at around 55 percent of the population. However, there has been an important reduction in the number of very poor, as illustrated by Chart 2.5 (very poor are households where consumption falls below the cost of the minimum food basket).

Chart 2.5. Incidence of Poverty

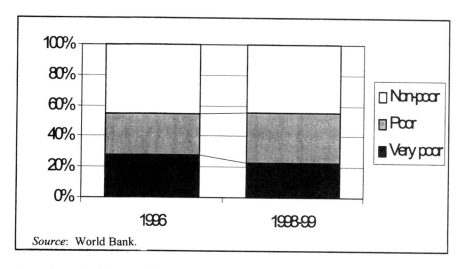

Source: World Bank.

As some people were escaping extreme poverty, the poverty depth has fallen from 21.5 to 19 percent (an average poor in 1996 had a consumption 40% below the poverty line, by 1999 he/she moved closer to the poverty line falling short by 34% percent), and a substantial reduction in the severity of poverty (from 11.1 to 9 percent) has occurred. Almost all groups shared in this improvement, but the largest gains were recorded for urban dwellers and for the rural population residing in the most productive agricultural areas (valleys). Two socio-economic groups have benefited most from the reduction in poverty depth and severity: full-time wage employees (whose risk of being very poor dropped from 25 to 15 percent), and self-employed (20 percent of them were very poor in 1996, by 1999 this share declined to 12 percent). Pensioners have improved their living standards, though only slightly. On the other hand, the risk and severity of poverty remained unchanged or slightly worsened for the unemployed and economically inactive.

The analysis below of employment and wage trends provides some insights why the recent growth has such limited impact on real incomes and poverty. In brief, it derived from highly unequal distribution of gains associated with recent economic growth:

- While the employed have benefited from economic growth, the growth did not lead to the increase in the number of jobs available;

- Growth had too narrow a basis – for instance, no growth in value added was recorded in industry, while growth was the most impressive in sectors with low employment;

- Growth did not lead to a sizable increase in the real wage bill in the largest (by employment) sectors.

While the average real wage in the economy grew at a higher pace than GDP, this gross was highly uneven across sectors, and was not accompanied by growth in total employment. The 1998 average real wage was about 60% percent higher than in 1995, while GDP (at factor cost) was only 12.2 percent higher. The economy-wide wage bill increased at a slower pace than the real wage -- by 44 percent in real terms – due to falling employment (by 9.4 percent). As a result, the non-employed labor force has surged by 54.9 percent.[19]

The sectoral breakdown of the above indicators is presented in Table 2.8. The following observations stem from the data:

---

[19] Probably overestimated due to emigration.

- Real wages have grown in all sectors except agriculture[20]; however, the improvement in wage levels has disproportionately benefited labor in a few relatively well-to-do sectors that employed a small percentage of total labor;

- The backbone sectors (agriculture and industry) that in 1998 employed 58 percent of workers, either kept the same amount of labor (agriculture) or intensively shed labor (industry). The total wage bill generated by these two sectors has declined;

- Well-paying sectors (construction, transport and communication), showed an increase in the total wage bill and yet shed a lot of labor. The best-paying financial sector almost halved its labor force while giving a very significant pay rise to the remaining workers. Its total wage bill fell by almost one-third;

- Another sector that generated the most significant percentage increase in the real wage bill was public administration. Its employment has slightly decreased while real wage has skyrocketed (implying a large increase in budget costs albeit from an extremely low relative level);

- Other primarily budgetary sectors (health and education) have generated a sound percentage increase in the wage bill but their wage levels remain extremely low and employment has sharply decreased.

Table 2.8. Wages and Employment by Sector

	Monthly Wage		Employment/contingent		
	1998 (AMD)	Real Growth 1995-98, percent	1998 thousand	Real Growth 1995-98, percent	Wage Bill: Real Growth 1995-98, percent
Labor force	--	--	1,860	3	--
Total Employment	18,000	59.3	1,337	-9.4	44.3
Non-employed labor force	--	--	523	54.9	--
Agriculture and forestry	10,206	-31.8	567	2.7	-30.0
Industry	21,278	101.5	209	-31.0	39.0
Construction	31,639	117	57	-25.0	62.8
Transport and communications	28,606	77.5	51	-3.8	70.8
Services and others Including:	14,309	179.2	453	-7.9	157.1
Public administration	20,616	293.8	29	-2.0	285.9
Credit, finance and insurance	41,918	873.6	5	-44.4	441.3
Health and social security	8,939	118.8	78	-9.3	98.5
Education, culture and arts	7,662	97.2	155	-13.9	69.8

Source: NSS and staff calculations.

---

[20] The accuracy of the wage estimate in agriculture raises doubts. The sector is composed of a large number of family farms with a leaning towards subsistence-type economy. A large portion of labor payments on these farms is either made in-kind or captured as proprietor's surplus. Under these conditions, the better way to single out labor share in output would be to calculate labor surplus rather than wages. No such data are available though.

Overall, large variations in rates of sectoral growth, inflation and employment combined resulted in a heavy concentration of winners from the recent growth in Armenia. Table 2.9 presents a decomposition of change in the sectoral real wage bill into changes in the share of wages in value added, the ratio of the sectoral price index to CPI, and the growth of sectoral value added.

Table 2.9. Changes in Share of Wages in Value Added, Price Ratios, and Growth, by Sector, 1995-98, Indices

Sector	Real Wage bill	Share of wages in value added	Ratio of sectoral price index to CPI	Growth in value added
GDP at factor cost	1.443	1.226	1.049	1.122
Including: Agriculture and forestry	0.70	0.765	0.834	1.097
Industry (manufacturing, mining, and energy)	1.390	1.387	1.005	0.997
Construction	1.628	0.998	1.130	1.444
Transport and communications	1.708	1.173	0.926	1.573
Services and other*	2.571	1.562	1.471	1.119

*Calculated as a residual and includes statistical errors.
Source: Staff calculations.

As seen from the table, an almost ten percent agricultural growth was offset by unfavorable price dynamics (prices for agricultural products lagged behind the CPI inflation, which was reflected in the sharply negative change in price ratio) and by a increase in labor share in output. As a result, total real wages generated in the sector decreased. In contrast, industry prices moved in line with CPI. An increase in the industrial wage bill resulted from an increase of labor share in value added, while output stagnated.

For industry and agriculture combined (with almost two-thirds of total employment), the wage bill declined, which was further aggravated by negative impact on real consumption of several external factors such as a reduction in foreign transfers (both remittances and humanitarian assistance) since late 1998 and a decline in implicit (non-cash) subsidies to population (e.g., in the energy sector). In the budget sector, the welfare impact of growth and salary increases was additionally reduced by significant wage arrears and payment delays.

The fact that growth disproportionately benefits workers in a few relatively well-to-do and relatively small sectors is not particularly surprising and is well documented in post-import-substitution economies e.g. in Latin America. Moreover, such a concentration of winners may signal ongoing economic restructuring[21] – adjustment according to emerging comparative advantage of the economy. A pronounced increase in industrial duality, e.g. emergence of high-wage high value added segments amid the stagnant majority of industries, could be a positive sign that may trigger new economic dynamics. The central policy questions in this respect are the following:

- How to promote linkages from these growing segments to the rest of the economy and avoid the enclave character of growth;

- How to ensure a decent degree of redistribution and expand a number of those who benefit from growth.

---

[21] But may also reflect an effect generated by a powerful distributional coalition.

Given some features of the Armenian economy (country isolation and existence of a number of highly-educated professional groups), one should not be surprised by the current concentration of winners in Armenia. About 1,000 employees in the Armenia diamond industry are currently responsible for US$70 million in manufacturing exports (30% of total manufacturing exports in 1999). Another thousand employees produce as much as US$18-20 million in exported software. While the economic impact of these sectors on overall living standards is rather modest at the moment, these and similar sectoral examples provide the greatest longer-term opportunity for Armenia, which relates to a prospect of emerging high value added export-oriented clusters.

The previous two sections help clarify "the mystery of growth without poverty reduction", which has been observed in Armenia over the last 5-6 years. The main explanation of the puzzle relates to a narrow sectoral and enterprise base of growth, when downsizing of traditional enterprises had a stronger impact on employment and average incomes than expansion of new companies. The established "Soviet" firms have continued to shed their labor, forced by further compression of traditional markets in the FSU and by tightening of budget constraints. The overall growth was generated by a limited number of new or fully-restructured firms with relatively high productivity and low demand for labor. Entry of new labor intensive SMEs was insufficient. In addition, potential income gains from growth in the agriculture and budget sectors were largely wiped out by respectively unfavorable changes in relative prices and wage arrears.

2.5.   Employment Trends

A rather disappointing outcome of growth in the period 1994-99 in terms of employment generation should be reviewed in the context of the macroeconomic development over the transition. Charts 2.6 – 2.8 compare trends in output and employment over the past decade in Armenia, Central and Easter Europe and Baltics and the CIS. A sharp contrast between CEE and the CIS is immediately apparent as well as the resemblance of Armenia to other CIS countries. In the CEE, the level of total employment has a similar U-shape pattern to GDP, but the recovery in employment took place about two years after GDP started growing again; in the CIS, the initial adjustment to aggregate employment was much smaller relative to the fall in GDP, and shedding of excess labor continued. These charts show that Armenia suffered from a larger fall in output at the outset of transition than CIS countries on average. This evidently led to a substantial labor hoarding on aggregate. Thus, falling employment in the context of economic growth of the late 90s can also be interpreted as a lagged result of low employment elasticity with respect to growth at the outset of transition.

Substantial labor hoarding still has been a characteristic of the Armenian economy in 1996. The survey revealed that up to one-third of listed employees in industry were not performing any work and have been on administrative leave for a prolonged period of time. The situation has been similar in 1999, though at a lower level of employment[22]. The existence of the gap between the number of listed employees and those who actually work means that there will remain a tendency to decline in the aggregate number of employees as the employment lists adjust to the actual labor market situation.

---

[22] In November 1996, out of 370,000 enlisted employees in industry only 200,000 were performing any work. In January-September 1999, among all enlisted employees 20 percent (96 out of 512,000) were on administrative leave.

Chart 2.6. Trends in Output and Total Employment in CIS

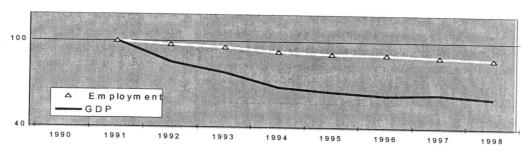

Notes: Right axis: GDP and Total Employment (index=100 at 1991 for CIS and 100 at 1990 for CEE).
Sources: Data for 1990-99 represent the most recent official estimates of emloyment and GDP as reflected in publications from the national authorities, the IMF, the World Bank and the OECD.

Chart 2.7. Trends in Output and Total Employment in CEF

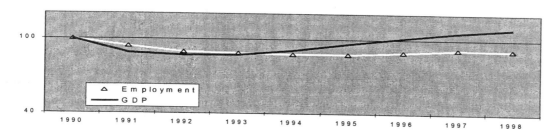

Notes: Right axis: GDP and Total Employment (index=100 at 1991 for CIS and 100 at 1990 for CEE).
Sources: Data for 1990-99 represent the most recent official estimates of emloyment and GDP as reflected in publications from the national authorities, the IMF, the World Bank and the OECD.

Chart 2.8. Trends in Output and Total Employment in Armenia

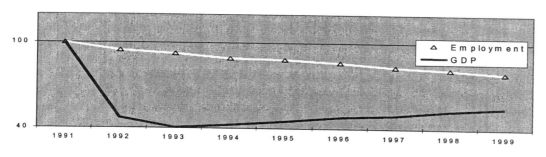

Notes: Right axis: GDP and Total Employment (index=100 at 1991 for CIS and 100 at 1990 for CEE).
Sources: Data for 1990-99 represent the most recent official estimates of emloyment and GDP as reflected in publications from the national authorities, the IMF, the World Bank and the OECD.

However, macroeconomic factors of lagged employment adjustment do not exhaust all developments on the labor market. Behind a relative stability of aggregate employment there has been a deep reallocation of employees between sectors; agriculture has absorbed labor released from other sectors. Between 1990 and 1995, agriculture absorbed 1/4 million new workers, while industry and construction have released 300,000 workers. Agriculture effectively acted as a safety net for the unemployed and displaced workers in the environment of a drastic fall in real incomes. The downside of this was a fall in the productivity in the economy, as more workers moved to a relatively low value added activity. After 1995, structural changes in official employment have been minor compared to continuing labor shedding in industry (which lost almost 100,000 workers between 1995 and 1998).

There are several important reasons to be careful while using official data on employment. Specifically, official employment statistics from CIS (and Armenia is no exception) fail to take into account the broad extent of adjustment of actual working hours. Consequently, a significant number of workers who are formally considered employed, in reality are either unemployed or have dropped out of the labor force altogether. On the other hand, the situation in the labor market has become more and more influenced by the informal sector. Given the weaknesses of the statistical system in capturing small-scale enterprises and individual start-ups (which are only covered by episodic surveys), it is not surprising that official estimates of employment have become less and less reliable. One possibility to address this difficulty is to use household survey data to gain insights into the actual labor market status of the population. Applying a set of internationally-accepted methodologies (recommended by ILO), we indeed find substantial differences between the official employment numbers and survey-based results.

The survey revealed that less people report employment than assumed by the statistical records. The gap is large: while official statistics report that around 1.4 million. people work, only one million respondents confirmed that they had employment (whether paid or unpaid) at the time of the survey[23]. On the other hand, unemployment, as measured by household surveys, stands at much higher levels than suggested by registration statistics (400,000 instead of 170,000 registered unemployed). The Chart 2.9 shows little change in the employment situation between 1996 and 1999.

Chart 2.9. Unemployment by Age Group

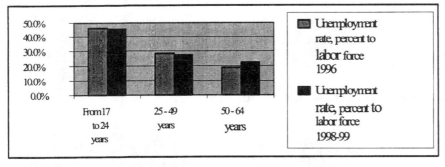

Source: World Bank

Not only is unemployment high, there is also a problem of low labor market activity, as many dropped out of the labor force. Table 2.10 is based on labor force survey results on the share of non-employment in population by age groups for selected countries in the region. It turns out that Armenia is an outlier in this group (which includes Bulgaria, a country with the worst labor market situation in CEE). Almost half of the prime working age adults (25-49 years old) do not have gainful employment.

Parallel to high unemployment there is also widespread hidden employment. The legal practice in Armenia is not to count as unemployed able-bodied members of rural households that own land (these people cannot register as unemployed and claim benefits). Around 200,000 working age family members of farmers reported being unemployed or inactive. On the other hand, there are many family members of the urban self-employed who presumably help their family heads, but report themselves as being out of "real" employment. This adds over 200,000 to the estimates of employment in urban areas. But even with these adjustments, over a third of the labor force is not gainfully employed. Chart 2.10 shows the distribution of the labor force in Armenia by labor market status.

---

[23] The estimate for the population for the period of the survey was put at 3.1 million instead of 3.8 million officially registered.

Table 2.10. Non-Employment Rates for Armenia and Selected Countries in the Region

Age group	Armenia				Russian Federation				Bulgaria			
	15-24	25-49	50-60	**Total**	15-24	25-49	50-60	**Total**	15-24	25-49	50-60	**Total**
Total	82%	48%	59%	**58%**	62%	20%	27%	**30%**	80%	25%	35%	**41%**
Male	77%	36%	45%	**47%**	60%	16%	16%	**27%**	80%	23%	37%	**40%**
Female	86%	58%	71%	**67%**	64%	23%	44%	**33%**	81%	28%	30%	**42%**

Note: Non-employed are unemployed and out of the labor force.
Source: Armenia - SDS 1996 HH survey, OECD (1998).

Chart 2.10. Armenia - Structure of Working Age Population by Labor Market Status

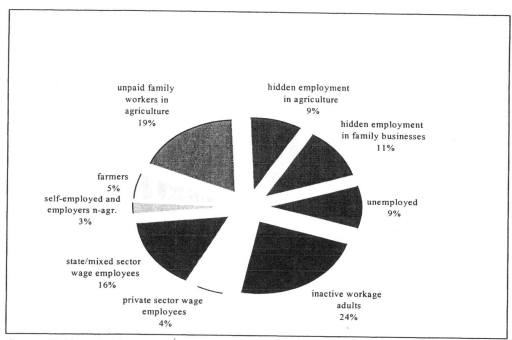

Source: SDS household survey 1998-88; working age is between 17 and 60 years.

Using the survey data and taking into account both the extent of "inflated" employment and hidden employment, we find that the share of the private sector in employment has increased from 57 percent in 1996 to 76 percent in 1998. However, this increase was driven primarily by the increase in the number of own-account workers (self-employed) and their family helpers both in urban and rural areas, but not by the expansion of paid employment in private firms. Though the latter group has increased substantially, it remains too small (from 2 percent of the labor force in 1995 to 4 percent in 1998) to influence overall trends at the labor market. In terms of absolute numbers of hired workers, private sector wage employment (around 90,000) lags behind the state and mixed ownership sectors (around 320,000). This employment is concentrated in urban areas (82 percent), primarily in Yerevan (60 percent), and in several economic sectors.

The serious weakness of formal employment in the enterprise sector (both public and private) is especially striking when one looks at the data on the structure of payroll taxpayers. These data, provided by Armenia's Social Insurance Fund, represent the core of country's formal employment and covered about 427 thousand employees (one third of the total employment) in 2000. Such data suggest that about a half of total formal employees were working in traditional budget-related sectors such as education, health, culture, and local government. At the same time, the combined share of industry and construction was only 17%.

As more families started their own businesses and new private firms expanded, the gap between official records of employment and the real situation has increased. To assess the extent and composition of informal employment, we make a comparison of the official structure of employment with the household survey generated estimates based on actual work performed during the reference week in 1998-99 (Table 2.11). Positive values for the discrepancy between official reports and survey data show sectors where actual employment is greater than recorded officially, arguably because of the existence of the informal sector. On the other hand, negative numbers point to the existence of inflated employment records in official reporting.

Table 2.11. Employment by Sectors: Survey-Based Versus Official Estimates for 1998-99 (thousand)

Sector	Household Survey	Official, 1998	Discrepancy
Agriculture and forestry*	763	*566*	+198
Industry and construction	95	*266*	-171
Transport, trade, communications **	229	*164*	+66
Other services (private and public)	227	*341*	-114
Total employment	*1,315*	*1,337*	-22

* Note: All inactive or working age unemployed members of rural households with land are counted as employed in agriculture.
** Note: All inactive or working age unemployed members of households with income from self-employment or valuable sales are counted as employed in trade.
Source: NSS and staff estimates.

Agriculture and trade correspond to two prevailing types of the informal sector in the economy: subsistence agriculture dictated by the need for survival and urban informal businesses often also of subsistence nature. In terms of sheer numbers, subsistence agriculture has the largest share of employment. It is a mere survival strategy (the value added per family helper in subsistence gardening in 1998 is estimated at around US$60 annually). The informal sector in the urban economy is characterized by a much greater productivity and a more complex structure than the rural informal sector.

The household survey gives a picture of the emerging small scale private firms in urban areas. There is a core group of individuals leading small businesses (according to survey estimates - around 50,000 active self employed, which fits with 47,000 individual entrepreneurs according to the official registry in late 1998). Many of them use help from their family members, almost 200,000 people. In addition, there are as many as 5,000 entrepreneurs who hire labor in urban areas, employing around 20,000 workers throughout the year, mostly on casual contracts (without a formal agreement), often invisible to official statistics. Thus, the size and number of microfirms in Armenia is indeed very small: on average 4 employees, covering not more than 5 percent of the total wage employment. The pool of workers that are in and out of this casual employment is much greater: an estimated 100,000 individuals who were unemployed in reference week of the survey had been temporarily employed during the course of the previous year. Some of these "marginal" workers also form a group of seasonal migrant workers employed abroad. Therefore, own account workers with their family helpers and small start-ups employed combined exceed number of those currently employed by formal private sector firms.

Armenia does not fully utilize the potential of non-agricultural self-employed and small entrepreneurs to generate employment: they account for only 4 percent of total employment, while in successful transition economies their share exceeds 10 percent (Poland - 14 percent, Hungary -12 percent). These numbers indicate existence of serious barriers for establishment and development of small scale enterprises, and thus for employment generation. The number of individuals who have tried in the past to establish a business exceeds 100,000 - twice the actual number of entrepreneurs and self-account workers.

So far, the dynamics of employment in Armenia have been determined by the absorption of labor in agriculture, small entrepreneurship and by labor shedding in industry. Thus, it is important to monitor closely future changes in the structure of employment rather than just follow aggregate employment numbers. A large segment of the labor market in fact is currently operated by intra-family relationships. It is also often a low-productivity and low earning segment. The existence of this segment of unpaid family workers means that the dynamics of employment in the future are going to be far too complex to fit into the simple scheme of employment generation by economic growth. Future changes to poverty would depend not as much on general employment trends but more closely react to the evolution of employment structure.

2.6. New Entry: Just Not Enough to Make a Difference

While an increasing role of the private sector in the economy has been a fundamental feature of transition to the market, recent analysis suggests that the structure of the emerging private sector is as important as the rate of its expansion. There is sufficient evidence to claim that the two main segments of the private sector – newly privatized traditional firms and entirely new, usually small, de novo companies – have rather a different impact on economic dynamics during the transition period.[24] Indeed, most of the growth in the leading economies in transition, including Poland, Czech Republic, Slovak Republic and Slovenia was due to expanded activities of small-scaled, owner-operated businesses.[25] In Russia, regional variations in economic growth reveal close correspondence between the number of small business legal entities and regional growth.[26] De novo firms just proved to be more productive and more innovative everywhere during the transition, and as such they became the main agents of the economy-wide restructuring. Reallocation of labor and capital from traditional to de novo firms proved to be a prominent source of increase in aggregate productivity and growth.

The recent empirical evidence from Central and Eastern Europe suggests that there is a threshold in the expansion of small businesses, which, if not achieved, makes the return to a sustainable growth path problematic. This threshold value seems to be around 40 percent for the shares of small firms in both total employment and value added.[27] This indicator permits the division of all transition economies in two groups. On the one hand, leading reformers in Central Europe and the Baltics have these shares higher than 50 percent, and in this respect their economic structure has become increasingly similar to that of such EU members as Greece and Spain. These economies have experienced high and sustained growth since the mid 90s . On the other hand, both shares remain low in most slow growing economies of the FSU and southeastern Europe. In these economies, labor shed from non-viable traditional enterprises did not migrate to new firms, but instead largely moved to low productive activities in the informal sector and especially into subsistence agriculture. The latter trend remains quite relevant to Armenia.

---

[24] Mitra and Selowsky (2000), Havrylyshyn and McGettigan (1999).
[25] Ernst (1997), Kontorovich (1999).
[26] Berkowitz and De Jong (1999).
[27] Mitra and Selowsky (2000).

While the incidence of small de novo firms in Armenia is much higher than in several larger FSU economies, such as Russia and Ukraine, the Armenian de novo sector remains too small to make a critical contribution to overall growth patterns. There is an insufficient number of active new companies and they do not grow sufficiently enough to absorb excessive labor. Also, as mentioned above, the incidence of urban self-employment in Armenia is at least 3 times lower compared to leading economies in transition. This is another indicator of fundamental weaknesses in recent growth, which is a reflection of existing barriers for both new entry and factor reallocation.

Table 2.12 shows changes in an overall number of registered companies in Armenia between 1994-2000. These are gross numbers on registrations, and they provide a positively biased picture. By late 2000, more than 44,000 business entities were registered in Armenia, which gives 14.2 businesses per 1,000 inhabitants. This is rather a decent level of entrepreneurship. However, too many of these registered firms do not operate. It is estimated that Armenia currently has only about 30,000 active businesses or less than 10 per 1,000 inhabitants[28], and the growth of the number of firms have been slow recently. Meanwhile, modern market economies generate many more SMEs: e.g. Germany has 37 registered SMEs per 1,000 inhabitants, Slovenia – 45, USA – 74.

Table 2.12. Number of Registered Business Entities, by year end

Years	1994	1995	1996	1997	1998	1999	2000
Number of registered business entities	5,089	21,238	29,836	37,687	41,241	43,327	44,164
Growth rate, percent		317	40	26	9	5	2

Source: NSS.

The current number of registrations accumulated due to two main processes. First, an intensive small privatization program, largely completed in 1995-96, increased the number of legal entities in the economy almost six-fold. Second, further expansion in 1997-2000, which has been going at a slower pace but still provided an additional increase in registrations of about 50%.

The real situation with a small business is, however, much less positive. As several business surveys revealed, most registered businesses do not operate at all. The surveys of small businesses conducted by the National Statistical Service (NSS) in 1997-98 showed that between 56 and 61% of participating businesses remained inactive during the year of survey. A similar 1999 survey showed a further increase in this share, up to about 80%[29]. Overall, as estimated by the NSS, Armenia currently has less than 9,000 operating businesses, not much more than it had in late 1995, and about 40% less compared to its peak in 1998.

It is also indicative that the net flow of new registrations slowed down considerably in 1999-2000. Moreover, the rate of company liquidation increased: in 2000, per each 3 new registrations, two companies were liquidated.

Table 2.13 gives a broad structure of the new private activity by value added created by its different segments. It reveals that in Armenia about 60% of GDP is produced outside of traditional enterprises. This is a high level that is similar to many leading transition economies. However, the structure of such a de novo private sector in Armenia is quite different. Less than a quarter of the overall business activity of the de novo sector is associated with registered companies. The rest derives from predominantly low productivity activities in agriculture, commerce, and urban services.

---

[28] However, it is more than in Russia, where has only 5.6 firms per 1,000 inhabitants.

[29] This may be compared to the data on Russia. In the mid 90s, 30% of business in Moscow did not operate without formal liquidation (Kontorovich, 1999).

Such a structure of the new private sector confirms two other main features of the Armenia business environment. The first relates to prevailing informality of business transactions. Entrepreneurs are frequently forced to stay in the informal sector by the existing regulatory regime and enforcement practices, especially by those in tax administration. Second, many active entrepreneurs pursue survival, defensive strategies. These are "forced entrepreneurs", who have been waiting for an opportunity to return to their traditional occupation as hired labor. Such businesses have a rather limited development potential.

Table 2.13. Share of Various Segments of the New Private Sector in GDP, percent

Family farms	25
Individual entrepreneurs	6
Informal (non-registered) business activity of households	16
De novo firms in industry	4
De novo firms in other sectors	9
TOTAL	60

Source: Staff estimates based on the various NSS data.

Table 2.14 gives a breakdown of the industrial sector by the "age" of operating firms. It suggests 8-fold gap in productivity between new and traditional firms. This productivity potential reflects unrealized potential for growth in the economy. Economy-wide barriers for factor reallocation keep this potential on hold.

Table 2.14. Traditional and De Novo Firms in Industry, 1999

	Number of firms	Output, billion dram	Total employment, thousands	Average employment	Productivity, thousand dram per employee
Traditional firms	928	169.73	81.20	87.5	2,090.3
De novo firms	249	113.76	6.84	27.5	16,631.6
Total	1177	283.49	88.04	74.8	3,220.0

Source: NSS.

The last section of this chapter provides additional evidence to confirm that, despite all existent weaknesses of new industrial firms, they as a group managed to over-perform the traditional large firm. This underlines both current costs of depressed new entry as well as potential gains of addressing barriers for their development.

2.7. Evolution of Industrial Structure, 1988-1999

In the early 80s, Armenia reached the level of the most industrialized Soviet republics with specialization in high technology sectors, such as electronics, mechanical and electrical engineering and chemicals. About 40% of GDP has been produced in industry (this includes manufacturing, energy, and mining), which has been the most dynamic part of the economy. However, the industrial structure of Armenia proved to be the most vulnerable to disintegration of the Soviet Union. As a result, the transitional shock was rather severe: industry was the sector of economy that was the most badly hit in the early 90s by both unfavorable moves in relative prices and the collapse of traditional markets. Also, the recovery in industry was the weakest among other aggregated sectors of the economy.

Evolution of the Armenia industrial structure in the 90s helps to clarify the overall scale of economic transformation as well as prospects for further economic recovery. Charts 2.11-2.13[30] show shares of individual industrial subsectors in 1988, 1994, and 1999. At its peak, Armenian industry was

---

[30] Note that the NSA does not produce any separate statistics on the software sector.

dominated by two sectors – machinery (engineering) and light industry (textile, garments, and footwear) – which produced more than 55% of total output. These were exactly the sectors which were hit the most everywhere in the FSU. These shocks related to collapse in demand (especially in defense production), opening markets to import competition (especially in consumer goods), and price liberalization that eliminated implicit energy and input subsidies. In Armenia, these common shocks were exaggerated by blockades, which made it even more difficult for Armenian enterprises to keep their traditional markets in the FSU. The share of the machinery sector declined from 31.6% in 1988 to 20.1% in 1994 and to only 3.3% in 1999. The compression of light industry was even greater: from 24.4% in 1988 to 1.4% in 1999.

Chart 2.11. Industrial Output Structure in 1988

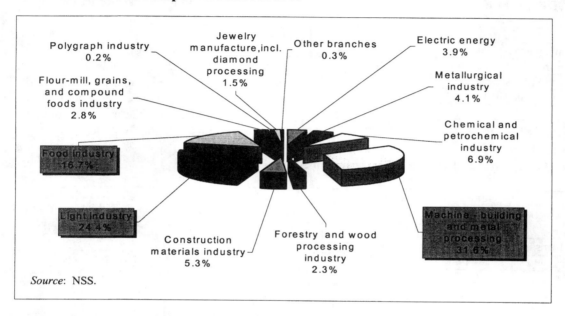

Source: NSS.

Chart 2.12. Industrial Output Structure in 1994

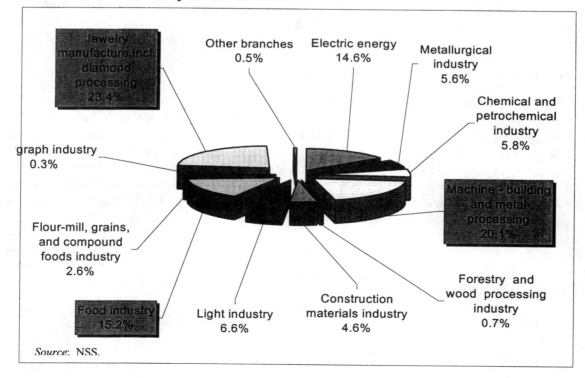

Source: NSS.

Chart 2.13. Industrial Output Structure in 1999

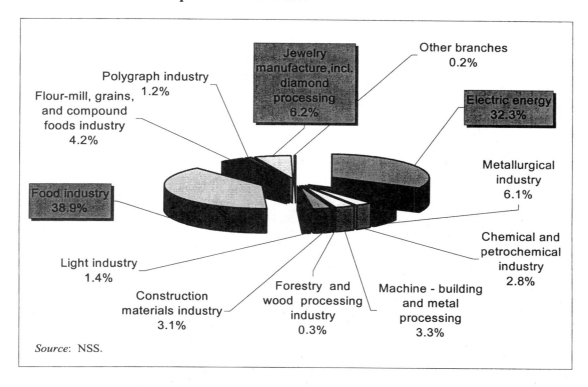

Source: NSS.

The winners of industrial restructuring were power generation and food processing sectors, which increased their combined share from about 20% to 38.5%. In addition, significant expansion also took place in three smaller sectors – jewelry, metallurgy (mining), and publishing.

Tables 2.15 and 2.16 present additional data on sectoral variation in real growth rates and relative price developments. By late 1994, total industrial production in Armenia declined to about 38% of its peak in 1988. Post-stabilization recovery was rather weak, and the index of industrial production increased by only 7% between 1994 and 1999. While most sectors expanded during this period, the machinery sector continued to decline. The growth was the strongest in mining and metallurgy (driven by a recovery of exports in ores after the cease-fire) and construction materials (pushed by expansion in public investments, which in a large part were externally funded).

The analysis of the data suggests that a significant disconnect exists between the current industrial and export structure and Armenia's potential longer-term comparative advantages. So far, the strongest growth took place in the subsectors where it would be quite difficult to sustain. For instance, in mining and metallurgy, Armenia does not have a sufficiently strong mineral base (Maraboli, 2000). In addition, high transportation costs could be a binding constraint for exports of ores and metals. In power generation, Armenia has benefited from the existing excess capacity (which is mostly a legacy from Soviet times) but it will not be able to stay as a low-cost producer of electricity beyond the lifetime of the existing power plants. In food processing, while there is still room for further import substitution, significant growth in food export would be difficult because, compared to its neighbors, Armenia, with its mountainous terrain, has serious comparative disadvantages in agriculture.

Table 2.15. Variation in Real Growth Rates Among Industrial Subsectors, 1988-99

	Real output indexes, 1988-99		
	88-99 (1988=100)	88-94 (1988=100)	94-99 (1994=100)
Total Industry	41.0	38.3	107.1
Electric energy	33.2	33.7	98.5
Ferrous metallurgy	142.1	28.9	492.4
Non-ferrous metallurgy	42.4	17.3	245.7
Chemical and petrochemical	28.4	23.2	122.0
Machinery and metal processing	12.3	40.0	30.7
Forestry and wood processing	38.4	23.4	164.3
Construction materials	29.9	16.1	186.0
Light industry	45.2	33.2	136.2
Food industry	34.5	26.9	128.3
Flour-mill, grains, and compound food	35.3	64.0	55.2
Polygraph industry	222.1	160.7	138.2
Jewelry (incl. diamond processing)	98.8	99.8	99.0
Other branches	313.2	310.6	100.8

Source: Staff estimates based on the data from the NSS.

Table 2.16. Variation in Price Growth Among Industrial Subsectors, 1988-99

	Price indexes, 1989-1999		
	89-99 (1988=100)	89-94 (1988=100)	95-99 (1994=100)
Total Industry	7,150,191	1,127,214	634.3
Electric energy	69,118,774	3,973,007	1739.7
Ferrous metallurgy	...	...	...
Non-ferrous metallurgy	13,178,111	4,015,691	328.2
Chemical and petrochemical	20,036,390	4,638,476	432.0
Machinery and metal processing	3,840,741	852,317	450.6
Forestry and wood processing	14,138,399	2,775,967	509.3
Construction materials industry	21,121,050	2,629,977	803.1
Light industry	5,586,095	652,388	856.3
Food industry, incl. flour-mills	14,002,434	1,122,099	1247.9
Polygraph industry	...	...	...
Jewelry manufacture, incl. diamond processing	...	...	182.7

Source: Staff estimates based on the data from the NSS.

At the same time, the performance of sectors that are expected to become broad areas of Armenia's potential advantage – high value-added and skill demanding, labor intensive, light-weight -- was disappointing. This is clearly a reason for serious concern that poses an additional risk of sustainability of current growth rates.

The strong expansion of the software sector in 1997-2000 (Box 2.2) represents one of the brightest spots in the recent industrial development of Armenia. It is estimated that during 1997-99, output and export of Armenia software companies has been at least doubling each year, and in 1999 it amounted to US$15-20 million. It is a widely held view that the sector has major potential and under favorable circumstances could produce a major spillover effect on the rest of the economy in terms of productivity and global linkages. There is strong interest from Western companies (often owned/managed by Diaspora Armenians), which face a global shortage of programmers and are aware of business opportunities in Armenia. However, at the moment, the software sector remains rather small (about 1,000 employees, not more than 7-8% of the overall merchandise export as officially reported[31]). If not addressed, the current pace of expansion could be undermined by serious constraints related to availability of telecommunication services, lack of institutional infrastructure to provide business development services, shortage of management skills, insufficient protection of property rights for software products, outdated software training in local universities, and a limited pool of available programmers. This is in addition to more general constraints that hamper private sector expansion in the economy – red tape, limited availability of financing, small size of local market, etc.

The Government considers the software sector among its top priorities for its industrial policy. It is expected that the Government IT Strategy would be finalized in the course of 2001.

Box 2.2. High Road to Competitiveness: Emerging Cluster in the Software Industry

Within the former Soviet Union, Armenia specialized in information technology and electronics. The Soviet legacy included a number of R&D facilities (academic institutes, educational and computer centers) and a 6,000-strong force of programmers. During the first years of independence, most traditional organizations stopped their operations, small private companies emerged in the sector, while a large number of programmers emigrated.

The recovery in the sector started in 1995-96 and accelerated since 1997. As in other emerging economies (e.g. Bangalore cluster in India), the Armenia software cluster consists of export-oriented firms (many of which are subsidiaries of Western corporations) doing contract work for the West, more fragile firms working for CIS countries and internal markets, and semi-formal project teams striving to set up formal firms to do contract work for the West. At least 12 US software companies are known to have their subsidiaries in Armenia at present. The number should grow in the coming months. European companies are said to be following suit, with several of them already present in the country. In the view of industry insiders, the low cost of skilled labor is the primary factor attracting foreign investors to the sector. Experienced programmers working for a US-owned firm in Armenia are paid an average of $500 a month, 20 times less than their counterpart in the US. In addition, software has two strong advantages compared to most of the other sectors in Armenia. First, it is basically unaffected by transportation problems. Second, the sector is left outside of interests of influential local clans, which substantially reduces costs of new entry.

The sector produces business, accounting and statistical applications (almost 50% of total sales), internet products as well as learning, entertainment and design-related products. There are already noticeable linkages to other sectors: locally-developed software has been installed in a number of the most advanced enterprises in diamond cutting, engineering, publishing, etc.

"Herein lies our future," says Aleksandr Adamian, deputy directory of HPLA, the Armenia subsidiary of the California-based Heuristic Physics Laboratories. Founded in 1995, HPLA is one of the pioneers of Western hi-tech investment in Armenia. It started off with just 5 programmers and now boasts more than 60. Company officials see the possibility of further expansion. HPLA specializes in the development of special software that is used for detecting defects in electronic microchips. In contrast, Bever Computers is one of those local firms that get most of its orders in Russia. Bever develops computer programs for financial management for Russian defense enterprises, capitalizing on its managers' old Soviet connections.

Source: Poghossian, Alexander and Vahram Stepanyan (2000).

---

[31] All numbers related to the software sector are based on indirect estimates, which in most cases derive from Poghossian and Stepanyan (2000). The official statistics do not distinguish the software sector from other manufacturing and does produce any regular data on sector developments.

2.8.   Export Performance

Export performance is universally accepted as the best benchmark of growth performance. Acceleration of economic development in a number of successful developing countries was export-driven (Boxes 2.3 and 2.4). In Armenia, trends in merchandise export represent the weakest element of Armenia's macroeconomic performance and a major source of macroeconomic vulnerability. The nominal volumes of merchandise export declined by about 15% between 1995 and 1999. Export has shown a stronger growth rate since the middle of 2000. Still, by the end of 2000 it amounted to only 16% of GDP. As a result, the Armenian trade deficit is rather large and amounted to 29% of GDP in 1999. In addition, export trends have been quite volatile, reflecting both the specific nature of some of Armenia's main export products (e.g. jewelry and processed diamonds), weak capabilities of the local private sector, as well as the instability of several of Armenia's main export markets.

Box 2.3. Best Practice in Export Promotion: World Market Trends and "Success" Factors

Many small developing countries (Chile and Mauritius among them) were able to turn-around disappointing growth performance since the 1980s. These success stories cover such diverse sectors as high-value agricultural exports, fish, garments, and assembling of electronic equipment. These country-specific "successes" are often clustered in specialized "niche" markets, which experienced especially rapid expansion. Leading examples are: Thailand (tuna and poultry); Taiwan (pork and fish products), Chile (fruit, tomato paste, fish products); Brazil (frozen concentrated orange juice), Kenya (vegetables). Box 2.4 provides a summary for successful export strategies that were developed in the garment industry in the late 80s.

While export industries differ greatly in terms of technology, international market structure, and market conditions, a number of common factors appear fundamental to export success, and they are quite relevant for Armenia. They include:

(a)   "export booms" coincided with macro-economic and trade policy reforms, which much improved export incentives;

(b)   the private sector has undertaken production, processing and marketing on a commercial risk basis;

(c)   the government's role has been critical in setting appropriate policies, but also in playing a facilitating role, e.g. by providing infrastructure, training and research facilities, and, at times, assisting in setting quality standards;

(d)   while local firms have been strongly involved, foreign investors – alone or often in joint venture with local partners – have played a key role in supplying technology, training, management and marketing capacity, as well as access to international markets;

(e)   industrial organization was characterized by both vertical integration (that linked producers of raw materials with processing companies and marketing in importing countries) and active competition between medium and larger local producers; contract-based production and inter-firm trade have been key to ensuring market information and access;

(f)   efficient, high-volume infrastructure capacity (especially in transport and communications) are vital to low spoilage and high profitability.

Source: Madagascar Private Sector Assessment. World Bank (1996).

On the one hand, Armenia continues to suffer from gradual erosion of its traditional markets in the FSU. On the other hand, Armenian companies proved to be incapable to expand their sales to new markets: merchandise exports to non-FSU countries remained roughly constant at the level of around 10 percent of GDP.

Exports to the FSU declined in part due to a continuing decline in incomes in the FSU states during the 90s. However, diminishing competitiveness of Armenian merchandise export seems to be a major explanation of decline. Armenian companies lost their market in Russia and in the rest of the FSU to competitors from Turkey, China and other leading producers of non-expensive consumer goods. High transport costs reduced opportunities for continuation of traditional exports in mining, metallurgy and chemical industry. In addition, Armenian participation in defense cooperation with Russian plants declined due to political factors.

Box 2.4. Garments Industry: Building Export Success on Global Market Trends

World apparel exports experienced rapid growth over 1980-91 – reaching a total of $98 billion in 1991. The top ten exporting countries (1) accounted for about 80 percent of total exports. In addition, a number of dynamic newly-industrializing economies (NIEs), notably in East Asia but also elsewhere, have achieved apparel export growth rates of 15-50 percent p.a. over 1980-91 – far higher than the industrial average. Those successful exporters included Thailand, Indonesia, Malaysia, Singapore, Sri Lanka, and Mauritius.

The success of these NIEs has been based upon strategies that have taken maximum advantage of both world market trends and global market structure:

- <u>Market dynamics</u>. All new entrants began with a strong labor cost advantage. This enabled them to enter the lower price end of the world apparel business, which is a highly competitive, diversified market with few barriers to entry. With increasing per capita incomes and labor costs, these NIEs are now moving up-market to produce higher value, less standardized garments. These require higher quality and faster delivery times, which accumulated experience enables them to attain. As they move up-market, they are freeing up a major market niche for new, lower cost producers such as China, Bangladesh, and Pakistan.
- <u>Manufacturing and Marketing Links</u>. Garment manufacturing in the NIEs is organized on the basis of: (i) sub-contracting (or contract manufacturing), which predominates; (ii) licensing; and (iii) direct foreign investment. In each case, it involves close contractual relationships between local producers, foreign investors and international marketing and manufacturing firms that are responsible for sales and distribution.
- <u>Improved infrastructure</u>. This is a key to expanding output, improving marketing and distribution, and thus to maintaining cost-competitiveness of exports. This includes notably services of telecoms, shipping and transportation, and efficient customs and trade documentation procedures.

(1) These are: Italy, Hong Kong, China, Republic of Korea, Taiwan, Germany, France, Great Britain, Portugal, and Turkey.

Source: Madagascar Private Sector Assessment, World Bank (1996).

In addition to general problems with exports to the FSU, Armenia's export was additionally hit by the Russia crisis in 1998-99. By the same reason, strong recovery in Russia in 2000 was quite beneficial for Armenian exports. Total 2000 exports increased by more than 15%, while merchandise exports to Russia and Ukraine expanded at higher rates than the average.

The trends in overall exports (including both goods and services) were more positive due to some expansion in export of services (telecom, tourism). Total exports amounted to US$367.5 million in 1999, which is a 22.7 percent nominal increase compared to 1995. Still, as a share of the GDP, total exports decreased from more than 23 percent in 1995 to 20.6 percent in 1997 and to about 19 percent in 1999. In 2000, it finally recovered to the level of 1995, i.e. 23 percent of GDP. In addition to weak export performance, it was due to a relatively high average GDP growth rate over the period and also because of real appreciation of the dram.

For a small country which is heavily dependent on import of raw materials and which has an economy that historically was closely integrated with its neighbors, the existing level of export is abysmally low and creates a major macroeconomic risk. Even though among Armenia has one of the most liberalized trade regimes in the CIS, its merchandise export is the lowest among CIS countries. For comparison, average export accounts for almost 40% in Moldova, and more than 30 percent in Kyrgyz Republic, Tajikistan, Turkmenistan, and Ukraine (Table 2.17).

Table 2.17. Merchandise Exports as Percent of GDP in CIS States, percent of GDP

	1997	1998	1999
Armenia	14.2	11.6	12.7
Azerbaijan	n.a.	14.7	23.2
Belarus	n.a.	26.5	22.1
Georgia	8.8	8.2	8.8
Kazakhstan	30.1	26.8	35.3
Kyrgyz Republic	37.5	31.2	36.4
Moldova	38.0	41.9	40.5
Russia	19.8	27.0	18.5
Tajikistan	66.6	58.6	36.9
Turkmenistan	41.4	34.0	49.9
Ukraine	30.9	32.0	30.0
Uzbekistan	n.a.	10.6	11.3

Source: World Development Indicators.

As business surveys suggest, Armenian enterprises are the second least likely to export in the region, after Azerbaijan. Only 4 of the 100 private enterprises in the 1999 survey export any of their products or services.

Significant Changes in the Export Structure

As opposed to a lack of expansion in merchandise exports, the export structure changed substantially. This relates mainly to the final destination of trade, although commodity composition also was affected. Structural shifts in exports are basically coherent with the increased share of new markets outside of the FSU. The positive sign is the increasing share of the private sector, which mostly reflects results of the mass privatization program. While the share of the private sector in overall exports comprised 33.7 percent in 1995, it increased to 68.5 percent in 1998 and to above 70 percent in 1999.

The structure of merchandise exports by both country and commodity has become more concentrated. Consumer and capital goods by now account for only small shares of exports. Consumer goods are destined mainly to CIS countries (cognac) and to some extent to the USA (garments), while the majority of capital goods is exported to Russia and Iran, as well as to Turkmenistan. The majority of total exports is intermediate goods (more than 50 percent), including diamonds (re-exported after initial processing and polishing), raw materials (ore, metals, electricity). The destination of intermediate goods and raw materials (other than diamonds) is more diversified.

Main trade partners of Armenia are Belgium, the Russian Federation, Iran, the United States, and Georgia. Analysis of broad export trends reveals that Armenia tends to shift its external trade from the CIS countries. In 1995, the share of external trade with non-CIS states was 37 percent, but in 1999 it exceeded 75 percent. In 1999, export to the CIS comprised only 33 percent of its 1995 level (Table 2.18).

However, it should be noted that when diamond export is measured on a net basis, the share of non-CIS countries is considerably lower: in 1999, it is roughly estimated to be in the range of 30-40 percent compared to more than 70 percent in Table 2.12. Therefore, while diversification of exports has taken place, it is still not far advanced. Overall, a considerable share of traditional Armenian exports (food, footwear, equipment), especially from SMEs, continues to go to Russia and other CIS countries. Many Armenian enterprises, especially those without foreign ownership, demonstrate inability to find strategic partners and new markets outside of the CIS.

Table 2.18. Exports: Top 15 Partners in 1995 and 1999

1999 Rating	Country	1995 Rating	1995 Export Share	1999 Export Share
1	Belgium	4	11.4	36.3
2	Iran	3	12.9	14.7
3	Russia	1	33.5	14.6
4	USA	14	0.2	6.9
5	Georgia	9	1.0	4.8
6	Germany	5	3.7	4.4
7	United Kingdom	12	0.5	4.1
8	Turkmenistan	2	25.4	2.6
9	Switzerland	8	1.1	1.6
10	UAE	18	0.2	1.1
11	Ukraine	7	1.7	0.9
12	Italy	27	0.1	0.6
13	Nagorny Karabakh	-	0.0	0.5
14	Canada	-	0.0	0.5
15	Turkey	10	1.0	0.4
	Total for top 15		92.5	94.0
	O/w: CIS		61.6	23.4
	Non-CIS		30.9	70.6

Source: Staff estimates based on the NSS data.

Sectoral and Commodity Composition of Export

Main winners of changes in sectoral composition of merchandise export were production of precious stones and metals as well as ores and energy, which together constituted about 60% of Armenian merchandise export in 1999 (Table 2.19). Thus, Armenian exports are highly-concentrated: processing of precious stones (43 percent of total), mineral production (nearly 16 percent of total, of which about 6 percent accounts for ores) and base metals (approximately 11 percent, of which the share of scrap was 7 percent). The share of precious stones and metals exceeded 40 percent of the overall exports in 1999, which is roughly equivalent to their share in 1995-96. Export of diamonds exceeded one-third of total merchandise exports in 1999. A successful restructuring and privatization of an old Soviet diamond processing company yielded increases. Electricity export expanded from practically zero in 1995 to 8.2 percent of total exports due to a major reform effort undertaken in the energy sector. However, it should be noted that net electricity exported amounted to only 3.3 percent of total exports.

The share of both machinery and chemicals sectors decreased two-fold, while the most dramatic losses occurred in two rather small sectors – furniture and toys (their share dropped more than 6 times) and glass and ceramics (almost 3 times). The share of the textile sector also decreased.

As a result, except for diamonds and gems, Armenian leading exports today are concentrated in sectors (energy, metallurgy), where the country does not have strong comparative advantages in the long term. Metal scrap remains a major part of overall exports. There has also been an increase in the market share of traditional Armenian exports: agricultural (more than 2 times) and food products. At the same time, except for software (See Box 2.1 in the previous section), no new significant export sector has emerged.[32]

With respect to the commodity composition of exports, Armenia still exports quite a limited number of products. Only about 60 types of products (according to a four-digit commodity classification) were exported in 1998-99. Fourteen top products represent 87 percent of total merchandise exports in 1999 compared to about 80 percent in 1995 (Table 2.20).

Table 2.19. Merchandise Exports: Top 11 Sectors

1999 Rating	Sectors	1995 Rating	1995 Export Share	1999 Export Share
1	Precious stones and metals	1	33.0	43.0
2	Total of mineral production, incl. Ores & energy	4	10.6	16.3
3	Base metals, incl. Scrap	3	11.4	10.8
4	Machinery	2	18.2	9.4
5	Prepared food	7	4.7	7.0
6	Textile, footwear and leather	6	9.2	6.6
7	Chemicals and plastics	5	9.6	4.7
8	Agricultural products	11	0.4	0.9
9	Wood and paper	10	0.4	0.6
10	Glass and ceramics	9	0.8	0.3
11	Furniture, toys, other	8	1.6	0.3
	TOTAL		100	100

Table 2.20. Top 14 Export Commodities

1999 Rating	Commodity	1995 Rating	1995 Export Share	1999 Export Share
1	Diamonds	1	26.3	36.1
2	Electricity	-	-	8.2
3	Ores (copper, zinc, molybdenum)	3	10.2	6.3
4	Knitwear	4	6.4	5.5
5	Gold	5	5.0	5.1
6	Aluminum and articles thereof (incl. Scrap)	10	2.9	3.9
7	Cognac	7	3.8	3.9
8	Electrical machinery and equipment	2	10.6	3.8
9	Rubber and articles thereof	9	3.3	3.8
10	Ferrous metals, incl. Scrap	6	3.9	3.8
11	Machinery, mechanical appliances, parts	8	3.3	3.7
12	Copper and articles thereof, (incl. Scrap)	11	2.3	2.4
13	Cement	13	0.3	0.5
14	Pharmaceutical products	12	1.2	0.4
	Total for top 14 commodities		79.5	87.4
Memo:				
Net electricity export			0.002	3.2
Net diamond export			7.5	1.3

---

[32] The official trade statistics (in all Tables of this section that derive from these statistics) do not reflect software exports.

Decline in Exported Value Added

The official merchandise export data per above are in fact overestimating the existing export potential of Armenian exporters. That is, the actual volume of value added created by Armenian exporters is considerably smaller that the official reports on exports, i.e. the existing weaknesses in export performance are even greater than the above analysis may suggest. This is because a relatively large portion of total export sales does not represent value added created by Armenian exporters.

There are three components in total exports that contribute to such an overestimation of the actual current export potential of Armenia. These include:

- Metal scrap. Export of metal scrap (aluminum, copper, ferrous) continues to be a major export commodity in Armenia (7 percent of total merchandise export). This is not a sustainable export – the existing stock of unused equipment and other metal products, inherited from Soviet times, will be exhausted rather soon and this source of "easy" export will disappear.

- Electricity export. More than half of electricity export in 1998-99 represents a seasonal swap with Iran. In other words, this export is conditional on Armenian commitment to import the exact amount of electricity from Iran. While somewhat beneficial for the power sector, such a swap is less favorable for the economy than regular export.

- Diamond export. Diamonds constitute a major export item in Armenia. Fluctuations in diamond production over the last several years had a significant impact on total export volumes.[33] However, it is important to notice that Armenian companies produce a relatively small share (about 17 percent) of total value of exported diamonds. Therefore, even large increases in diamond export have a moderate impact on GDP growth, domestic incomes, and balance of payment.

Due to these three factors, it seems important to complement a traditional analysis of export trends by more accurate estimates of actual value added by Armenian exporters. Table 2.21 suggests such a proxy estimate for a combined impact of all three factors, described in the previous paragraph. Overall, about 47 percent of the total Armenia merchandise exports in 1999 did not represent the actual capacity of the Armenian economy to sell domestic goods abroad and earn foreign currency. More than US$90 million in export earnings (about 25 percent of total exports and 40 percent of total merchandise exports) represented just a swap-type trade in electricity and diamonds, which is neutral for purposes of GDP growth and improvement of balance of payments.

Analysis of export trends, based on this proxy measure of value added in the export sector, revealed a much larger export decline. Total "value added" of export declined by about 44 percent during 1995-99, compared to a nearly 15 percent decline of merchandise export as reported by official statistics.

2.9. Investment Performance

According to official statistics, total investments in Armenia amounted to about 19-20% of GDP per annum over the last several years (Table 2.22). Average annual real growth for investments was close to the GDP growth, i.e. to about 5% for 1997-98. This expansion in investments was to a large extent

---

[33] In addition, the net export of diamonds in 1999 was quite small due to considerable purchases of raw diamonds to refill the stock.

driven by a growth in FDI. The official data suggest that in 1999 the flow of FDI almost reached 6.6% of GDP and was about 5 times higher than in 1996.

Table 2.21. Proxy Estimates for Exported Value Added, million US dollar

	1995	1999
Total merchandise export	270.9	231.7
O/w: - Gross electricity export	0.003	19.1
- Gross export of diamonds	71.2	83.9
- Gross export of metal scrap	0.1	16.1
Memo: Net electricity export	0.002	7.6
Net export of diamonds	20.4	3.1
Total "value added" in the merchandise export sector, adjusted for 3 factors above	219.8	123.3
Value added as % of total merchandise export	81.1	53.2

Source: Staff estimates.

Table 2.22. Total Investments and their Sectoral Breakdown, 1996-99

	1996	1997	1998	1999
Total investments, million AMD	132,282.6	153,350.6	182,824.5	181,218.8
- as % of GDP	20.0	19.1	19.1	18.4
- Nominal growth rates, %		15.9	19.2	4.4
Sectoral Shares, % :				
Industry	33.5	29.7	21.7	18.8
Agriculture	9.2	16.4	18.1	16.4
Transport (1)	6.9	11.9	7.2	11.2
Communication	12	14.5	8.8	9.4
Housing	19.5	15.8	23	21.5
Others	18.9	11.7	21.2	22.7

(1) - Includes investments in road construction/rehabilitation.
Source: Staff estimates based on the data from the NSS.

However, the investment data as reported in Armenia's National Accounts seems to be considerably overestimated, probably by 4-5% of GDP. This comes as a combined result of several statistical distortions:

- Domestic private investments seems to be inflated due to a used approach to an adjustment for the scope of informal activities in construction. It is assumed that the share of informal investments is as high as a share of informal activities in other sectors, including manufacturing and services. However, because a major part of investments in Armenia is funded either by budget or by donors, and these investments are quire well recorded, there is a relatively smaller scope for under-reporting of investment-related transactions.

- FDI volumes are inflated because of the confusion between two different concepts of foreign direct investments, those as related to the balance of payments and to a category of national accounts. In Armenia, almost a third of total FDI for 1995-98 derived from privatization transactions, especially from sales of companies in telecom and gas distribution. In contrast with conventional FDI, privatization proceeds do not necessarily constitute investments in the real sector. In Armenia, most privatization proceeds have been frozen before mid-2000 at the special budget account, while a smaller portion (including gas received as payment for gas distribution companies) were spent to finance current Government consumption.

- Budget investments are somewhat overestimated because of remaining problems in the budget classification, which does not distinguish properly between donor-funded investments and other spending under donor programs, e.g. on technical assistance.

Thus, the actual level of investments in Armenia is likely not to exceed 15% of GDP, which is just insufficient relative to restructuring needs of the country. In contrast, Gross Domestic Investment in leading economies in transition in both Central Europe and the Baltics has been significantly above 20% of GDP in the second part of the 90s.

The sectoral structure of investments (Table 2.22) reflects high shares of housing, utilities and infrastructure. The combined share of industry and agriculture is modest (about 35% in 1999, while these sectors contribute to about 52% of GDP) and declined in 1996-99. Such a imbalanced investment structure reflects both supply (availability of donor financing) and demand (weakness of the private sector, needs of the Earthquake Zone) factors.

Structure of investment financing. Available data describe only sources of financing of capital construction in the formal sector of the economy (Table 2.23). They do not cover financing of capital repair, stock accumulation, and investments made by the informal sector. Thus, the data presented below relate to just about a half of the officially reported investments. However, this is the most visible and statistically the most reliable part of the overall investment flow.

Table 2.23. Sources of Financing for Capital Construction, Percent of Total

	1996	1997	1998	1999
Total capital construction, o/w:	100	100	100	100
Consolidated Budget	22.4	8.6	19.3	18.5
Main donors, o/w:	26.9	24.6	14.4	30.9
- IBRD	18.2	7.0	9.1	18.5
FDI	10.4	28.2	11.2	2.1
Local private sector, o/w:	37.9	36.3	52.5	45.4
- Enterprises	18.2	12.2	8.6	16.6
- Households	19.7	24.1	43.9	28.8
Others	2.4	2.3	2.6	3.1

Source: NSS.

Donors and Armenian households are the main sources of investment financing. Their combined contribution amounted to almost 60% of the total in 1998-99. The Armenian Government contributed an additional 18-19% of the total from its own budget funds (excluding donor financing). The share of the local private enterprise sector remains low, below 15% of total. As mentioned above, FDI contributes relatively little into real sector investments.

The commodity composition of fixed investments reflects a low share of machinery and equipment, which on average was below 10% of the total in 1997-99 (Table 2.24). The major share of investments still goes to the construction and rehabilitation of fixed structures (construction, repair). This is a direct reflection of dominance of donors and households in investment financing, who have been channeling most investments in housing and large infrastructure projects (roads, urban development, irrigation networks), with a high construction content.

Table 2.24. Structure of Fixed Investments, Percent of Total

	1996	1997	1998	1999
Total of fixed investments, o/w:	100	100	100	100
Construction works	79	82	80	87
Machinery and equipment	14	12	11	6
Other components	7	6	9	7

Source: NSS.

Overall, the data above suggest low levels of investment activities. In addition, the development impact of current investment patterns is even lower than investment volumes could suggest. Investments are heavily concentrated in public and household sectors, while little is invested in support of enterprise restructuring and productivity growth.

Role of Foreign Direct Investments

While the existing investment levels are low and the investment structure is not efficient, Armenia's investment needs are huge. As a result of disintegration of the FSU and following developments through the 90s, only small segments of the industrial structure inherited from the USSR are still viable. Most of Armenia's industrial assets were created as part of a technological network that by now has mostly disappeared. Armenia is facing a challenge of re-industrialization: existing assets (both capital and labor) need a deep restructuring and upgrade (recombination of assets) in order to join new global and regional value chains. This will require considerable investments, including investments in managerial skills. There are only two theoretical sources of investment financing: FDI and domestic savings. The problem with domestic savings is that, under the most optimistic scenario, the rate of its potential accumulation in Armenia is still too slow relatively to existing needs. There is a risk that the country may lose even a larger part of its population quicker than its benefits from domestic savings become significant.

Therefore, strategically FDI in Armenia is the only way to ensure a sufficient rate of job creation and economic growth, and therefore social and political stability. While at the moment Armenia does not have many competitive advantages for attracting FDI, this report assumes that there is considerable room for attracting FDI in various sectors, such as software, jewelry, mining, tourism, textile and garments, etc.

Armenia has had modest successes in attracting foreign savings. By FDI per capita, Armenia keeps a leading position among non-oil FSU states (Table 2.25). However, these data are somewhat misleading. In Armenia's case, FDI numbers (and total investment volumes) are inflated by rather high privatization proceeds received from privatization of infrastructure companies in telecom and gas distribution. About a third of the total reported FDI received by Armenia in 1992-99 derives from these transactions. The flow of small and medium investment transactions, i.e. actual investments into the real sector, including those in start-up companies, is very low. As Table 2.25 suggests, even when large privatization transactions are included, per capita FDI in Armenia in the 90s were 6 times below those in Poland and 10 times lower than in Estonia. The existing opportunities for FDI promotion have been grossly underutilized.

Barriers for foreign investments (as well as for domestic) remain numerous as surveys of private entrepreneurs have shown[34]. There is still considerable opposition to FDI from influential interest groups that are openly concerned that new investors would ultimately reduce their political role and their market share. The critical role of FDI (at least in the short term) for economic and social recovery in Armenia is not acknowledged or accepted. While top Armenian officials have been making numerous statements about the importance of FDI, little effort has been made to build an adequate infrastructure that would try to attract investments and support foreign investors during the early stage of their ventures. In particular,

---

[34] See Chapter 3 for a detailed discussion of barriers for private investments.

the Government mostly failed to transfer the investment potential of the Diaspora and the ongoing flow of Diaspora-funded humanitarian assistance into real sector investments.[35]

Table 2.25. FDI Per Capita, US dollar

	Annual average, 1994-99	1999
Albania	17.9	13.2
Armenia	18.8	40.5
Azerbaijan	73.8	104.0
Belarus	9.1	18.5
Bulgaria	33.4	83.3
Croatia	91.7	163.0
Czech Republic	178.5	339.8
Estonia	183.3	233.3
Georgia	6.6	17.8
Hungary	218.6	156.9
Kazakhstan	51.8	53.3
Kyrgyz Rep.	13.9	13.9
Latvia	105.7	60.0
Lithuania	75.9	108.1
FYR Macedonia	14.2	14.3
Moldova	13.4	39.5
Poland	109.3	168.4
Romania	36.2	59.8
Russia	17.2	23.9
Slovak Rep.	60.6	92.6
Slovenia	88.5	75.0
Tajikistan	2.6	4.9
Turkmenistan	11.9	20.8
Ukraine	8.4	12.0
Uzbekistan	5.9	9.4
Total for the region	40.4	57.2

Source: FIAS.

2.10. Performance of Large Industrial Enterprises in Armenia[36]

The objective of this section is to review the trends occurring in the sector of large traditional industrial enterprises since economic liberalization and stabilization have been largely completed in Armenia. In order to answer the key question: "Are large industrial enterprises in Armenia worth banking on in terms of their ability to generate growth and employment?", performance indicators of 100 largest industrial enterprises for 1997-99 were analyzed and contrasted with 100 largest industrial enterprises in Kazakhstan and Lithuania.

The analysis presents evidence of the overall rather weak performance of large enterprises, which has further deteriorated in 1998-99 compared to 1997. Although the Russian financial crisis was probably the major factor underlying the serious decline in the 1998-99 financial and output performance, there were other factors, such as a jump in real interest rates (exceeding 40%) after close to zero inflation in 1998-99[37], and the substantial hike in energy/electricity tariffs.

Overall, 1998 was a "bad year" for the entire Armenian industrial sector. Total industrial output declined by 2 percent, and total gross profits from sales declined by more than 30%, as compared with 1997, and reached a level as low as 1% of GDP. While industrial output increased by 5% in 1999, it did not lead to a stronger financial performance. The share of loss-making enterprises in industry increased from 31% in 1997 to 47% in 1998 and to 53% in 1999.

---

[35] Amirkhanian (1997) describes a complexity of relationship between the Armenian Government and the Diaspora. With respect to prospects for Diaspora's investors in Armenia he points to a demand side of the process: "Significance of the Diaspora will come down to whether the local Armenians can afford to share their limited resources and opportunities with the outsiders" (p. 21) So far, there is little evidence that the political elite in Yerevan is ready for such a sharing.

[36] This section is based on *Grigorian, David, "Restructuring of Large Industrial Enterprises in Armenia: A Comparative Analysis"*, World Bank (2000).

[37] Registered for the first time since Armenia independence in 1991.

Moreover, the largest enterprises were disproportionately hit by the overall deterioration in performance. Contrasting the performance of the largest enterprises with the rest of the Armenia industrial sector leads us to believe that the overall modest industrial expansion reported in the second half of the 90s has not been due to industrial giants, which were slow to restructure and hard to adjust to the harsh conditions of the Armenian economic landscape. Similarly, given the current state of aggregate demand and new markets for large enterprises, as well as realistic assessment of the stock of available managerial skills, it remains unlikely that the sub-sector could become a major engine of future economy-wide growth.

Largest Industrial Enterprises: Main Performance Indicators

The data used in the analysis was provided by the Armenian Statistical Agency and contains performance indicators for 100 largest (based on the employment data for each year, excluding energy sector companies) industrial enterprises in Armenia for 1997-98[38]. The share of the chosen enterprises in the total industrial output amount to 28% in 1997 but it dropped below 20% in 1997. Practically all enterprises in the sample did exist before the transition, i.e. the sample indeed represents a core of the traditional enterprise sector.

Table 2.26 compares performance of the largest enterprises with the overall trends for the industrial sector. It provides for a straightforward conclusion: industrial giants have seriously under-performed in 1998 compared to the rest of the sector. While the overall industrial output declined by about 2%, large enterprises faced a 40% reduction in output. All industrial sub-sectors show similar differences in performance. This suggests that a substantial growth (above 10%) took place outside of this core of traditional companies that were presented in the sample.

The extent of labor shedding by traditional enterprises, when compared to a decline in the output, would provide for an indirect and highly simplified indicator of accumulated restructuring effort and downsizing. The pre-transition employment data were available for a sub-set of 75 enterprises in our sample. In 1987, these 75 enterprises employed over 137,000 workers[39], while the reported employment for the sample of 90 enterprises in 1999 was only 55,180. This suggests that average employment has dropped from over 1,800 employees per enterprise in 1987 to only 613 employees in 1999, or by the factor of 3. This should be compared with the decline in output, which ranges from at least 4-5 times for the largest enterprises in textile and chemicals to at least 8 times in machinery. Thus, as large reductions of employment as these numbers suggest, they still do not fully reflect the extent of labor redundancies in the sector. Despite well-known excessive labor hoarding practices in the FSU, during the years of transition labor productivity further declined within the sample of largest traditional companies. Anecdotal evidence suggests that workers prefer to stay on the payroll without getting paid rather than quitting, fearing to lose their "association" with the enterprise just in case production is revived or the enterprise is privatized in which case there is a chance they may be offered some enterprise stock.

---

[38] For 1999, we obtained the data for 90 companies – those which were presented in the sample for both previous years.
[39] Unfortunately, the data do not provide distinction between productive and non-productive workers.

Table 2.26. Dynamics of Real Output and Employment by Sub-Sectors, 1997-99

	Total Industry	Metallurgy	Chemicals	MEEE*	Light Industry	Food Processing	Other**
Sample characteristics:							
Number of Enterprises	90[40]	12	5	29	29	6	9
Output, million Drams							
1997	74,537	10,800	10,931	8,231	4,311	22,471	17,794
1998	44,752	11,938	6,868	5,565	2,121	16,888	2,718
1999	40,135	13,577	5,359	4,101	2,171	12,095	2,822
Change in Output, 1997-98 deflated, %	-40.0	10.5	-37.2	-32.4	-50.8	-24.8	-84.7
Change in Output, 1997-99 deflated, %	-46.1	25.7	-50.9	50.2	-49.6	-46.2	-84.1
Change in Employment, 1998-99, %	-10.2	-21.6	-14.8	-11.3	-3.1	0.3	-4
Change in Employment, 1997-99, %	-16.3	-24.4	-18.4	-19	-8.6	-5.5	-12.7
Memo Items:							
Implicit 1998 inflation index	5	7	-1.5	-1	9	-0.5	3.9
Change in total Industrial Output, 1997-98, deflated, %	-2.1	47.5	-12.9	-25.6	5.5	7.4	-19.2
Change in total Industrial Output, 1997-99, deflated, %	+3.0						

- Machinery, Electrical Equipment and Electronics, ** - Other sectors include Furniture, Medical Equipment, etc.
Source: Grigorian, David (2000).

Table 2.27 shows distribution of 100 largest industrial enterprises by categories A-E[41]. Contrary to common expectations, 64 out of 100 large industrial enterprises in the sample were profitable as of end-1997. These enterprises represented approximately 70 percent of the labor force employed and revenues generated by those 100 enterprises. The share of profitable companies declined to 41 percent in 1998 and to one-third in 1999, with the bulk of profitable enterprises leaving category A for categories D and E. In total, 15 enterprises improved their performance in 1998, while 40 enterprises did worse than in 1998. The share of companies, which were not capable of paying wages (category D), increased drastically in 1998 and reached 37 percent, while the share of revenues received by these enterprises exceeded 20 percent. In addition, in 1999, approximately 22 percent of the labor force was employed in 20 value subtracting enterprises (category E) that all together generate 17 percent of output.

---

[40] A balanced panel of 90 enterprises is used to estimate the growth rates for the sample.

[41] Hereafter enterprises are classified in groups according to their financial performance using the following criteria (see Pohl, Gerhard, Semion Djankov, and Robert Anderson (1996). *"Restructuring of Large Industrial Enterprises in Central and Eastern Europe"*, World Bank Technical Paper 332). World Bank, Washington, D.C.

  A   (profitable) if profit before tax is greater than zero;
  B   if enterprise cannot finance depreciation (i.e. although cash flow after debt service is positive, its profit before tax is negative);
  C   if enterprise cannot service its financial debt (i.e. cash flow after debt servicing is negative);
  D   if enterprise cannot pay salaries (i.e. operating cash flow is negative); and
  E   (value subtractor) if enterprise cannot pay to suppliers (i.e. value added is negative).

Table 2.27. Distribution of 100 Industrial Enterprises by Performance Categories, 1997-1999[42]

	A			B			D			E		
	1997	1998	1999	1997	1998	1999	1997	1998	1999	1997	1998	1999
Number of Firms:	64	41	30	9	8	9	13	37	30	10	13	20
Employment, percent	69.0	42.1	23.5	10.4	8.6	6.5	9.6	38.1	40.1	8.8	10.3	22.4
Output, percent	70.9	57.8	33.2	7.9	16.5	1.6	18.6	20.5	47.7	0.5	2.0	17.1

Note: the 1999 sample contains 90 companies.
Source: Grigorian, David (2000).

Table 2.28 describes sectoral differences in performance. A vast majority of enterprises belonging to group A as of 1997 were from Machine Tools, Electronics/Radio, Textile/Clothing/Leather, and Food and Beverages sub-sectors. While enterprises in Food and Beverages, Textiles, Clothing and Production of Electronics sub-sectors at the very least retained their profitability in 1998 (largely remained in group A), those in Machine Tools Production, TV and Communication Equipment, and Furniture sub-sectors mostly migrated to loss making categories in 1998-99.

Table 2.28. Distribution of 100 Industrial Enterprises by Sub-Sectors and Performance, 1997-99

	All			A			D			E		
Industrial Sub-Sectors	1997	1998	1999	1997	1998	1999	1997	1998	1999	1997	1998	1999
Total (1+2)	100	100	90	64	41	30	13	37	30	10	13	20
1. Mining industry	4	4	4	1	1	1	1	1	3	1	1	-
2. Processing industry	96	96	86	63	40	29	12	36	27	9	12	20
Of which:												
Food and beverages	8	7	6	5	6	3	2	-	2	-	1	-
Textile	18	18	18	6	5	8	4	9	4	4	2	5
Clothing	6	9	6	6	8	4	-	1	-	-	-	-
Leather	5	5	5	4	1	1	1	3	1	-	-	2
Chemicals	4	4	3	3	2	1	1	2	1	-	-	1
Rubber and plastic	4	3	2	3	1	1	-	1		-	1	
Other non ferrous mineral production	3	4	1	2	2	1	1	1	-	-	-	-
Ferrous metallurgy	3	3	3	1	1	-	-	-	1	2	2	1
Metal processing industry excluding machine tools	5	5	4	4	2	-	-	2	2	-	-	1
Machine tools production (not included in other categories)	18	17	17	13	6	3	1	7	7	2	2	5
Production of electronics and computers	7	7	7	6	5	3	-	2	3	-	-	1
Communication and medical equipment	9	8	8	5	-	2	2	6	4	1	2	2
Furniture and others	6	6	6	5	4	2	-	2	1	-	2	2

Source: Grigorian, David (2000).

Table 2.29 provides some additional insights into the performance story as it relates to differences in ownership. It is worth mentioning that as of end-1998 only 17 enterprises in the sample were fully privatized, while the state still retained full ownership rights in 12 and partial ownership (presumably

---

[42] Non-balanced sample, i.e. not all enterprises are the same in both annual samples.

small residual shareholding) in 71 enterprises[43]. These numbers suggest that while the GOA has made considerable progress with privatization since the mid 90s, the privatization agenda, at least as it concerns the largest enterprises, is still unfinished.

Table 2.29. Distribution of 100 Industrial Enterprises* by Ownership and Performance, 1997-99

	ALL			A			B			D			E		
	1997	1998	1999	1997	1998	1999	1997	1998	1999	1997	1998	1999	1997	1998	1999
Total	100	100	90	64	41	30	9	8	9	13	37	30	10	13	20
Fully State	11	12	10	4	3	2	2	1	-	1	4	7	4	4	1
Fully Private	16	17	13	9	8	7	2	-	2	3	6	1	1	2	3
Mixed	73	71	67	51	30	21	5	7	7	9	27	22	5	7	16

* - Unbalanced panel.
Source: Grigorian, David (2000).

Only 4 out of 64 (slightly more than 6 percent) of profitable enterprises were fully state-owned in 1997. On the other hand, 4 out of 10 (or 40 percent) of value subtractors were state-owned enterprises. In contrast, 9 out of 16 fully private enterprises (over 55 percent) were profitable in 1997, and this share remained broadly unchanged in 1999. Share of profitable enterprises with mixed ownership declined dramatically: from 70 percent in 1997 to slightly over 30 percent in 1999.

Overall, there seems to be sufficient evidence to claim that within the sample both fully private and enterprises with mixed ownership outperform fully state-owned enterprises. However, it does not suggest that the performance of private companies was sufficiently strong to be sustainable. The data do not support a possible argument that continued privatization, not complemented by other policy interventions, could resolve most problems that large enterprises have been facing.

Cross-Country Analysis

This section develops a comparative analysis between performance of large industrial enterprises in Armenia, Kazakhstan and Lithuania[44]. Why is it of interest to compare these countries? The answer lies in the different features of the transition process in these countries.

Lithuania witnessed a rather successful reform path compared to most of the FSU states. Budget deficit was put under control as early as 1993. Proximity to Western European markets, successful liberalization, and significant technical assistance from Scandinavian neighbors prepared a solid ground for both supply and demand driven restructuring in the enterprise sector. Lithuanian growth rates have been positive since 1994. Most large enterprises had been privatized in 1995-1997.

In contrast, in Kazakhstan, stabilization was delayed, the investment climate was much less supportive, and restructuring processes were much slower than in Lithuania. Soft budget constraint was still a major issue for most of the 90s and even accessibility of large markets like Russia and China did not result in any significant performance improvements by the industrial sector.

---

[43] Little change occurred in 1999. Also, it is worth noting that none of the fully private or mixed enterprises reported any foreign ownership.
[44] The data on Kazakhstan (for 1997-1998) and Lithuanian (1996-1997) enterprises derived from the enterprise databases provided by the Statistical Agencies of the respective countries. For the purpose of this study, 100 largest industrial enterprises (excluding energy producing and energy distributing companies) were selected from the databases, based on their reported employment.

Armenia represents a case that falls somewhere in between Lithuania and Kazakhstan. While macroeconomic reforms of 1994-95 were rather swift and effective, enterprise restructuring was undertaken at a much slower pace. Also, similar to Kazakhstan, Armenia has lagged behind advanced transition economies in establishing both market-friendly institutions and an investor-friendly business environment, which led to a weaker supply-side response. In addition, Armenia's efforts to privatize state assets were conducted, owing to geopolitical and other problems, in the environment of striking lack of interest from external investors.

Yet, despite the apparent differences, the restructuring process in these three countries has some common patterns: privatization led to strong insider dominated ownership structure with resulting weaker ability and willingness to restructure. Also, in none of these countries did foreigners receive a significant role in corporate governance (with the only exception of the oil sector in Kazakhstan).

Table 2.30 presents data on the role of the pre-transition industrial sector in each of these three countries. The data on labor productivity (measured by a ratio of industrial output to industrial employment) for 1987 suggest that Lithuania was leading with approximately 22,000 rubles worth of goods produced per employee, followed by Kazakhstan with 21, and Armenia with 18. At the same time, Armenia and Lithuania were much more industrialized countries: about 31% of total employment was concentrated in industrial establishments. Also, the Armenian industrial structure was highly skewed towards the machine building sector.

Table 2.30. Pre-Transition Indicators of Industrial Concentration, 1987

	Industrial Employment ('000)		Percent of total Employment	Industrial output (mln. Rubles)	Percent of total Output***	Productivity (1000 Rubles)	Share in Industrial output percent	
	1987	1998					Machine building	Consumer goods**
Armenia	483	209	31	8,277	55	18	32	26
Kazakhstan	1,514	756	21	31,763	20.5*	21	11	12
Lithuania	582	306	31	12,559	37	22	23	22

* - 1990 figure, Kazakhstan Industrial Statistics Bulletin (1999). ** - 1990 data.
*** - Total Gross output in the enterprise sector.
Source: USSR Statistical Handbook. All data are for 1987 unless otherwise indicated. Numbers for 1998 are from the Economist Intelligence Unit and World Bank.

Table 2.31 suggests that an average large industrial enterprise in Armenia is currently much smaller than those in Lithuania and Kazakhstan if measured by employment and book value of total assets[45]. Furthermore, in US dollar equivalent the total output generated by the average enterprise in Armenia is less than one-tenth (1/10) of those generated by its Lithuanian counterpart and less than one-thirteenth (1/13) generated by its Kazakh counterpart.

---

[45] Corresponding figures for book values of total assets of 100 largest companies are $249 mln, $5,533 mln, and $1,545 mln for Armenian, Kazakh and Lithuanian enterprises respectively.

Table 2.31. Sample Characteristics: Armenia, Kazakhstan, Lithuania – 1997

	No. of Enterprises	Average Number of Employees	Total output, million USD	Employment share in Total Economy	Output share in Total Industry
Armenia	100	687	162.1	0.05	0.28
Kazakhstan	100	2,829	2,170.6	0.04	0.20
Lithuania	100	994	1,645.0	0.06	0.30

Source: Grigorian, David (2000).

Table 2.32 shows distribution of the largest enterprises by performance categories. Although in 1997 the number of profitable enterprises in Armenia was roughly the same as in Lithuania, a 1998 drop in the number of profitable enterprises in Armenia (as well as in Kazakhstan) was more pronounced than in Lithuania. Also, in 1997, only one out of every 50 enterprises was a value subtractor in Lithuania, while that number for Armenia was one out of every 10. At the same time, in Kazakhstan, a country with a shorter record of macroeconomic stabilization and enterprise restructuring than Armenia and Lithuania, enterprises' financial performance was even weaker than in Armenia: more than half of the sample belonged to either category D or E in 1997 (in Armenia – 23%). This share increased in Kazakhstan to 72% in 1998 (in Armenia – 50%).

Table 2.32. Distribution of Enterprises by Performance Categories

		Total	A	B	C	D	E
	1999	90	30	9	1	30	20
Armenia	1998	100	41	8	1	37	13
	1997	100	64	9	4	13	10
Kazakhstan	1998	100	20	6	2	28	44
	1997	100	34	7	2	20	37
Lithuania	1997	100	62	13	7	16	2
	1996	100	68	12	3	16	1

Source: Grigorian, David (2000).

A summary of productivity indicators is reported in Table 2.33. An average enterprise in Lithuania was about 8 times more productive in 1997, when measured in sales per employee, compared to those in Armenia. This gap seems to be even wider in 1998-99. Even large enterprises in Kazakhstan turned out to be in 1998 on average at least 7 times as productive as their Armenian counterparts. In addition, in all sectors in Armenia, productivity indicators (measured by both value added and revenues per employee) declined between 1997 and 1998, while those in Kazakhstan and Lithuania increased[46]. While enterprises in Kazakhstan face a much softer budget constraint than those in Armenia, still their pace of restructuring, as measured by productivity trends, has been higher.

It is interesting to note that the only sector where the difference between productivity indicators across countries is not so pronounced is food processing. In Armenia, food processing is currently the sector with the strongest presence of both successful start-ups and first movers among traditional enterprises who have undertaken restructuring, as well as with a significant import substitution effect.

---

[46] The exception is the Chemical sub-sector in Kazakhstan.

Table 2.33. Productivity Indicators for the Largest Enterprises

	Armenia			Kazakhstan		Lithuania	
	1997	1998	1999	1997	1998	1996	1997
Sales per employee, $	2,304	1,514	1,401	9,498	10,730	15,745	17,823
Value added per employee, $	835	480		1,351	2,008	4,469	4,680
Total taxes to sales	0.05	0.04	0.04	0.05	0.14	0.03	0.02
Memo Items:							
Number of firms	90	90	90	100	100	100	100
Total Employment	65,907	61,435	55,180	203,670	203,670	104,476	104,476

Source: Grigorian, David (2000).

Table 2.34 contains liquidity indicators for sample enterprises. The first ratio is a ratio of working capital to total assets[47]. A low (or negative) working capital ratio is indicative of the fact that operations are financed by mainly short-term borrowing, including arrears. The second – acid test ratio - is defined as a ratio of sum of liquid assets and accounts receivables to current liabilities. This ratio shows to what extent enterprise's short-term liabilities are covered by its liquid assets and accounts receivables, i.e. whether or not the enterprise is sensitive to "liquidity crises". An acid test ratio which is less than one, is indicative of the fact that even if the enterprise sells all its liquid assets and is paid back all its receivables, it will still not be able to pay for all liabilities which are soon becoming due.

Table 2.34. Liquidity Indicators: Comparative Analysis

	Armenia			Kazakhstan		Lithuania	
	1997	1998	1999	1997	1998	1996	1997
Working capital/ Total assets	0.06	(0.13)	(0.2)	0.04	0.06	0.18	0.19
Acid test ratio*	0.36	0.20	0.25	0.55	0.56	0.77	0.87

* Acid Test Ratio is defined as a ratio of sum of liquid assets and accounts receivables to current liabilities.
Source: Grigorian, David.

The data show that Lithuanian enterprises emerge as clear leaders in their ability to attract long term financing and service their short term debts. Enterprises in Armenia and Kazakhstan generate somewhat identical liquidity patterns. The table provides additional confirmation of deteriorating liquidity position of Armenian enterprises between 1997 and 1999. The working capital ratio for the whole sample turned negative in 1998-99, with practically all sub-sectors reporting significant drops. The acid test ratio also decreased, leaving only 25 percent of current liabilities in 1999 covered by liquid assets.

Implications for Economic Growth and Policy Agenda

The above cross-country comparison of average size and average productivity of large enterprises suggests a rather low level of capacity utilization in Armenian firms. Combining these findings with the data on financial performance one may conclude that such utilization levels are not sustainable. But attaining much higher capacity utilization levels for Armenian traditional industrial enterprises is rather difficult. Old CEE markets have either disappeared entirely (most of defense production) or lost to

---

[47] Working capital is defined as the difference between current assets and current liabilities.

competitors from the rest of the world. Unless and until new product markets are discovered, financial viability of most large companies is highly questionable. Getting new or partially recovering old markets would take time, serious investments in technologies and training, and major policy efforts that are described in the following chapters.

The analysis above also seems to suggest that with time, restructuring and competitive challenges become even more difficult. The longer the "waiting period", the productivity gaps to be bridged are becoming even wider, which makes it more difficult for Armenian enterprises to compete with foreign companies, even within the CIS.

In addition to structural factors, the deterioration of performance in 1998-99 reflected a cyclical effect related to the Russia crisis. It is possible that the data for 2000, when available, would show some improvement in performance relative to the results reported above. This does not question, however, main conclusion of this section: the performance of the large enterprises in Armenia is weak compared to their competitors in other economies in transition as well as to the performance of smaller, often newly-established Armenian enterprises.

Based on the experience of more advanced economies in transition, it is likely that only a small portion of large companies could be capable of joining global supply chains without even larger downsizing and/or major restructuring. While in the last two years, Armenia saw several examples of successful restructuring in large companies, as a group the largest enterprises did not contribute to recent growth. This trend is likely to hold in the medium term[48]. For various historical, geopolitical and structural reasons, prospects for traditional companies are not encouraging. This is another justification for the Government to refocus its policies on improvement of the environment for new companies.

It is worth emphasizing that in contrast to many FSU states, the core constraint for enterprise restructuring in Armenia is not related to budget subsidies. Since 1994, the Government managed to eliminate the most budget and quasi-budget subsidies. Compared to several other countries in the FSU, Armenia's enterprise sector is relatively subsidy-free[49]. But as this section shows it proved to be insufficient. Too many large enterprises are allowed to operate for years by accumulating debts to the budget, energy sector, employees and banks. This erodes the hard budget constraint and incentives in the entire enterprise sector as well as could become a serious problem for the banking sector.

At the same time, the recent Armenian and regional experience demonstrates that the problem of large traditional enterprises could not be resolved by introducing an aggressive program of their massive liquidation. While the government's capacity to undertake bankruptcy and liquidation procedures is in urgent need of expansion, a comprehensive strategy for largest enterprises should be based on the combination of liquidation and market-based restructuring of these enterprises. Chapters 5 and 6 present a possible approach to a design of such a strategy. Its key elements include:

- Case-by-case liquidation of large non-viable companies through mechanisms that would encourage formation of start-ups and spin-offs to utilize assets and infrastructure of traditional firms.

- Encouraging SME creation through reduced barriers for new entry, which facilitate reallocation of assets from traditional to the new economy.

---

[48] While the sharp deterioration in performance in late 90-s had its cyclical component related to the Russia crisis, the report argues that the basic factors determining such a deterioration were not of a temporary nature.
[49] The next chapter provides a review of the subsidy incidence in the enterprise sector.

- Promotion of partnership arrangements with foreign companies, who would facilitate integration into global markets, including a transfer of commercial know-how, and encourage transition to more effective forms of corporate governance.

- Better training opportunities for local managers.

- "Damage control" and limit accumulation of bad debts and inter-enterprise arrears. The policymakers should limit direct or indirect flow of public resources to enterprises with a poor record of performance and restructuring.

3. MAIN CONSTRAINTS FOR INVESTMENTS AND GROWTH

3.1. General Political and Institutional Barriers for Enterprise Restructuring and Growth

This report argues that the general environment for enterprise restructuring in Armenia is rather weak, which resulted from a combined effect of several factors:

- General weakness of public sector institutions, many of which have emerged from scratch less than 10 years ago in the extraordinary situation of military conflict.

- The war and blockade resulted in high investment risks and uncertainties, which had a further detrimental impact on incentives.

- Mass privatization that gave Armenia a standard set of its benefits and problems. The latter includes insider control, weak corporate governance, and insufficient incentives and skills for restructuring.

- Political mobilization during the war had also affected the formation of the business environment by over-expanding the role of both various controlling agencies and "power" structures, and resulted in intensive involvement of military establishment in business activity.

Political Economy: Elements Relevant to Economic Restructuring

The main political challenges to reform progress in Armenia relate to the fragmentation of the political process, serious tensions within the political elite, and uncertainties associated with the unresolved Karabakh conflict. The political events of 1999 revealed that the political process is highly vulnerable with high risks of external shocks. Political coalitions are unstable and are consolidated more by their leaders' personalities than by the political programs of participants. Political parties and consultation mechanisms remain weak, which complicates and delays a policy response to a possible crisis.

Extreme mobilization of the Armenian society in the early 90s during the Karabakh war could still be traced in several core features of both policy making and public administration (Bremmer, 1996). This over-mobilization has been detrimental to the reform process through the following channels:

- In public administration, it supported establishment of an excessive control and inspection structure, and more generally delayed deregulation of the business environment.

- In policy making, it limited opportunities for public participation in discussions over reform priorities; lack of dialogue between main stockholders makes it much more difficult for the Government to maintain public support for reforms and creates additional problems with implementation.[50]

---

[50] Rodrik (2000) underlines the importance of effective consultative mechanisms for generating necessary policy adjustments and containing adverse consequences of shocks.

- In the economic area, close links between existing leading firms (both recently privatized SOEs and start-ups) and power ministries and influential politicians became a major source of non-competitive behavior and barriers for entry.

Fragmentation of the political elite had its manifestation in the high turnover of Armenian Governments. Since 1991, Armenia had 10 Prime Ministers.[51] These personnel changes in most cases produced very little change in economic policy. However, they contributed to uncertainty and instability.

Armenia Institutional and Governance Review (IGR), completed by the World Bank in 2000, identifies two more important institutional issues confronting Armenia today: unbalanced development of policy capacity, and underdeveloped institutions of accountability. The IGR notes that the demand for good policies is constrained by weak expenditure controls, pervasive informality, overarching pre-eminence of the executive over other branches of state resulting from the weak checks and balances system, as well as from underdeveloped civil society and media.

Lack of communication between the public and authorities, weakness of political parties and other "voice" mechanisms (e.g. trade unions), which all relate to this underdeveloped accountability of the executive branch, gradually eroded public trust in authorities and core public sector institutions. For instance, the results of the public awareness survey suggest that the majority of the population have little trust in the judicial system. And the public's opinion on courts performance and more broadly on law enforcement agencies at large is strictly negative. (Box 3.1).

Box 3.1. Public Attitude Towards the Legal and Judicial System

A survey of public awareness and public attitude towards the legal and judicial system in Armenia has been carried out in the course of the preparation of the World Bank Judicial Reform Project. The survey was conducted by the Armenian Center of Ethno-Sociological Studies Akunq in December of 1999. Almost 1,100 people were interviewed and additional meetings with 20 focus groups were conducted.

The survey revealed that public opinion on both law enforcement agencies and their staff is strongly negative. Agencies that were rated the worst included courts, prosecutor's office, units of the Ministry of Internal Affairs as well as tax inspections. The public's image of judges, staff of the prosecutor's office and police lacks the characteristic of honesty. Public awareness is very low with respect to ongoing judicial reforms, enforcement mechanisms for judicial decisions, and provision of legal services.

The majority of the population (53%) considers the current judicial system as not affordable. People, even in emergencies, prefer not to turn to the protection of courts because they are considered "useless", "troublesome", and "untrustworthy". According to the results of focus-group interviews, this system is described as "corrupt". A general attitude is rather negative: "Let nobody ever face them". Almost all the focus groups believed that the laws were not equally enforced for all the social layers, and the interests of the wealthy and senior officials are much better protected. These factors together make many individuals feel they do not have adequate legal protection.

Source: World Bank.

Frequent government reshuffling combined with weak participation mechanisms also inflated private perceptions of Armenia's business and investment risks. By the late 90s, popular Investment Risk Indexes tend to overestimate Armenia's political risks and somewhat discount actual economic reform progress. In particular, Armenia was viewed much lower (relatively to several other FSU states) by private sector rankings compared to the assessment of the leading donors (Table 3.1).

---

[51] Collier (2000) suggests a correlation between success of reforms and government's tenure in power.

Table 3.1. Difference in Perceptions: 1998 Assessments by the IBRD and WSJ

	World Bank Assessment, 1998		Wall Street Journal Assessment, 1998	
	Rank (out of 27)	Average Score (max = 5)	Rank (out of 27)	Average Score (max = 10)
Hungary	1	4.6	1	8.3
Estonia	4	4.5	5	7.5
Latvia	5-6	4.2	6	7.0
Lithuania	8	3.9	7	6.8
Armenia	14	3.6	18	4.2
Georgia	15-16	3.5	16	4.5
Azerbaijan	18	3.2	17	4.4
Moldova	20-21	2.9	11	5.1

Note: The objective of WSJ ranking is to assess relative "quality of doing business" in a particular country, while the IBRD assess a broader set of macroeconomic and structural reforms.
Sources: World Bank, Wall Street Journal.

Insufficient Capacity of Core Public Sector Institutions and Unfinished Deregulation Agenda

In the early 90s, the Armenian Government was very decisive in advancing its broad liberalization agenda. As a result, it was quite successful in removing various trade, price, exchange and interest rates restrictions. From the macroeconomic perspective, after 1996, the Armenian macroeconomic environment has contained little distortions associated with Government regulations, nominal tax regime, and budget subsidies. Thus, the notional business environment (which is reflected in laws and regulations) is relatively good. However, at the microeconomic level, the situation is different. The state has no capability (and little incentives) to enforce this favorable legal framework, i.e. to transform the notional business environment into an effective business environment.

Despite considerable progress with structural and institutional reforms, Armenian basic institutions in support of the market environment remain weak. This is not surprising given the scale of the task and the severe resource limitations Armenia faces. At the same time, Armenia has been suffering from institutional segmentation – attempts to build too many new institutions simultaneously, without proper prioritization and sequencing (World Bank, 2000c). This excessively broad institutional agenda, which at least in part is donor-driven, resulted in weakening of several core functions of economic management and additional problems with inter-agency coordination.

The lesson from Armenia and several other economies in transition suggests that liberalization and de-regulation do not bring tangible benefits if they are not supported by sufficient government capacity to protect a liberal economic regime. If this capacity is lacking, then one may expect that central regulations would be replaced by decentralized regulations and harassment, which could be more costly that the original ones. The regime of decentralized regulation, imposed by local governments, special interest groups, sectoral agencies, and criminals is much less predictable and leads to all kinds of wrong expectations. In its extreme, economic costs of uncertainty could exceed costs of administrative controls. That is, a distortive but predictable policy regime could be preferable for economic agents than a volatile regime with smaller average number of notional distortions. In Armenia, with its divided political elite, frequent changes in the government, numerous competing controlling agencies, and a weak central oversight, one should not be surprised to see such a "decentralized model" of excessive regulation, driven less by a policy of the central Government but largely by all kinds of special interests.

Overextended powers of various inspections and regulators seem to be a single major failure of the Government's program to establish a liberal, business-friendly environment. First, the Armenian

Government is just too large and produces too much daily pressure on the relatively weak and small private sector. According to World Bank estimates, Armenia's budgetary sector employment in 1998-99 comprised almost 10% of the Armenia population[52], while in the OECD states the similar share on average amounts to 7.7% and in the FSU states – about 8%. Second, the overall inspection and controlling function of the Government is too fragmented with individual inspections enjoying little central oversight. According to Presidential Decree No. 352 of August 1, 1994, 17 separate state agencies were granted the right to conduct business inspections. The Decree was effective until the summer of 2000, when the new Law on Inspections somewhat reduced the number of inspecting agencies and introduced a new, more transparent framework for state inspections of businesses.

Given the massive state failure, enforcement of an investment-friendly business framework becomes the responsibility of the private sector. This happens in two main forms:

- A heroic entrepreneur, who takes advantage of a permissive legal framework and creates a tolerable business environment for himself by bribing his way out and by using mass media to get rid of state and criminal racket.

- Second, 'old boys' networks and established interest groups get access to scarce-services of the state (investor protection, competition policy, etc.). Note that this is different from a usual view of interest groups obtaining special favors from the state. Here, 'old boys' networks do not receive any special treatment but rather services to which they are entitled by law anyway. This is a plausible interpretation of why Armenian first movers (the most successful local firms) are quite happy with the local business environment. Through connections they are able to enforce and enjoy the notional business environment.

In both cases, the emerged business environment has not provided a level playing field and tends to support further traditional networks and personal links between business and political leaders. In a small economy this leads to strong non-competitive pressures,[53] non-market constraints for new entry, and excessive costs for all sorts of outsiders, including foreign investors. One example relates to massive tax evasion by a small group of powerful importers, closely linked to the military leadership. Such importers have been paying a lower effective tax than domestic producers, which delays import substitution.

Legacy of Mass Privatization

Overall for the CIS, mass privatization did not, as yet, bring significant improvements in enterprise performance.[54] However, statistical analysis revealed that a different ownership structure of privatized firms has quite a different impact on performance. Foreigners, banks, concentrated individual owners, and to a smaller extent managers tend to be the most effective owners, while ownership by workers, and more generally diffused ownership or ownership by insiders has the least impact on performance improvements.

This cross-country perspective helps to explain at least partially weak enterprise restructuring in Armenia, where two of the most effective ownership classes (banks and foreign investors) have very limited scope. At the same time, it presents a puzzle of inefficient management ownership in Armenia.

---

[52] Includes employment in the health sector to make it comparable to other countries. Armenia's total population is assumed to amount to 3.1 million.

[53] McKinsey (1999) report argues that non-equal treatment of businesses is an equivalent of redistribution from more to less productive firms.

[54] Djankov and Murrell (2000) provide a detailed statistical analysis of factors that influence enterprise restructuring in transition.

While on average in the CIS the management ownership is rather supportive of restructuring, it is not the case in Armenia yet. In a surprising number of cases, the strategy of incumbent managers has been based on exporting the existing equipment and keeping companies idle most of the time.

In contrast to many CIS countries, in Armenia highly diffused insiders' ownership, which emerged after mass privatization, was relatively quickly consolidated by incumbent managers. For instance, in the sample of 145 large joint-stock companies analyzed by the Securities Market Inspectorate of RA in 1999, on average 2-3 largest shareholders held about 70% of company stock.[55]-[56] And in almost all cases, these largest shareholders were companies' insiders. Holdings by outsiders were rather small.

Several explanations could be the reason why in Armenia the managers were active in consolidating their control over privatized companies but they were not successful in pursuing restructuring. First, as Djankov and Murrell (2000) describe, managerial turnover in state-owned and newly-privatized companies as well as competition with new entry constitute two additional significant determinants of enterprise restructuring in economies in transition. In Armenia, the effect of strong management ownership has been weaker because it is not complemented by sufficient management change (bringing new human capital into old firms) and competition with new entry.

Second, as suggested by Desai and Goldberg (2000), uncertainty and lack of market control undermine managerial incentives in both maximizing firm value and longer-term restructuring. If managers are certain that they neither would be able to preserve control in firms they own, nor would be able to sell its control profitably as a future exit strategy, they do not want to invest in company restructuring. Potential benefits for managers from appreciation of company value are smaller than could be obtained through asset stripping. Overall, uncertainty with respect to economic prospects of Armenia as well as political uncertainty undermine longer-term incentives of existing managers/owners and at the same time reduce incentives for new owners for coming in.[57]

Third, as this report argues at a number of occasions, many managers/owners may have sufficient incentives for restructuring but do not have capabilities to implement any sustainable restructuring strategy. What could be done to address this problem represents the main theme of Chapters 5 and 6.

The rest of this chapter reviews in some detail several more specific constraints for enterprise restructuring. The next section presents perceptions of major constraints for business development as they are seen by managers who participated in various business surveys. Then we report on main obstacles for enterprise development in the areas of:

- Financing
- Management skills
- Budget constraints
- Blockade of Armenia's Borders
- Corporate Governance

---

[55] At the same time, these companies continue to have a large number of small shareholders. The average number of company shareholders exceeded 200, and about two-thirds of company personnel remained a shareholder.
[56] In contrast, in a typical Russian firm in 1999, managers controlled about 15% and employees – 36% of the stock, Desai and Goldberg (2000).
[57] The Armenian public views its economic and political environment as highly uncertain. In 1999, 45% of participants of the large household survey answered "do not know " when asked about their economic forecast.

3.2.   Main Problems in the Business Environment as Seen by the Private Sector[58]

In Armenia, as elsewhere in the CEE, the central challenge of transition relates to the facilitation of private sector entry, growth and productivity. A key first step is to remove leading constraints in the business environment to private sector development. Typically, the foremost experts on these constraints are entrepreneurs themselves, who daily confront these constraints in operating and expanding their firms. This section identifies main problems in the business environment in Armenia, based primarily on an enterprise survey conducted in April 1999[59]. In addition, more evidence is brought in from several other enterprise surveys. The key findings of the 1999 survey include:

- The leading constraints to business development as rated by Armenian enterprises are taxes and regulations, policy instability and uncertainty, the exchange rate, inflation and financing.

- Like other countries in the CEE, tax rates and regulations are the leading regulatory problem. Tax administration problems may derive not only from government policies, but also from the accounting practices and financial capacity of firms.

- Political and policy uncertainty may not only derive from events but from the routine practices of government in not providing businesses advance information about changes in laws, regulations and policies affecting them, and failing to consult affected businesses before making critical decisions.

- High interest rates are currently identified as the dominant financial constraint, and help to explain why banks provide only a small percentage of finance to firms. Firms, especially small firms, rely heavily on family and friends for finance.

- Firms are quite concerned about competitors evading taxes and regulations, apparently a common problem.

- Roads are identified as the leading infrastructure constraint, via the poor rating of the public services in this area. Customs processing delays imports more than in other countries of the region.

- Finally, businesses appear to hold government in poor regard in terms of its helpfulness to businesses, efficiency and the quality and integrity of a number of public services.

Previous Surveys. A number of business surveys were conducted in Armenia between 1996 and 1999 that have examined various challenges confronted by Armenian private enterprises.[60] A number of profound findings emerged from this work.

- Firms identified financing as their leading constraint. 74.5 percent of surveyed firms in 1998 responded that they did not apply for available bank loans because of high interest rates. Instead, firms depended heavily on internal financing and traditional networks of family and friends. Expectations for future financing from special funds were abnormally elevated.

---

[58] This section is based on the background paper prepared by Geeta Batra and Andrew Stone.
[59] Annex 3.1 provides a description of the sample, which included 125 firms.
[60] Grigorian (1996), Hurwitz (1996), IRIS (1997), Najarian (1997), Sharafian (1997 and 1999), World Development Report (1997). In addition, IRIS (1997 and 1999) reports on factors inhibiting FDI based on interviews with foreign investors.

- Armenian firms felt over-taxed, but objected almost as strongly to administrative practices associated with taxation. Responses suggest a feeling of unfairness, due to stringent or arbitrary behavior of tax agents; complex requirements; and other firms' ability to evade their full tax liabilities. Both taxes and customs were reportedly subject to wide evasion and corruption, and firms suggested difficulties with competitors who avoided VAT and customs duties. There was a lack of information regarding changes in tax laws and regulations.

- The informal sector clearly played an important role in the economy – both in terms of firms themselves engaging in a degree of evasion of rules, and in terms of perceived competition from firms that did not meet obligations with regard to VAT and income taxes, customs duties and regulations, and labor regulations and payments.

- Armenian firms sell to the domestic market to a remarkable extent, yet feel very constrained by demand. In 1998, 44% of respondents identified low demand as a leading obstacle. In spite of this inward orientation, the heavy reliance on imported inputs meant that 70% of firms felt their costs increased because of the blockade imposed by Armenia's neighbors.

- The surveys identified serious problems in the lack of marketing expertise, marketing intelligence, and information on foreign markets. Technical assistance programs, training, study tours and other forms of assistance had reached only 20% of SMEs covered by the 1997 survey.

A direct comparison of two similar surveys conducted in 1996 (for the World Development Report) and in 1999 (IBRD/EBRD survey) suggests that the role of constraints related to taxation, policy instability, financing, and inflation and foreign exchange constraints has gone up or remained broadly unchanged. At the same time, the role of corruption, infrastructure supply, crime, trade and labor regulation, licensing and registration, and safety/environmental regulation diminished.

The most recent regulatory cost survey (2000), sponsored by the World Bank, suggests that the complexity and non-transparency of government policy is the leading business environment constraint, surpassing taxes and tax administration. Also, its results prove that the time costs of regulatory compliance are inordinate, averaging almost a quarter of managers' time, placing Armenian firms at a competitive disadvantage with countries with lower compliance costs. Inspections, led by tax inspections, fire inspections, sanitary inspections and pension inspections, average 6.6 per firm per year. And the burden of regulatory compliance is regressive, weighing more heavily on SMEs, which given Armenia's history, would logically be a more important source of growth and jobs than traditional privatized large enterprises. Tax administration, inspections, and start-up procedures all pose disproportionate costs on SMEs.

General Constraints. Table 3.2 summarizes businesses' general assessment of constraints to their operation and growth. The first leading constraint is tax regulation and administration. This is identified as a "major" constraint by small and medium firms and a "moderate" constraint by large firms. The second leading constraint is policy instability – which is found most constraining by medium-sized firms. Inflation is the third leading constraint, with firms in agriculture especially highlighting its effects, and firms in services identifying it as only a "minor" constraint. The exchange rate is identified as a moderate constraint by firms of all sizes, but those in commerce and industry find it more constraining than firms in agriculture and services (who rate it only a "minor" constraint). Lack of financing (in stark contrast with earlier surveys) ranks only fifth (also a "moderate" constraint) and affects firms of different sizes almost equally. Firms in commerce and industry find finance a bit more constraining than those in agriculture and services. Anti-competitive practices of rivals or government are singled out by industrial firms as somewhat more constraining than firms in other sectors, but still is rated only a "minor" constraint.

Table 3.2. General Business Constraints

(scale : 1=no obstacle, 3= moderate, 4=Very severe obstacle)

General Constraints	Small	Medium	Large	Agric.	Indust.	Commerce	Services	Overall Mean
Tax Regulation/Administration	3.5	3.6	2.9	3.4	3.4	3.6	3.1	3.4
Policy Instability	2.9	3.3	2.6	3.3	3.2	2.8	2.8	2.9
Inflation/Price Instability	2.8	3.0	2.6	3.3	2.9	2.9	2.2	2.8
Exchange rate	2.8	2.8	2.6	2.4	2.8	3.0	2.2	2.8
Lack of Financing	2.4	3.2	3.1	3.4	3.1	2.5	2.1	2.6
Anticompetive practices	1.7	2.3	2.3	1.0	2.3	1.8	1.8	1.9
Corruption	1.8	2.1	1.9	1.5	1.9	1.9	1.9	1.9
Streets Crimes/theft/disorder	1.8	2.2	1.5	2.2	1.4	1.9	2.1	1.8
Infrastructure	1.7	1.9	1.9	2.7	1.9	1.7	1.6	1.8
Organized Crime	1.4	1.9	1.4	1.2	1.5	1.5	1.9	1.5
Functioning of the judiciary	1.4	1.5	1.8	1.2	1.5	1.4	1.8	1.5

Source: World Bank.

Comparing Armenia to the average results of 22 economies in transition (Chart 3.1), it becomes clear that within its region, Armenian firms rate taxes and regulations distinctly worse than average, while policy uncertainty and exchange rate uncertainty are ranked slightly worse than average. A number of constraints appear far less severe in Armenia than in the region, including all crime-related constraints, corruption, and anti-competitive practices, as well as inflation and even finance. Not surprisingly, Armenia has a ways to go before attaining the positive conditions of the 9 OECD countries in which this survey was administered, but the positive rating of the judiciary is noteworthy. Finally, it appears that many Latin American firms evaluate a number of their countries' conditions worse or no better than do Armenia firms, with the notable exception of taxes and regulations.

Chart 3.1. General Constraints to Armenian Firms and Regional Comparators

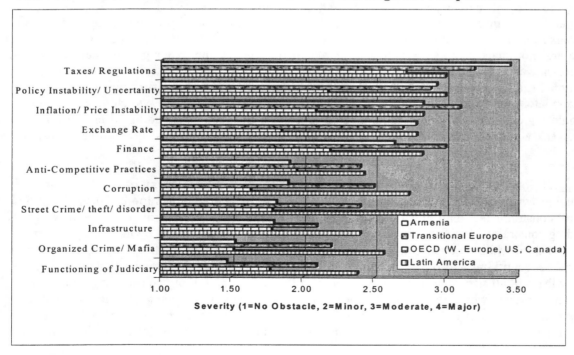

Source: World Bank.

Taxes and Business Regulations. In contrast to taxation, most other areas of regulation are at least slightly less constraining than the average. Labor regulations are especially unconstraining, evaluated as no problem at all. However, it should be noted that large firms find customs and trade regulations more constraining than do other firms.

Small firms find both taxes and tax administration somewhat more constraining than larger ones, lending some credence to Sharafian's analysis that part of the problem lies in the inexperience of firms in dealing with issues of financial management. However, such a result might also be found in a country either having unnecessarily complex tax rules (such that there are scale of economies for firms to deal with their complexity), taxes biased against smaller firms, or a system subject to the influence of larger and more influential firms.

Large firms find competitors' avoidance of duties and trade regulations and their receipt of subsidies as moderate constraints. The complaints about competitors' tax avoidance draw attention to the fact that there is substantial evasion. Although nearly 40% of firms estimated that the typical firm pays all of its taxes, the remaining 61% suggested that at least some taxes are avoided. Roughly 39% of firms suggested that the amount of income hidden from authorities for tax purposes amounted to more than 10% of the value of sales, and just over 20% of firms estimated that the typical firm hides more than half of its sales from the government. In spite of the seemingly high frequency of evasion, Armenia rated below the regional average for self-reported evasion, with the third highest rate of reporting at least 99% of income to tax authorities.

Foreign currency regulations rank as the second least favorite form of regulation among Armenian firms, and customs regulation place a close third. Customs and other aspects of import processing appear unnecessarily time-consuming for Armenian firms (Chart 3.2). For those firms importing goods directly, it takes an average of over 8 days from the time they arrive at the point of entry to the time they can be claimed, as opposed to a regional average of fewer than six days. By contrast, in Singapore, goods can generally be claimed within about three hours of their arrival in port.

Chart 3.2. Average Number of Days from Goods arrival at Port of Entry to Customs Clearance

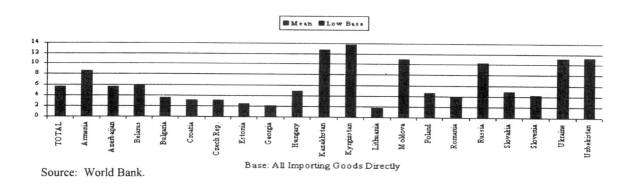

Source: World Bank.

Political Uncertainty and Policy Instability. The survey predates the assassination of Armenia's Prime Minister and other key political leaders in late 1999, so the "moderate" rating is likely reflective of the underlying level of political and policy instability. Results indicate that businesses find economic policies affecting them hard to predict. Over 60% of firms rated changes in economic policies as either "fairly", "highly", or "completely" unpredictable.

Other responses make it clear that an important source of policy uncertainty is the failure of government to adequately communicate changes in advance and consult the private sector. First, in a region with a markedly poor record for informing businesses in advance about legal, regulatory and policy changes affecting them (an average of 62% say they are never or seldom informed in advance), Armenia does even worse. Over 70% of enterprises state they are never or seldom informed in advance, and another 10% say this only "sometimes" happens.

Beyond not receiving information, many businesses are not consulted by government about changes affecting them and feel they have no "voice" in government decisions. For example, the average firm says the government "seldom" takes into account concerns voiced by the firm or its business association in decisions affecting them. The failure to consult may reduce compliance, reduce the quality of decisions and add to the unpredictability of the policy and regulatory environment for investors and managers.

Table 3.3. Financial Constraints to Armenian Enterprises

(scale : 1=no obstacle, 3= moderate, 4=Very severe obstacle)

Financing Constraints	Small	Medium	Large	Agric.	Industry	Commerce	Services	Overall Mean
High interest rates	2.8	2.6	2.7	2.6	2.8	2.9	2.4	2.8
Lack access to LT banks loans	1.6	1.9	2.2	2.0	2.0	1.8	1.2	1.8
Excess of paperworks/bureaucracy	1.4	2.3	2.0	1.4	2.1	1.5	1.3	1.7
Collateral requirements of Fin. Inst.	1.3	2.1	1.8	1.6	1.9	1.4	1.1	1.5
Banks lack money to lend	1.3	1.7	2.1	1.7	1.8	1.4	1.0	1.5
Inadeq. Credit info. System	1.3	1.7	1.6	1.6	1.7	1.4	1.1	1.4
Need special connections with banks/Fin. Inst.	1.3	1.6	1.7	1.2	1.7	1.4	1.0	1.4
Lack access to foreign banks	1.2	1.4	1.5	1.4	1.5	1.3	1.0	1.3
Lack access to lease finance for equipment	1.1	1.5	1.6	1.4	1.6	1.2	1.0	1.3
Lack access to equity investors or partners	1.1	1.4	1.7	1.4	1.4	1.3	1.0	1.3
Corruption of banks officials	1.1	1.3	1.5	1.3	1.2	1.1	1.0	1.2
Lack of access to specialized export finance	1.0	1.3	1.3	1.0	1.2	1.1	1.0	1.1

Source: World Bank.

Financing. After taxes and regulations, policy instability and inflation, financing is the fourth leading constraint identified by Armenian firms (Table 3.3). Across all firm sizes and sectors, the leading financing constraint is high interest rates. Persistent lack of access to long-term loans is the second leading constraint overall, but for medium-sized firms, excessive paperwork required and the collateral requirements of banks rank ahead of this constraint. Interest rates stand out as the leading financial constraint for more firms in Armenia than in any other country in the sample. This is not entirely surprising given the combination of current account deficits and tight money policies in place which, at the time of the survey, yielded a real interest rate of close to 40%.

It is not clear why the financing constraint has declined in importance between the 1998 and 1999 surveys, but it is evident that firms rely very little on banks (Table 3.4). Firms derived only 2% of their finance from local banks. Small firms derive no finance at all from banks, but even among large firms, only 13% have any finance from domestic commercial banks. By contrast, money from family and friends (presumably heavily influenced by foreign remittances) is the leading source of external finance for small firms and an important source for medium and large firms. Nearly half of the small firms derive some finance from family and friends, while more medium and large firms get financing from family and friends than from banks. Small and medium firms derive more finance from family and friends than from banks, but for large firms banks provide a somewhat higher percentage of total finance (6.1%).

Table 3.4. Structure of Financing, by Company Size

	Percent w/Commercial Bank Financing	Percent w/Friends and Family Financing
Small	0	46
Medium	6.7	30
Large	13.3	20

Source: World Bank.

Public Services: Quality and Integrity. Table 3.5 shows the efficiency ratings assigned to a number of public services. One discouraging result is that most of the agencies rank in the "slightly bad" category (3.5 to 4.49). The Roads Department and Parliament are rated worst, with central government close behind.

Table 3.5: Quality and Efficiency of Public Services

(scale : 1=very good, 3= slightly good, 6=Very bad)

Effic./Quality Public services	Small	Medium	Large	Agric.	Indust.	Commerce	Services	Overall Mean
Roads Department	4.35	4.50	4.77	5.14	4.67	4.22	4.47	4.43
The Parliament	4.40	4.42	4.07	4.80	4.57	4.34	3.86	4.36
The Central Gov't	4.20	4.35	3.60	4.00	4.31	4.13	3.93	4.15
Customs	4.10	4.06	3.92	4.33	3.91	4.13	4.00	4.07
Public Health/hospitals	4.06	3.92	4.00	4.00	3.69	4.11	4.38	4.02
Education Services/schools	4.07	3.76	3.82	3.50	4.00	3.91	4.45	3.97
Courts of Justice	4.17	3.42	3.40	3.50	3.62	3.98	4.21	3.90
Water/Sewerage Services	3.61	3.53	4.07	4.29	3.51	3.63	3.73	3.65
Telephone Services	3.41	3.60	4.67	5.00	3.37	3.59	3.71	3.61
Postal Services	3.50	3.18	4.14	4.83	3.32	3.31	4.00	3.50
The Police	3.59	3.14	3.64	2.75	3.59	3.34	4.13	3.49
Electric Power Company	3.15	3.30	3.40	3.29	3.26	3.18	3.24	3.22
The armed forces	2.94	2.47	2.77	2.40	2.63	2.70	3.69	2.82

Source: World Bank.

The government is perceived to be unhelpful to private enterprises. While the largest number of firms find the government to be neither helpful nor unhelpful to businesses, 48% find the central government to be either mildly or very unhelpful to businesses, and 43% place local government in these unhelpful categories. Only 7% find the central government mildly or very helpful to firms and 9% place local government in these favorable categories.

In addition to not being helpful, the government is regarded as inefficient in delivering public services. In a region marked by weak public service delivery, Armenia nonetheless stands out for the high percentage of firms ranking the government from mostly to very inefficient (85%).

One factor highly associated with weak governance and public service delivery is corruption. In a notably corrupt region, Armenia nonetheless rates slightly worse than average in the frequency of corruption. Over 40% of firms place it in the frequency of "informal payments to get things done" in the three highest categories: "frequently", "usually" or "always". The data makes it clear that the frequency of bribery declines with firm size, and that payments are made more often by firms in commerce and services.

Table 3.6 shows that bribery imposes a significant tax on firms, averaging around 7% of total revenue. Small firms are far more likely to pay in excess of 10% of revenues in "additional payments" to public officials, medium firms are most likely to pay less than 1% (although none say 0%), and half of the large firms estimate that between 2 and 9% of revenues go to bribes. By sector, it appears that commercial and service firms pay more in bribes than industrial firms, who pay more than agricultural firms.

Table 3.6. Percentage of Total Sales Paid as Bribes

Percentage of total sales as bribes	Small	Medium	Large	Agric.	Indust.	Commerce	Services	Overall Frequency
0%	0.00	0.00	0.00	0.00	0.00	0.00	0.00	0.00
Less than 1%	41.86	69.23	12.50	66.67	50.00	40.00	37.50	43.75
1-1.99%	9.30	7.69	37.50	33.33	5.56	11.43	25.00	12.50
2-9.99%	9.30	15.38	50.00	0.00	27.78	14.29	0.00	15.62
10-12%	9.30	0.00	0.00	0.00	0.00	8.57	12.50	6.25
13-25%	20.93	7.69	0.00	0.00	16.67	20.00	0.00	15.62
Over 25%	9.30	0.00	0.00	0.00	0.00	5.71	25.00	6.25

Note: (% of firms in each category)

Source: World Bank.

With what activities are unofficial payments most often associated? The data below suggest a general ordering of public services, based on the frequency with which different activities were reported by firms to "frequently", "usually" or "always" require a bribe. Two patterns are apparent: first, that dealing with taxes, obtaining licenses and permits, dealing with courts, gaining government contracts and dealing with customs all involve a significant frequency of extra payments. Second, in each of these cases, Armenian firms report a higher frequency of bribes than did the average firm in the region, especially with regard to taxes, licenses and courts. Third, the data (Table 3.7) suggest that Armenian firms face much less predictability regarding unofficial payments that they have to pay.

Table 3.7. Percent of Firms that Rated at 1, 2, 3

(1 always, 2 mostly, 3 frequently, 4 sometimes, 5 seldom, 6 never)

	Irregular additional payments made to Government	Advance knowledge of amount of additional payment	Service delivered as agreed if additional payment made	If payment made to one official, another Gov. official will request payment for same service	If Gov. official acts against rules, can go to superior and get correct treatment without recourse to unofficial payment
OECD	0.12	0.26	0.62	0.17	0.45
CIS	0.29	0.46	0.75	0.35	0.38
CEE	0.33	0.48	0.73	0.28	0.36
Armenia	0.40	0.51	0.73	0.36	0.37

Source: World Bank.

3.3.   Skill-Based Constraints to Growth

Armenia is a small, landlocked and resource-poor country. In addition, due to the Soviet legacy, it lacks either a set of established viable economic links with the global economy or a sufficient capacity for a rapid development of such links. Also, as in many other economies in transition, underdeveloped management skills represent the weakest element of labor and human capital.[61] These unfavorable endowments, combined with the current political risks, support the existing patterns of isolationism. Due to a severe shortage of modern management skills on the supply side and limited interest from foreign investors on the demand side, there are major barriers for expanding export and, more generally, for joining the global economy. As it is argued elsewhere in this report, establishment of knowledge, trade,

---

[61] Alacacer (2000).

and financial linkages with more advanced economies should be the central policy focus of the Government policy.

A Parable of Skill-based Constraints for Restructuring

The problems and opportunities for skill-based growth in Armenia could be told as a parable of two small software firms in Yerevan. They share the same history and are almost identical in their endowments of human and fixed capital. Yet, one is prospering and working with a leading multinational in Silicon Valley, while the other is struggling to survive. The successful firm was able to plug-in into worldwide networks of information technology. Through this collaboration, it takes advantage of design and marketing capabilities of leading firms in the USA. More generally, it learns about product differentiation and the importance of just-in-time delivery. Given rapidly changing needs of customers and demanding production and logistics disciplines, needed to keep pace with these changes, the successful firm is becoming a part of the new, knowledge-processing economy. Its small size and modest resources are not obstacles to success precisely because manufacturing and marketing skills, demanded by the market, largely reside in networks, not in individual firms.

In contrast, the struggling firm is at risk, in a great part because, like almost all Armenian firms, it is trying to survive on its own, mostly cut off from both leading foreign corporations and from other domestic companies. All the knowledge-induced changes that create opportunities for the first firm are threats to its neighbor. For the same disruptions of routine and habit that allow the first firm to convert inexperience into open-mindedness and the ability to take a fresh approach, create daunting risks for the second. While the first firm is trying to become a global market participant, the second one, left without connections, financial resources and relevant experience, is relegated to the CIS market and local public sector demand.

With regard to skills, the story is similar. When it comes to hands-on experience in programming, both owners-entrepreneurs are comparable. The successful one has a team of qualified programmers working for the firm full time. The surviving firm has a couple of moonlighting students, so that when a potential order from the US arrives, the firm is unable to meet the tight deadline and quality standards. Caught in yet another vicious circle, the failing firm has a hard time showing prospective customers that it could make good use of its high quality human capital if given the chance to use it.

Worse yet, the first firm is learning how to learn, the second only how much it does not know. The first firm embarks on *a virtuous circle of learning* (success breeds success -- inclusion in knowledge networks brings new expertise and makes subsequent learning more productive), while the second one falls into a *vicious circle of poverty* (failure breeds failure: exclusion from knowledge networks diminishes further chances to catch-up). In a global economy, which is increasingly characterized by rapid changes from unexpected sources, the success of individuals, firms, regions and national economies is based on their capability to learn by entering virtuous circles, while of course avoiding or rapidly extricating themselves from vicious ones. Put bluntly, capacity to learn is critical when changes are massive and fast.

On the surface, the fundamental differences in the firms' trajectories derive from pure chance: the successful firm had obtained access to foreign orders and capital at a crucial moment of its development through the owner's wealthy uncle who emigrated to the USA in the early 90s. In contrast, the owner of the failing firm was not favored by rich relatives. Moreover, the government's lending programs, administered by Armenian commercial banks, were not available to him either. The banks have so much trouble assessing the prospects of turning the firm around that they hesitate to make a loan.

From the perspective of this report, the example above presents a major policy issue to be addressed by the Armenian Government: How can those entrepreneurs who do not have a wealthy uncle be helped? How to support economic agents that face broadly correct incentives to learn and restructure but lack knowledge on new markets and market opportunities and capabilities to act on such incentives? The challenge is establishing business linkages – linkages between potential investors and potential local recipients of such investments as well as linkages between local firms, which would help them to reduce costs of both learning and entering the global market. The perception that establishment of such linkages is mostly a matter of luck (rich uncle from the Diaspora) is counter-productive; there is quite a lot that the Government could do in this field.

Experience of Enterprises Breaking Into New Markets (first movers)

The nature of skill-based constraints for export-oriented growth can be further gleaned from business practices of relatively successful enterprises breaking into new markets – first movers. The 'first movers', such as both software firms described above, are companies that are trying to do things differently from others. The section below is based on detailed case studies of 27 Armenian manufacturing firms, which were identified as first movers.[62]

(a) Characteristics of First Movers

- what distinguishes the first movers from the rest is their success in addressing "binding constraints", related to financing, marketing and other managerial knowledge, transportation and exports, and ability to get protection from harassment;

- even the first movers in Armenia are quite unsophisticated firms -- the sample contains a limited number of examples that describe a fundamental change in the product mix; observed examples of entrepreneurial spirit reflect mostly organization of rather traditional production units in non-traditional circumstances; the break-through that we see relate not to new product or marketing ideas but to new (for this country) arrangements to ensure both financing and political protection;

(b) Business Environment for First Movers

- availability of financing (thanks to credit lines sponsored by donors) seems reasonable; active people with sufficient expertise to develop a decent business plan are likely to get financing; many others may need additional help with preparation of business plans and other start up arrangements;

- access to subsidized credit lines is a critical factor in many cases; there is a concern that such access is correlated with political connections;

- first movers don't complain on the quality of the business climate; it is likely that they enjoy rents from their political connections and a special local status (outside of Yerevan); level playing field is a problem; entry costs are uneven and could be prohibitively high for too many;

- factor markets seems to work: case studies suggest sufficiently mobile reallocation of labor and capital from less efficient to more efficient firms; first movers are able to get equipment through asset-stripping; no big problems with access to real estate (land, building, office space); the system is open enough for takeover by outsiders; asset prices are depressed;

---

[62] The case-studies were prepared by Alex Poghossian and Vahram Stepanyan in the second half of 1999. Annex 3.2 provides a description of the enterprise sample.

(c) Support Programs and Linkages from First Movers

- very little reference could be observed to any value added from current programs of technical assistance that do not seem to address real needs of the private sector in terms of shortage of managerial skills; there is a need to reshape technical assistance with more emphasis of promotion of business linkages with the rest of the world, to have demand driven programs that support self-selection of recipients;

- the business environment remains quite segmented, no institutions for collective learning and sharing costs (only one reference to participation in an export association), no real impact of business associations;

- replication of the first successes happens but not very frequently and exclusively in sectors with low costs of entry; expansion of success along technological lines is the most noticeable in food industry: retail trade, food processing, packaging, agriculture, some equipment for food industry; there is a clear potential in a diamonds-gems-gold-watches cluster but this may need much more investments with a possible need for the Government's targeted investment promotion program;

- supply chains do not emerge even in the simplest situations: by unclear reasons molybdenum is imported from Mongolia not from a local mine; similarly copper is imported from Russia for local wire production;

(d) Links that First Movers Benefit From

- existence of traditional links with the Russian market seems to be a major comparative advantage; business links with Russia as a resource is as important as links with the non-CIS Diaspora;

- expansion to non-CIS markets is going rather slowly even for those firms which are successful in Russia; a clear skill gap here, a need for public intervention in support of business linkages;

- the Diaspora, when it is involved, operates mostly a source of financing (credits, FDI) and much less as a source of market information and expertise; not a knowledge bridge;

To summarize the above analysis, the single most important stylized fact about the sample is continuing isolation of the first movers, both from each other and from international value chains. This implies promotion of business linkages (marketing, managerial, financial, supply chain linkages) represents the first order of the policy agenda. This business linkages agenda is further illustrated by an example of the former SOE garment factory that represents a 'low' road to competitiveness, characterized by low value added (Box 3.2).

Box 3.2. Glass Half-Full or Half-Empty? Example of Contract Manufacturing in an Apparel Industry

On the face of it, the company is a highly successful paragon of market transition. This is a privatized firm with 51% of stock owned by the firm's manager, 20% by a US businesswoman of Armenian origin, with the rest of the equity belonging to the workers. 90% of output (waterproof nylon jackets) is exported to the USA. Compared to 1990 (the peak output), level of employment remains almost stable (around 500 people), although most of the work force is now employed part-time, labor turnover is very high and wages are low even by Armenian standards (US$10 per month). The firm's manager/owner admits that a large share of qualified personnel has left (many emigrated), and the current personnel is of poor quality, often undernourished. The firm has two competitive advantages. First, it has relatively modern Italian equipment installed in 1990. Second, there is an energetic and forceful management, who appears to be learning, albeit slowly, new management techniques and is determined to find profitable sales contracts.

The major share of capacity utilization comes from a contract with a single American distributor, who purchases waterproof jackets, puts on them its own trademark and sells them in the USA. All apparel inputs come from Turkey. The enterprise receives US$1.30 for manufacturing one coat, approximately one percent of the US retail price. Those $1.30 cover more than 70 operations, each of them involving a separate employee. This price barely allows for survival of the enterprise. However, the problem is not so much a low unit price, as current stalled opportunities for learning and acquisition of marketing skills because the current sale contract relegates the enterprise to assembly only and precludes moving into marketing and distribution.

The company's experience could be summarized as follows. First, the firm is clearly a first mover: it did break in into new markets and established new business contacts. Although focusing on low value-added activity, the firm is doing well compared to similar firms in the industry. Second, serendipity – fortunate constellation of circumstances – played an important part in discovering new business opportunities. In 1992, on a business trip abroad, the manager made contact with wholesalers from Holland, who from 1992 to 1997 purchased most of the firm's output and shipped it by air taking advantage of low air tariffs at that time. Third, many business opportunities were missed. For instance, many employees of the factory emigrated to the West. Although they still maintain close contacts with their relatives in Armenia, no attempts were made to convert them into the factory' marketing and sales force. Obviously, this is a non-trivial task but this opportunity was not even considered. Fourth, there are still signs of managerial learning that suggest that the 'glass is half-full rather than half-empty'. After an extensive search, the firm is about to sign a contract with another western wholesaler, which would be based on a profit-sharing arrangement. This would present more opportunities for learning of crucial marketing skills. Paradoxically, it is a perspective of a looming crisis (because of increased energy prices, $1.30 per coat the firm receives from the American distributor would not cover even operating costs), which prompted the manager to look for other opportunities. Sixth, it is intrinsic motivation that largely explains why the firm is still in business in an apparently inhospitable business environment: although business barriers are high, the management is unusually motivated to overcome them. The management identifies themselves with the firm, thus, closure of the enterprise could imply loss of their identity.

The major impediments for deeper restructuring of the company are quite typical of Armenia and relate to a pervasive lack of business information and marketing skills. (The manager was not even aware of various credit programs, sponsored by the World Bank and other donors.) It should be noted that subcontracting in apparel industry could be a relatively high-value activity, provided the output is sophisticated, based on the latest designs and shipped ready for sale. This move to higher value added subcontracting (exemplified by countries such as Turkey or Mexico) would require reliable access to relevant information and serious investments in management training. As a low income country, Armenia has received significant (compared to the current levels of exports) quotas for textile export to both EU and USA, which could be another potential incentive for strategic investors in this sector.

3.4. Private Credit: Limited Access at High Costs

In the late 90s, Armenia was characterized by a relatively well-regulated banking sector, which, however, remained small in size and rather segmented. The level of confidence to national currency and to the banking sector remained limited, and the economy is highly dollarized. Various estimates of cash dollars accumulated by Armenian residents put their amount in the range of 10-15% of GDP, while dram money supply is still at the level of 7% of GDP. According to the IMF, in the late 90s the currency substitution ratio, defined as a ratio of foreign currency deposits to broad money, was 15-20 percentage point higher than the median for CIS.

The Government banking and financial policies have been consistently liberal, and by the mid-90s the Government removed most restrictions on interest rates, capital flows, and foreign ownership in banking. In June 1997, the Law introduced stronger protection for owners of banking accounts, and evoked rights of any Government agency to freeze money at bank accounts without a Court decision.

This created a limited boost in confidence in banks. The share of cash in the total dram money supply still amounted to 70% in late 2000. While growth in total bank deposits was high recently, it was mostly due to hard currency deposits. Also, increase in deposits was fueled primarily by expansion in household deposits, while growth in deposits made by firms accounted for only 20% of the total deposit increase in 1999-2000. The latter reflects the fact that a large part of business transactions are still made outside of the banking system.

Despite considerable expansion in the late 90s, total assets of the banking sector amounted to just about 20% of GDP and total credit to the economy was about 9% of GDP at the end of 1999 (Table 3.8). Moreover, out of the total outstanding credits, only 57% were recorded as allocated to the enterprise sector, while the rest was reported as loans to households, which included both consumer credits and commercial credits to family businesses (micro credit).

Table 3.8. Several Monetary Indicators (End of Period Stock), Million Dram and Percent

	1997	1998	1999
Net Domestic Assets	42,652	80,686	81,088
Growth rate, %	-12.6	89.2	0.5
Credits to the Economy	48,486	81,601	90,127
Growth rate, %	30.4	68.3	10.4
Share, as % of GDP	6.0	8.5	9.1
Credits to the enterprise sector	37,560	45,828	51,690
Growth rate, %	17.2	22.0	9.8
Credits to non-state enterprises	12,175	17,828	25,869
Growth rate, %		46.4	45.1
Share, as % of GDP	1.5	1.9	2.6
Credits to the enterprise sector funded by the Credit lines	2,000	4,769	10,132
Share of total, %	5.3	10.4	19.6
Credits to the enterprise sector funded by Domestic sources	35,560	41,059	41,558

Source: Central Bank of Armenia.

There are 31 commercial bank in Armenia, most of rather a small size. The concentration of the banking system is relatively low for such a small economy, with the largest 3 banks accounting for 35 percent and the largest 10 banks for about 75 percent of its assets in mid-2000. 12 banks are either fully-owned subsidiaries of foreign banks or foreign banks have controlling interests in them. Foreign participation in the banking system increased following the removal in June 1995 of the 35 percent limit on foreign ownership of banks and reached 45 percent of aggregate banks' shareholders' equity in 1999. These 12 foreign banks accounted for about 44 percent of total assets of the system at the end of 2000.

The main trends with respect to enterprise credit could be summarized as follows:

- Public enterprises remained main recipients of banking credits until 1999. Their share was about 64% of the total outstanding credit in 1997, and declined to 50% in 1999.

- Loans to the enterprise sector were heavily concentrated in a few sectors, primarily in energy (Table 3.9). Credits to the publicly-controlled energy sector were allocated under heavy government interventions and at discounted rates (usually at 50% of market rate). These credits, which amounted to 50% of the total stock in 1998, have been similar in nature to non-commercial direct credits. In addition, about 20% of total credits in 1997-98 were backed by government guarantees. Almost all guarantees were granted to state-owned enterprises. The share of credits granted to manufacturing increased in 2000, however, because of much larger disbursements under donor-sponsored credit lines.

- Even in the recent period of high growth in credit, expansion in credits to the economy lagged behind growth in banking deposits, which reflects the limited intermediation capabilities of banks; e.g. accumulated growth of deposits amounted to 50% in 1999-2000, while net credits to the economy increased by about 25%.

- 80-85% of all loans are dollar denominated, while, given low export volumes, few borrowers have access to hard currency proceeds; this results in rather significant currency risks for the entire banking system.

- Since 1996, Armenian enterprises have been getting expanding access to donor-funded credit lines. The share of credit lines increased from 5% of the total credit in 1997 to about 20% in 1999. The overall expansion in the outstanding enterprise credit in 1999 derived exclusively from increased disbursements under credit lines. However, different types of borrowers have unequal access to the credit lines. Small newly established firms are disqualified in many cases.

- The high incidence of credit lines created additional distortions in the financial system. Average reported interest rates have been about twice lower under credit line loans compared to regular bank lending.[63] In addition, many of the credit lines have implicit government guarantees for commercial banks that administer them.

- The share of bad loans in the total outstanding credit dropped from 24.2% in 1996 to 10.6% in 1999 despite deterioration in enterprise performance after 1998. This happened due to tightening of banking supervision by the Central Bank, as well as because of concentration of credits within a smaller group of largest borrowers with the established credit history.

---

[63] At the same time, there is strong evidence that banks charge their clients with various informal fees for access to donor-funded credit lines. Thus, contrary to donors' intentions, most credit line subsidies were received by commercial banks, not by final borrowers.

Table 3.9. The Sectoral Structure of Enterprise Credits, Percent

	Loans in USD			Loans in AMD			Total loans		
	1998	1999	July 2000	1998	1999	July 2000	1998	1999	July 2000
Total	100	100	100	100	100	100	100	100.0	100
Industry	11	18	26.8	25.9	31.8	49.8	13.5	21.4	31.0
Energy	55	47	31.7	23.3	12.4	1.4	50.4	39.1	26.2
Agriculture	8	10	13.7	11.8	11.4	20.6	8.2	10.5	15.0
Construction	3	1	3.0	13.2	12.4	14.3	4.1	3.5	5.1
Transport and communication	2	2	2.8	2.0	0.4	0.5	2.1	1.5	2.3
Trade	15	10	21.9	20.0	9.8	13.5	16.1	9.8	20.4
Others	6	12	0.0	3.8	21.9	0.0	5.6	14.1	0.0

Source: Central Bank of Armenia.

Overall, while private credit has been growing with the annual rate in excess of 40% in 1998-99, availability of credit to the private sector still remains quite limited. The total stock of credit to the formal private sector (which is the only truly commercial banking credit in the system) amounted to 2.6% of GDP by the end of 1999[64]. Also, despite some recent decline in interest rates, most of this credit is still expensive – 30% and more in dollar terms (Table 3.10).

Table 3.10. Average Interest Rates for Various Types of Loans, Per Annum

	1998	1999	2000
Interest on loans in AMD:			
- Households and individual borrowers	54.6	33.9	30.7
- Legal entities	44.0	35.1	36.9
Interest on loans in USD:			
- Households and individual borrowers	47.5	47.2	35.3
- Legal entities	38.0	35.3	29.4
Interest rates under Credit lines	12-18	12-18	12-18

Source: Central Bank of Armenia.

A major positive development of the last two years relates to a noticeable increase in the average maturity of bank loans. The share of loans with a maturity of 1 year and longer has increased from 10% in 1996 to 62% in 2000 (Table 3.11). This is also a reflection of the recent expansion in credit line disbursements, which on average have longer maturities. Also, there is growing differentiation between borrowers: a limited number of (often large) companies with an established credit history have been able to get longer-term credits, while most of the private sector continues to face limited access even to short-term borrowing.

Table 3.11. The Composition of Banking Credits by Maturity, by Year End, Percent

	1995	1996	1997	1998	1999	2000 Preliminary
Total credits, o/w:	100	100	100	100	100	100
- less than 1 year	84	90	88.2	64.9	55.5	37.9
- 1 year and more	16	10	11.8	35.1	44.5	62.1

Source: Central Bank of Armenia.

---

[64] Excluding individual entrepreneurs.

Structural Problems in the Banking Sector and Economic Growth

Various empirical growth studies suggest a strong positive correlation between financial depth and long-term growth rates[65]. In Armenia, the economy remains heavily undermonetized and development of the financial system lags seriously behind progress on the macroeconomic side. In particular, M2/GDP ratios in Armenia are still much lower that those in e.g. Moldova and the Kyrgyz Republic, which are the countries with significantly weaker macroeconomic fundamentals.

However, as this report argues, the low level of monetization seems to be more an indication of various economy-wide constraints for growth and less a bottleneck for growth acceleration on its own. Furthermore, experience of other developing economies suggests that it is not uncommon when financing of the early stages of enterprise restructuring does not rely on banks, especially domestic banks.[66] Instead, it is usually coming from other sources, such as commercial credit from suppliers and other partners. Successful companies often manage to get export contracts first, and only then banks are ready to provide them with loans, not the other way around.

The recent review of Armenia's financial sector, conducted by the World Bank[67], pointed out several factors that hinder improvements in both mobilization of financial savings and efficiency of financial intermediation. These could be summarized as follows:

- High operational costs of Armenian banks, associated with the small size of most banks, drive up lending rates. In this context, there is a need to facilitate consolidation of the banking system.

- High incidence of informal activities reduces the share of total financial savings available for the formal financial sector.

- Inefficiency in domestic borrowing by the public sector has pushed up economy-wide interest rates.

- Limited presence of leading international financial institutions and non-sophistication of local banks resulted in an undeveloped menu of financial instruments available for domestic investors.

While Armenia has been rather advanced in terms of financial sector liberalization, the financial reforms (as a number of similar reforms in other sectors) did not produce adequate investment response and financial deepening as yet. The core reason for this failure relates to remaining distortions in the business environment, which, among other things, is mostly responsible for an excessively high share of informal activities. Informality reduces volume of resources available for mobilization by the financial sector and at the same time increases risks for banks' lending. In this sense, the leading constraint for financial deepening lies outside of the financial sector and financial policy and should be addressed through a broader policy package.

Overall, there is a potential for a low equilibrium trap in the financial sector, where several adverse factors have a mutually re-enforcing negative impact on development prospects:

---

[65] Levine (1997).
[66] World Bank (1998b). Mexico: Strengthening Enterprise Finance.
[67] World Bank (2000a). Armenia: Targeted Financial Sector Review.

- much more funding is potentially available (credit lines) than is actually utilized due to demand constraints (quality of business plans, low transparency of borrowers, not properly registered property rights, etc.);[68]

- those funds which are utilized are too expensive because of high costs of intermediation related to the small size of banks, weak judicial protection of lenders' rights, unresolved property rights issues (e.g. for urban land) that limit the scope of potential collateral, etc;

- low "recycling" of funds due to informality and the confidence crisis – a low share of funds channeled by banks to the real sector returns back as private sector deposits.

Still, there is still no full explanation of persistently high real interest rates in Armenia. As discussed in the macroeconomic section above, in addition to structural problems in the sector, interest rates were affected by the inconsistency between fiscal and monetary policy. Government policy targets in the past (1997-99) combined running substantial budget deficit with low inflation targets and a stable exchange rate. As in many other countries in such a situation, this led to rather a tight monetary policy and high interest rates. Some improvements in the institutional arrangements, relaxed monetary supply in 2000, and reduced Government net borrowing helped to reduce TB interest rates substantially in the course of 2000. But the prevailing interest rates are still excessively high.

3.5. Additional Costs to Business Associated with Blockade and Regional Conflicts[69]

Since the breakup of the USSR, the South Caucasus region had experienced a range of political conflicts resulting in a number of wars and border closures. A decade old dispute between Armenia and Azerbaijan over Nagorno-Karabakh (NK) had led to an undeclared state of war between the two countries. In 1994, a cease-fire was reached but the borders between the two countries are closed and trade, officially, does not exist.

A key economic consequence of the NK conflict - the closure of two-thirds of Armenia's borders (those with Azerbaijan and Turkey) - had cut off Armenia's rail links with countries other than Georgia (and because of an internal rift in Georgia, the rail link north from Armenia does not currently extend through to Russia). Trans-shipment of Armenian goods though Georgia is compromised by weak management, corruption, inefficiencies, and theft resulting in high costs for all modes of transport (road, rail and port), which creates a serious setback for Armenia's competitiveness. For instance, the first 700 km of the 2,200 km between Yerevan and Moscow account for 80 percent of the total cost of moving a consignment. The limited trade with Iran provides little opportunity for trans-shipment to the rest of the world.

As a result, disrupted traditional transportation routes stifle the export and import capabilities of Armenia, inflicting substantial visible economic losses and leading to sub-optimal geography of trade. In the 1998 survey (Sharafian, 1999), participating firms suggested that their costs were increased by an average of 70% due to the blockade. The general effect of blockades on Armenian exports can be illustrated by the dynamics of the overall freight factor (the ratio of freight costs to the value of merchandise) in the BOP. As shown in Table 3.12, as the most geographically isolated country, Armenia

---

[68] Share of credit to the economy in total bank assets stayed below 50% since the middle of 1997. In addition, a significant increase in foreign assets of Armenian banks in 1999-2000 provides another indication that banks face serious problems with bankable investment projects within the country.

[69] This section is based on Polyakov, Evegeny (2001).

registers the highest freight factor[70] in the Southern Caucasus. Overall, total annual direct extra costs of transportation in Armenia, which could be attributed to closing borders in the region, estimated to be in a US$ 6.4-8.4 million range.

Table 3.12: The Overall Freight Factors in the South Caucasus, 1995-99, Percent

	1995	*1996*	*1997*	*1998*	*1999*	Change between first and last year
Armenia	12.0	11.3	12.3	10.1	9.3	-2.7
Azerbaijan	10.5	8.6	9.4	13.5	7.4	-3.1
Georgia	N/A	7.9	3.9	8.2	8.3	0.3

Source: Polyakov, Evgeny (2001).

In addition to the direct additional transportation costs, the blockade affects the economy through a number of other channels, increasing overall price levels for various tradables, eliminating potential incomes from transit, and inflating both risks and uncertainty of economic transactions. This section provides analysis of various elements of total costs and then examines a related question: what would be the likely short-term impact of the resolution of regional conflicts and lifting the associated economic blockades on Armenia.

At the same time, it is worth noting that, despite no visible progress of political settlement of NK and other conflicts, the current economic impact of blockades eased considerably compared to what it used to be in the early 90s. In the five years since the cease-fire, trade flows have somewhat bounced towards normalization. Table 3.12 provides additional evidence for this: it shows a considerable decline in the freight factor between 1995 and 1999. According to the information from Armenian forwarders, standard rates for shipments from Yerevan to Western Europe declined by a quarter in the last several years.

Trading partners found ways to conduct trade despite the closed borders and economic blockades, albeit still at extra cost. This can be attributed to several factors: improved political stability in Georgia, which made it a major transit route for Armenian exports and imports; increased cooperation with Iran; gained trading experience; and some "erosion" of border control. Even in the case of Armenia and Azerbaijan, anecdotal evidence indicates that some unofficial trade between these two countries is taking root.

Excessive Transportation Costs and Potential Savings

There are considerable barriers at all transportation routes that link Armenia with its main partners.

While there are no trade barriers between <u>Armenia and Georgia</u> that arise from political conflicts, the trade flow is affected by high non-tariff barriers related to corruption. According to anecdotal evidence, the unofficial payments on the roads through Georgia account for from a quarter to a third of the official highway tariffs. In turn, the official transit fees are considered to be high. The most common carrier -- a truck with a capacity of 10-20 tons – transiting the Georgian territory must pay $245 equivalent in local currency. And Georgian railways charge Armenian shippers 50% higher tariffs than on cargo originating in Azerbaijan. Because most Armenian trade has to travel through Georgia, where the port of Poti serves as the main regional seaport and is linked to Armenia by a railway, the costs of Georgia transit has a fundamental impact on costs of Armenia exports and imports.

---

[70] The overall freight factor is estimated as the ratio of freight costs (defined as the sum of freight debit and credit) to merchandize value (the sum of merchandize debit and credit) in the balance of payments.

Trade between <u>Armenia and Russia</u> goes by road via Georgia and by railway via Azerbaijan. When using the railway through Azerbaijan, the consignments are assigned to a Georgian intermediary, a scheme that is used in the trade between Armenia and Turkey, with the same increase in costs. In case the blockade is lifted, the affect on Russian transit to Armenia via Georgia would be only minor, since the majority of Russian exports are energy (natural gas and nuclear fuel), which do not use sea or rail routes. The transit of Armenian exports to Russia currently sent via Azerbaijani railway through Georgian intermediate addresses would become easier and quicker to arrange. Nevertheless, substantial cost savings would arise only if Armenia were to enter railway tariff agreements with Azerbaijan.

Transportation between <u>Armenia and Iran is conducted</u> by road through a mountain Megri region, which is usually shut down for most of the winter months. Ground transportation costs would go down by at least one-third if the railway via Azeri enclave of Nakhichevan were re-opened.

Since the border between <u>Armenia and Turkey</u> is officially closed, trade between the two countries is conducted via Georgia intermediaries. These arrangements raise transaction costs substantially, and do not allow trade in construction materials (due to high transport costs) and energy. Straightening current trade routes and using Turkish ports for transshipments will create direct and immediate benefits for Armenia (see Box 3.3).

Box 3.3. Comparison of Port Usage

If the Turkish port of Trabzon were to be used for the transshipments of Armenian goods instead of the Georgian port of Poti, the ground share of container transport costs would decrease by one-fourth. Currently, about 5,000 containers per year pass through Poti on their way to/from Armenia. At a transshipment cost of $1,400 for a 20 foot container and a $1,800 cost for a 40 foot container, the savings would range from 1.8 to 2.0 million dollars a year. General cargo would probably continue to flow through Poti or would switch to Mersin, since Trabzon has no rail link.

If the Turkish port Mersin on the Mediterranean coast were used instead of Poti for general cargo, it will help to eliminate transshipments from/to Mediterranean ports en route to North America, Western Europe, and Asia. The shallow-water port Poti on the Black Sea cannot accept large ocean-going vessels, which requires transshipments in smaller, so-called feeder, ships. This might result in as much as 65 percent transport savings for general cargo[71]. However, the inability of Turkish railways to handle the massive transit of general cargo probably would not allow for a full switch of Armenian trade to this route in the short term.

Source: Polyakov, Evgeny (2001).

Non-direct Transportation Costs and Savings

In addition to direct savings, the direct link between Armenian and Turkish road and railway systems would increase the availability, predictability, and reliability of shipping services. These features, currently unavailable for Armenian traders, are at least as important as transportation costs. Opening the Turkish boarder would make Armenia a transit country rather than "the end of the line". The major transport initiative, TRACECA, aims at developing the East-West corridor through the Caucasus and the Caspian Sea to Asia.

The potential gains of transit could be even larger for Armenia in the case of possible strategic shifts in trade flows from the currently dominant East-West route to a North-South direction to support

---

[71] Elliott Hurwitz' estimate quoted in The World Bank (1995). *Transport Sector Review for Armenia.*

the growing trade of Russia and other countries in the region with India and the Gulf states. There is interest in this issue among such countries as Russia, Iran, and India, who have recently signed a protocol on the development of the North-South transport corridor through the Caspian Sea. The existing (but currently blocked) Nakhichevan-Iran rail link could be an important element of the North-South route. However, after years of blockade, significant investments will be needed to restart even a modest regular service, which must increase manifold to upgrade this link to handle higher cargo volumes.

Price Effects

Table 3.13 presents a sample of relative average prices of main commodity groups, among Armenia, Azerbaijan, Georgia, and Turkey. Despite the fact that these data refer to 1998, and do not take into account a scalable currency devaluation in Georgia after the Russia crisis[72], it still provides some interesting insights. As the data suggest, with respect to Azerbaijan, Armenian energy and agricultural prices are twice as high; prices for fertilizers and timber are on par; the price of cement is a third lower than in Azerbaijan and a fifth lower than in Turkey. With respect to Georgia, Armenian energy prices are higher, and agricultural prices are at the same level.

Table 3.13. Comparison of Selected Wholesale Prices in Armenia, Azerbaijan, Georgia, and Turkey, averages for 1998, as percent of prices in Turkey

Commodities	Unit	Azerbaijan	Armenia	Georgia
Energy Products				
Average		**20%**	**44%**	**32%**
Electric power	KWh	33%	39%	33%
Gasoline	Ton	18%	32%	29%
Diesel oïl	Ton	27%	49%	
Natural gas	M3	10%	55%	33%
Agricultural Products				
Average			**104%**	
Wheat	KG	67%	111%	101%
Barley	KG		131%	85%
Sunflower seed	KG		218%	89%
Beef and veal	KG	16%	34%	
Poultry	KG		113%	158%
Wool	KG	6%	33%	42%
Eggs	Unit	123%	163%	85%
Butter	KG		41%	46%
Crystal Sugar	KG	69%	55%	61%
Wheat flour	KG	87%	144%	177%
Fertilizers (average)		**74%**	**67%**	**149%**
Timber (average)		**62%**	**36%**	
Copper	Ton		51%	
Portland Cement	KG	126%	78%	62%

Source: Polyakov, Evgeny (2001).

---

[72] Due to Georgia's devaluation, the relative prices in Georgia today vis-à-vis Armenia and Azerbaijan are lower today than in 1998.

It is easy to conclude from the above data that trade blockades play a significant role in pushing Armenia's energy prices upward, which constitutes an implicit tax on both production and consumption in the country. The large price differential of Armenian cement with respect to both Azerbaijan and Turkey signals that Armenia could restart its traditional exports of construction materials to the neighbors, despite the high transportation costs of these products. At the same time, the agricultural sector of Armenia would likely come under competitive pressure from Azerbaijan, if the regional market becomes more integrated, and could negatively affect rural incomes and rural poverty in the Armenia.

Export Opportunities in an "after-crisis" Environment

A World Bank analysis assessed the potential for export expansion for countries in the South Caucasus based on the gravity model[73]. The model links intensity of international trade with countries' GDP levels, populations, and distance between two countries. Table 3.14 suggests that at the moment Armenia exports much less than one may expect from its GDP level, size, and other characteristics. The overall ratio of potential to actual exports is 2.4.

Table 3.14. Armenia - Average Annual (1995-98) Actual and Potential Export Volumes

Trading partners	Exports (million USD)			Partner's share, percent (sample = 100)	
	Actual	Potential/Actual ratio		Actual	Potential
		Current incomes	Higher incomes, as assumed by the WB growth scenario		
Azerbaijan	--	--	--	0.0	0.6
Georgia	7,478	3.0	5.9	3.3	4.0
Turkey	4,692	7.6	14.0	2.0	6.4
EU	63,223	3.7	6.2	27.6	41.6
Russia	72,457	1.1	1.5	31.6	14.3
USA	5,916	17.2	30.2	2.6	18.4
Iran	38,233	1.2	2.0	16.7	8.0
Other CIS	38,300	2.4	1.6	16.3	6.7
Subtotal	**230,299**	**2.4**	**4.1**	**100**	**100**

Source: Polyakov, Evgeny (2001).

Such low export volumes can at least partly be explained by the physical restrictions on the movement of goods. A number of case studies show that better opportunities for export can be directly associated with the opening of borders. For instance, there may be a good market for Armenia's building materials industry (cement, building stone, tile) in Turkey and Azerbaijan. If the production capacity were more fully utilized, production in this sector could increase by 40 to 80 million dollars a year.

However, as it is argued elsewhere in this report, a more important reason for weak export performance relates to insufficient capabilities of Armenian companies. While it is likely that regional trade may be boosted by conflict settlements, a sustainable expansion in manufacturing exports would not happen without a major industrial restructuring and improvements in the business environment.

---

[73] The gravity model was developed by Baldwin to assess potential changes in trade flows due to European integration. (Baldwin, Richard E. (1994). *Towards an Integrated Europe*, Centre for Economic Policy Research, London). The model describes more accurately international trade in manufactured goods, while it is less efficient in explaining trade in either natural resources/energy or agricultural products.

Benefits for the Energy Sector

As already mentioned, trade blockades play a significant role in pushing Armenia's energy prices upward. Being an importer of oil products, natural gas, and nuclear fuel, Armenia is very dependent on fuel imports: disruption of fuel supplies in the early 1990s brought the economy to a near total collapse. Subsequently, the high energy dependence contributes substantially to Armenia's investment risks.

At the same time, trade in energy presents the most obvious export and import opportunities for Armenia, since it has the largest surplus electric power generation capacities in the region. Armenian exports to Turkey could increase by as much as US$230 million, which equals total Armenian manufacturing exports in 1999. High import content of Armenia's power export would require an increase in fuel import that would stand at US$100 million a year. If the unit costs of gas decrease by 25 percent (in the case of the substitution of Russian gas by Azerbaijani[74]), the import content would go down to US$75 million.

However, the top efficiency in power generation and distribution systems would only be achieved if the Southern Caucasus countries and their neighbors operated as one system. There are a number of reasons why it is not happening: Armenia cannot trade electricity directly with Turkey or Azerbaijan for political reasons while Armenia and Georgia cannot safely operate in parallel with Russia and Iran unless Azerbaijan joins in for technical reasons. The latter requires a level of cooperation between Armenia and Azerbaijan that has not yet been achieved.

Total Benefits

Overall potential benefits of the trade normalization are summarized in Table 3.15. The potential new export volume would equal 15 - 19 percent of GDP. Assuming a (modest) multiplier effect of export growth on GDP of 2.0, the increase in exports may lead to up to cumulative 30 - 38 percent of the GDP growth.[75]

Table 3.15. Selected Potential Effects of Trade Normalization (million US dollar)

Transport savings	6.4-8.4
Savings from using lower-cost energy	45
Potential growth in exports	268.9-342.4
O/w: - gravity model	38.9-72.4
- natural resources/energy	255-296
Total effect	320-395.8
Complementary imports	80-100
Total effect minus complementary imports	220.3-315.8
As percent of 1999 trade deficit	38-54

Source: Polyakov, Evgeny (2001).

Impressive as they are, these estimates fall far short of the widespread overoptimistic expectations in the region about the size of peace benefits and the ease of their realization. It is hardly debatable that political settlement of the conflicts in Southern Caucasus and subsequent rationalization of trade routes will provide a one-time positive systemic impetus for regional development, and Armenia is holding the leading position in the queue. Absence of conflicts and blockades will

---

[74] In addition, full substitution of Russian gas and oil products by those from Azerbaijan would result in about US$45 million savings a year.

[75] Based on the sample of 95 countries, Burney (1996) estimated the coefficients of elasticity of GDP with respect to its major determinants, including exports, for the period between 1980 and 1990. He found that elasticity coefficients for exports vary considerable across regions with the lowest value (recorded for Africa) equal to 0.082 and the highest (recorded for Asia) -- 0.254. The export-GDP multiplier of 2.0, used in our analysis, corresponds to the elasticities obtained for faster growing Arian economies. In other words, our estimates for potential growth impact of export expansion are based on rather optimistic assumptions regarding a high growth development pace.

undoubtedly decrease the associated investment risks, cut the transportation costs, etc. Nevertheless, the political settlement per se will not provide a panacea to the multitude of economic and social problems, nor will it guarantee a stable long term development path.

The current poor business environment and incomplete industrial restructuring that represent a major hurdle to export performance will not disappear overnight following the political rapprochement. The realization of the peace dividend will depend on appropriate policy reforms aimed at strengthening supply response to demands of opening markets.

3.6. Fiscal and Quasi-Fiscal Subsidies: How Binding is Budget Constraint?

Over the last several years, the Armenian Government has been rather successful in sustaining macroeconomic stabilization by pursuing a tight monetary policy, strengthening control over budget expenditures, and accelerating reforms in public utilities. The budget fiscal deficit on a cash basis was rather stable and fluctuated between 5.2% and 6.6% of GDP in 1996-99 and was fully financed from non-inflationary sources. Budget subsidies to the enterprise sector remain relatively low. Most cross subsidies through tariffs (discounted tariffs to privileged groups of population) in electricity and utilities have been eliminated in mid 1997.

Accumulated experience with transition since 1990 suggests that hard budget constraints for enterprises are not just a critical element of macroeconomic stabilization, they are also necessary for both enterprise restructuring and the credibility of reforms (Pinto et al., 2000). Overall, and especially when compared to several largest CIS economies[76], it seems that the budget constraints in Armenia were modestly tight for most of the enterprise sector in the late 90s. While the level of quasi-fiscal subsides (tax and utility arrears) remained high, those were heavily concentrated in a limited number of largest companies (SOEs and recently privatized). However, within the sample of largest industrial enterprises, as was shown in the previous chapter, a relatively large share of firms were able to operate only due to accumulation of debts to the budget, energy companies, and labor. The Government should accelerate liquidation and/or forced restructuring of these firms, which would have a beneficial impact on the entire enterprise sector[77]. However, there is no evidence so far that softness of budget constraint for a few largest companies was among the major factors that had slowed down the overall enterprise restructuring process. Arrears and implicit subsidies in Armenia are much more fiscal than a restructuring problem.

From the macroeconomic perspective, the process of fiscal adjustment is still far from completed. The level of quasi-fiscal deficit, especially in the energy sector (power, gas, heating), while reduced, is still significant and could be a potential threat to the imposition of the hard budget constraint in the enterprise sector. The purpose of this section is to review the structure and main trends in major types of subsidies remaining in the Armenian economy, to identify their main recipients, and to justify the earlier statement that this residual flow of subsidies was only marginally detrimental to restructuring of the enterprise sector.

Table 3.16 provides a summary of main estimates for annual subsidies. It reveals that the incidence of subsidies remains high and most subsidization has been kept outside of the regular budget. In 1996-98, quasi-fiscal financing of subsidies amounted to 4.3-5.4% of GDP, which was 4-10 times

---

[76] For instance, in Russia, heavy hidden and untargeted subsidies, provided through a system of tax and energy non-payments, amounted to 7-10% of GDP annually in 1995-97. Adding explicit budgetary subsidies brought the total in excess of 15% of GDP a year. It is not surprising that such softness of budget constraints stifled enterprise restructuring and growth and made a major contribution to the 1998 crisis through accumulation of public debts, Pinto et al. (2000).

[77] See also the section on corporate governance below.

higher that the volume of budgeted subsidies. This level of quasi-fiscal financing is comparable with the size of official cash-based deficit of the annual budget. Subsidization through tax arrears was rather modest (on average amounted to about 1% of GDP, Chart 3.3).

Table 3.16. Subsides in Armenia, as percent of GDP

	1996	1997	1998	1999
1. Budgeted subsidies	1.3	0.8	0.5	2.4
2. Increase in tax arrears	0.6	0.7	1.8	1.3
3. Total fiscal (1+2)	1.9	1.5	2.3	3.8
4. Quasi-fiscal financing of subsidies	5.4	4.3	5.3	2.9
5. Total financing of subsidies (3+4)	7.3	5.8	7.6	6.7
Net Recipients of subsidies (on consolidated basis)				
- Population	2.6	2.2	2.9	2.2
- Energy (power and heat)	2.3	-1.5	-0.3	1.86
- Infrastructure (water, transport, and irrigation)	0.03	0.5	0.5	1.0
- Commercial enterprises, without agriculture	1	1.6	1.1	1.6
Memo: Gross quasi-fiscal subsidies	8.7	5.8	7.0	3.4
Memo: implicit tariff subsidies		2.0	1.5	less than 0.5

Source: Staff estimates based on the data from the MOFE, Statistical Agency and public utilities.

Chart 3.3. Budgeted Subsidies, Quasi-Fiscal Subsidies and Tax Arrears (1996-99)

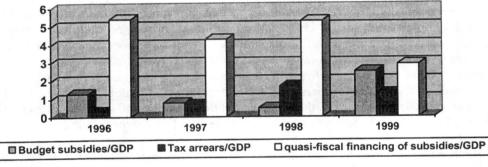

Source: Staff estimates.

Table 3.16 reflects two main channels of subsidy financing: a) explicit budget subsidies; and b) subsidies received by economic agents through accumulation of arrears to public and publicly-controlled companies in the utility/energy sector. Table 3.16, however, only partially covers another source of subsidization – subsidization through tariffs – that derives from a combination of low tariffs for utility services and insufficient budget compensation of utilities with explicit subsidies. This somewhat distorts our estimates regarding the allocation of total subsidies between different recipients: it underestimates the amount of subsidies received by final consumers of energy and utility services (population and enterprise sector) and overestimates net subsidies received by intermediaries (energy and utilities).

At the same time, the data in Table 3.16 seems to reflect pretty accurately the overall volume of subsidies in the economy, i.e. it does not underestimate seriously the incidence of subsidies. This is because main energy inputs were imported to Armenia at non-subsidized prices. As a result, non-budgeted tariff subsidies to Armenian consumers were mostly reflected through additional accumulation of arrears for energy inputs by service providers, and they are reported in Table 3.16 as subsidies to these service providers.

The main source of funding of quasi-fiscal subsidies was the operational cash flow of (mostly publicly-owned) energy companies – first of all in the gas and power sectors. Heating and water companies provided smaller amounts of subsidies in particular years. In turn, gas and power companies financed their operational deficit by building debts to their suppliers and commercial banks as well as through under-maintenance of companies' assets. Overall, accumulation of debts related to import of energy inputs (natural gas and nuclear fuel) made a significant contribution to the build-up of Armenia's external debt in 90-s.

The Government introduced a major change in its budgeting policy in 1999, when a much larger share of total subsidies was actually budgeted (2.5% of GDP). It was the first year when total fiscal subsidies (budgeted and tax arrears) exceeded subsidies financed by public utilities. Still, the level of quasi-fiscal subsidies (2.9% of GDP) remained high.

Better budgeting of quasi-fiscal subsidies in 1999 was accompanied further by the Government's efforts to increase cost recovery in tariffs and improve payment discipline. As a result, one may assume that tariff subsidies have been mostly eliminated in 1999. Also, comparison of the flows for 1999 and for earlier years helps to get rough estimates for tariff subsidies in preceding years: it is likely that the volume of tariff subsidies in 1997 amounted to 2% of GDP and in 1998 – 1.5% of GDP. Households received at least two-thirds of this amount, while commercial enterprises benefited from the rest.

At the same time, despite a positive development in 1999, there is no clear trend towards a decline in the overall volume of subsidies (both fiscal and quasi-fiscal): it changed from 7.3% of GDP in 1996 to 7.6% of GDP in 1998 and to 6.7% in 1999.

Non-payments by consumers for energy and utility consumption were a single main form of quasi-fiscal subsidization. The culture of non-payment is well rooted in Armenia and it supports long-chains of overdue payables within the economy. This is reflected in the line "Gross quasi-fiscal subsidies" in Table 3.16. The overall annual flow of non-payments in main utilities amounted to 8.7% of GDP in 1996, 7.0% of GDP in 1998, but it was reduced considerably in 1999 (3.4% of GDP) due to a stronger Government reform effort.

Therefore, various economic sectors may be grouped as the following:

- Main donors in the energy sector.

- Intermediaries: sectors (heating, water, irrigation) that receive budget and quasi-budget subsidies but transfer most of them to the final recipients.

- Final recipients (households and the enterprise sector) of quasi-fiscal/fiscal subsidies.

- Minor recipients of budget subsidies (transport, publishing).

The gas sector has been a major source of net quasi-fiscal subsidies in the economy. From the gas industry, subsidies have been diverted to power and heating companies, while the power sector channeled most of them further to irrigation, water, and industry. Finally, all major sectors such as power, water, irrigation, and heating were involved in subsidization of households (Table 3.17).

Table 3.17. Intersectoral Flows of Subsidies in the Economy, 1998 And 1999, Billion Drams

1998	Total net subsidies received	Total fiscal net	Budget subsidies	Increase in tax arrears	Total quasi-fiscal net	Energy subsidies	Water subsidies	Irrigation subsidies	Heat subsidies	Gas subsidies
Total, net	**22,103.1**	**22,103.1**	**4,941.0**	**+17,162.1**	**0.0**	**0.0**	**0.0**	**0.0**	**0.0**	**0.0**
Net sub./GDP	2.3%	2.3%	0.5%	1.8%						
Net Recipients:										
Transport	759.1	759.1	736.0	23.1	0.0					
Culture	410.0	410.0	410.0		0.0					
Energy	-850.0	7,447.2		7,447.2	-8,297.2	-25,158.0				16,860.8
Drinking water	-2,429.1	2,097.4	2,000.0	97.4	-4,526.5	3,769.2	-8,295.7			
Irrigation	6,188.9	1,387.6	1,795.0	-407.4	4,801.3	5,370.4		-569.1		
Heating	-1,579.8	327.3		327.3	-1,907.1				-4,526.9	2,619.8
Gas sector	-24,506.9	3,728.0		3,728.0	-28,234.9	-28,234.9				-28,234.9
Population	27,713.3	2,166.2		2,166.2	25,547.1	12,205.3	7,380.9	569.1	4,147.0	1,244.8
Industry	10,385.0	2,133.6		2,133.6	8,251.4	862.1				7,389.3
o/w: Nairit	7,356.6	313.2		313.2	7,043.4	485.2				6,558.2
Budgetary organize	1,465.1	0.0			1,465.1	1,344.9				120.2
Other	4,547.4	1,646.6		1,646.6	2,900.8	1,606.1	914.8		379.9	
memo: Gross subsidies	47,668.5	22,510.5	4,941.0	17,569.5	66,784.6	25,158.0	8,295.7	569.1	4,526.9	28,234.9
Gross sub./GDP	5.0%	2.4%	0.5%	1.8%	7.0%	2.6%	0.9%	0.1%	0.5%	3.0%
memo: Quasi-fiscal financing of subsidies					42,965.7					
as % of GDP					4.5%					
GDP=	955,791.0									

1) In 1996, 1997, budget subsidies to the heating sector were subsidies in kind/provision of humanitarian mazut.

2) In 1997, 26.5 billion. Dram payables to the gas sector were written-off

3) Includes also arrears to the Pension Fund.

Table 3.17 Continued

	Total net subsidies received	Total fiscal net	Budget subsidies	Increase in tax arrears	Total quasi-fiscal net	Energy subsidies	Water subsidies	Irrigation subsidies	Heat subsidies	Gas subsidies
1999										
Total, net	36,713.9	36,713.9	23,991.2	12,722.7	0.0	0.0	0.0	0.0	0.0	0.0
Net sub./GDP	3.8%	3.8%	2.5%	1.3%						
Net Recipients:										
Transport	573.7	900.2	900.0	0.2	-326.5	-326.5				
Culture	577.8	577.8	577.8		0.0	0.0				
Energy	-3,324.5	5,616.2	2,688.0	2,928.2	-8,940.7	-9,698.3				757.6
Drinking water	-1,354.6	5,607.6	5,061.0	546.6	-6,962.2	869.0	-7,831.2			
Irrigation	10,836.3	8,270.2	7,764.4	505.8	2,566.1	3,589.7		-1,023.6		
Heating	-2,207.6	2,289.5	2,600.0	-310.5	-4,497.1				-6,997.6	2,500.5
Gas sector	-8,247.0	165.0		165.0	-8,412.0					-8,412.0
Population	21,762.4	1,300.6		1,300.6	20,461.8	6,771.0	7,803.9	1,023.6	3,590.4	1,272.9
Industry	15,748.1	10,665.7	4,400.0	6,265.7	5,082.4	-1,524.3			3,097.0	3,509.7
o/w: Nairit	9,919.4	4,161.6	4,400.0	-238.4	5,757.8	150.3			3,097.0	2,510.5
Budgetary organize	1,228.3	0.0			1,228.3	829.7	27.3			371.3
Other	1,120.9	1,321.0	1,321.0	1,321.0	-200.1	-510.3			310.2	
memo: Gross subsidies	70,676.6	36,713.9	23,991.2	12,722.7	33,962.7	9,698.3	7,831.2	1,023.6	6,997.6	8,412.0
Gross sub./GDP	7.1%	3.7%	2.4%	1.3%	3.4%	1.0%	0.8%	0.1%	0.7%	0.8%
memo: Quasi-fiscal financing of subsidies					28812.0					
As % of GDP					2.9%					
GDP=	991,549.7									

Source: Staff estimates.

Subsidies to the Population

The household sector is a major recipient of net subsidies. In all years it exceeds 2% of GDP – about 35% of total subsidy financing. These include household payables to the energy, water, heat, and gas sectors as well as an increase in land tax arrears. In addition, in 1997-98, households received tariff subsidies, which could be roughly estimated as 1% of GDP.

Chart 3.4 compares the amount of quasi-fiscal subsidies with the volume of public cash expenditures on social assistance and social insurance (pension, poverty benefits and similar programs). Quasi-fiscal subsidies to the population amounted to 36-57% of social public expenditures in 1996-99.

Chart 3.4. Quasi-Fiscal Subsidies to Population and Public Expenditures on Social Protection/Insurance, 1996-99.

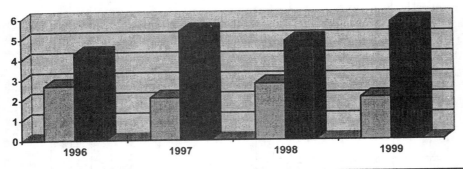

Source: Staff estimates.

In nominal terms, gross subsidies to the population reached their highest level in 1998 (26.5 billion dram, an increase of 60% compared to 1996). The structure of household debts shows that overdue payables to the energy and water sectors constitute around 70% of the total quasi-fiscal subsidies received by population. As of the end of 1999, household debts amounted to 48% of total receivables from the energy sector. However, the composition of indirect subsidies has changed recently towards an increased share of water and heating sectors. This to some extent reflects considerable improvements in payment discipline that occurred in the energy, gas and irrigation sectors in 1998-99, while collection levels in heating and water remain below 30%.

Subsidies to the Enterprise Sector

The enterprise sector is the second largest recipient of net subsidies (Chart 3.5). When tariff subsidies are included, commercial enterprises received about 2.5% of GDP in subsidies in 1997, about 2% in 1998 and 1.8% in 1999.

Most enterprise subsidies were of quasi-fiscal nature until 1999. In 1999, the GOA introduced fiscal tightening to clear arrears of public sector enterprises to the utility sector through direct budget subsidies/discounted loans. Thus, the ratio of fiscal–to–quasi-fiscal subsidies has been reversed from its 20%:80% proportion in 1998 to 68%:32% in 1999. This was a major positive shift to more transparent budgeting/financing. But as of mid-2000, the sustainability of such a policy remains of serious concern.

Enterprise subsidies are heavily concentrated. Nairit is the only industrial enterprise that is a recipient of direct budget subsidies. Nairit is considered by the authorities to be too large to fail. Total average annual subsidies (explicit and implicit) received by Nairit in the last 4 years amounted to 0.6% of GDP. In dollar equivalent, every one of the 4000 employees was a recipient of an annual subsidy that amounted to about $2,500. This should be compared to an average industrial wage of about $600 a year, and the average salary of a teacher of $350 a year.

Chart 3.5. Fiscal and Quasi-Fiscal Subsidies to the Enterprise Sector and Households, percent of GDP

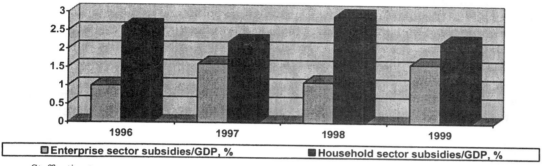

Source: Staff estimates.

As far as tax arrears are concerned, they are also heavily concentrated in a few companies. Tax debts of the seven largest debtors amount to about 30% of total tax arrears[78] with the leading role of energy sector enterprises. The share of the 10 largest debtors outside of the energy and utility sector was about 20% of total tax arrears. This corresponds to an overall subsidy of 0.5-0.8% of GDP received by these 10 companies over 1997-99.

Arrears and Barter

There are no available systematic data on the incidence of arrears and barter in Armenia's enterprise sector. In the course of the preparation of this report, we have developed a proxy estimate, based on the reports of 90 largest industrial non-energy enterprises for 1997-98.[79] Our analysis suggests that after a major expansion in arrears in 1998 (real annual growth of about 60%), the overall stock of arrears by the end of 1998 amounted to about 7% of GDP. Overdue payments to suppliers and bad debts to banks made most of the total arrears, while wage and tax arrears were relatively low. And arrears were heavily concentrated in several enterprises. In the sample, almost 90% of total arrears were concentrated in just 6 chemical companies (including Nairit). And practically the entire growth in arrears in 1998 was concentrated in the chemical sector [80]. Overall, the comparison of these sample data with available sectoral information on arrears from the energy sector, the Central Bank, and tax authorities once again suggests that while non-payments for energy supply, tax and credit arrears are relatively common, non-payments are relatively rare in transactions between Armenian enterprises outside of the energy and utility sectors[81]. In other words, the average Armenian company in manufacturing/services is largely arrears free (with respect to its payments to suppliers and employees), at least in comparison with other countries in the FSU. While wage arrears economy-wide are still a problem in Armenia, wage arrears are concentrated in the budget sector (health, education). This is quite different from the recent Russian experience, where accumulations of arrears along technological chains had been a common phenomenon.

---

[78] Excluding land tax arrears.

[79] The enterprise sample was described in the last section of the previous chapter. It was assumed that these largest traditional enterprises are responsible for a quarter of total arrears and barter in the enterprise sector.

[80] The available partial data for 1999 seems to suggest that the overall stock of arrears in the enterprise sector somewhat declined in 1999, following again by a 20% decline in arrears in the chemical sub-sector.

[81] However, barter made up to 60% of total enterprise payments for electricity before 1998.

Similarly, as the sample data suggest, the incidence of barter is not high either. The largest enterprises from the sample reported that on average only 10% of their revenue were obtained through barter operations in both 1997 and 1998. But the chemical sector again was the outlier: in chemical companies about 45% of revenues came through barter.

To sum up, there is no evidence that non-payments and barter are a serious constraint for development of either enterprise sector (by eroding a budget constraint) or of the financial sector (by crowding out the banking credit). This lower incidence of non-cash transactions could be explained by two main inter-related factors:

- small and very open size of the economy; and

- major trade shock of early 90s that resulted in destruction of traditional Soviet economic links (barter emerged in Russia initially along these traditional Soviet supplier relations).

As a result, the Armenian market is just too narrow to make barter arrangements liquid and attractive. A relatively large part of all businesses has either to import inputs from the countries where barter is not acceptable or to sell their outputs to households for cash. There is no large domestic market for intermediary goods to support barter deals.

In addition, the Armenian Government has been much more responsible in its policy of not encouraging non-cash payment schemes in the economy. This was in striking contrast to Russia, where federal and regional governments were major initial "creators" of the market for non-cash instruments (they organized tax offset schemes, issued bonds and veksels, helped local enterprises to clear mutual arrears on a non-cash basis). This "innovative" Government activity for issuing money substitutes was then further expanded in Russia by commercial banks and large companies.

3.7.   Corporate Governance Regime and Disincentives for Investments

Poor corporate governance practices[82], lack of transparency and management accountability, as well as the underlying legal framework that lacks sufficient mechanisms of shareholder protection is rather a common problem in the CIS economies and generally it is detrimental to the investment potential of local companies. In Armenia, this general problem has several specific manifestations. For instance, in Armenia, the business environment demonstrates even stronger dependence on personal relationship and political connections that creates obstacles and increased uncertainty for external investors. Also, Armenia's legal and regulatory framework shows a clear tendency to over-regulation.

At the same time, as discussed earlier in this Chapter, the ownership structure of Armenian corporations is, to a remarkable degree, concentrated. While the voucher privatization led to some initial dispersion of ownership, it then has been quite quickly consolidated by managers/owners. High concentration of ownership, at least in principle, creates more favorable pre-conditions for improvements in corporate governance. However, these pre-conditions are not sufficient yet for strengthening incentives of managers/owners to restructure and maximize the value of the firm, which is a result of various factors, especially uncertainty in the business environment.

The Government of Armenia has been making some progress in several key areas of the corporate governance agenda. In particular, several core pieces of legislation were enacted, including the 1999 Civil Code, 2000 Securities Market Regulation Law, and the 2000 Law on Accounting. An

---

[82] The section benefited from an earlier note on corporate governance in Armenia, prepared by Sue Rutledge.

independent market regulator – the Securities Commission – was set up. Also, a central share registry (central Depositary) was established and made fully operational, registration with which is mandatory for all companies with number of shareholders, exceeding a minimum established by the Law.

The Joint Stock Company Law (JSCL) is a key law that influences corporate governance practices in Armenia. The JSCL contains several fundamental provisions that support good corporate governance: (i) the requirement that company managers must have less than half the seats at the company board; (ii) specific liability provisions for the board members and the company executives; and (iii) the requirement for independent audits for all open joint stock companies.

The strengths in the JSCL are undermined, however, by other weaknesses in the business environment or legal framework. For instance, with respect to liability for board members and company managers, the current legislation does not include a detailed description of specific roles and responsibilities of directors and managers, beyond the provision of official information. In the absence of such defined roles and responsibilities, it would be rather difficult to determine the extent of liability of specific individuals.

Other important weaknesses of the JSCL relate to the following areas of corporate governance:

- Rules for decision making at shareholders' meetings and shareholder participation;

- Approval of large transactions by the company board; and

- Approval of compensation of auditors by the company board.

Shareholder participation. The JSCL allows important decisions (i.e. changing the company charter) to be made by 75 percent of votes of shareholders participating in the shareholders' meeting. International best practice requires that key decisions be made by shareholders representing not less than a minimum percentage of shares, regardless of actual attendance at the meeting. Potentially under the Armenian Law, major decisions could be approved by shareholders representing as little as 23 percent of total shares. This may provide incentives for potential abuse: minority shareholders could try to make it difficult for others to attend the meeting.

Large transactions. The JSCL allows the company board to make decisions on transfer of large parts of company assets without calling a shareholders' meeting. Up to 50 percent of the total assets (book value) may be sold or transferred to other parties by an unanimous decision of the board. While the Law includes some mitigating provisions, such as identified procedures for determining asset values, international norms suggest that any transfer in excess of 25 percent of the company's assets should require the approval of the shareholders.

Audit framework. The JSCL requires the shareholders' meeting to approve both the company's annual financial statements and the selection of an auditor. However, the law authorizes the company board to determine the compensation level for the auditor. Because the quality of work undertaken by an external auditor maybe affected by the allocated compensation level, it create a possibility for the board to manipulate the quality of the audit. In Armenia, such a risk maybe significant, given current weaknesses of the auditing profession. Thus, it seems important to amend the law and transfer the authority over auditor compensation to the shareholders' meeting.

Barriers for Investments

The current legal framework makes outside investments in the existing corporations too complicated and time consuming for investors, mainly because it over-regulates the investment process[83]. It is a potential barrier for investments and it also undermines the efficiency of capital market mechanisms (e.g. it would reduce the threat of a takeover).

The Law contains several economically and legally unjustified technicalities that combined could lead to a substantial increase in transaction costs. Infusion of new capital in the company is difficult, because making respective amendments to the Charter could take up to three months. The delays derive from over-complicated procedures for holding shareholders' meetings, for registering the amended Charter, for issuing the shares, etc. The equity investment also requires a full pre-payment of any increase in charter capital, i.e. investments are expected to be frozen at the company's account until the Charter has been re-registered and new shares are issued.

Another example of legal deficiencies relates to debt-for-equity swaps, which is a convenient investment and corporate restructuring instrument. For reasons unknown, the Armenian Law does not allow for this kind of transaction. Also, the established debt-asset ratio (1:1) is too low and limits opportunities for company financing, especially given the fact of artificially low valuation of many companies derived from valuation methods used during mass privatization.

Contradictions in the Bankruptcy Framework

As of the end of 2000, the corporate governance regime in Armenia was still affected by a major inconsistency in bankruptcy legislation. This has significant negative implications for corporate governance, budget constraint, and contract enforcement. The exit of non-viable companies is limited, and so far was promoted through Government sponsored liquidation of bankrupt state enterprises[84], but not through court-led regular bankruptcy procedures. The continuing presence of non-viable companies has delayed formation of an even playing field in the economy, as loss-making companies are permitted to accumulate arrears in their payments of taxes and energy/utility bills, while profitable firms are required to pay their obligations in full. While there is plenty of evidence that secondary markets for equipment, industrial and office space, and other assets are rather advanced and provide noticeable reallocation of capital from loss-making to profitable firms, the weak exit of bankrupt companies clearly makes this process less efficient than it could be potentially. The latter results in higher asset prices for efficient companies and constitutes a tax on their development.

The Armenian Bankruptcy Law was adopted in December 1996 and took effect in March 1997. While there are some procedural weaknesses of the Law, overall it is considered as a rather solid piece of legislation. The problem, however, relates to a contradiction between the Civil Code and Civil Procedure Code, both of which became effective in January 1999.

The Civil Code requires that bankruptcy be handled exclusively by provisions of the Civil Procedure Code, while the latter does not have any bankruptcy section. This makes the initial Bankruptcy Law, which is not a part of any Code, somewhat "illegal", i.e. in direct contradiction with core legal acts. As a result of this inconsistency, in early 1999, the Council of Court Chairmen (CCC) adopted a decision, advising courts to stop hearing bankruptcy cases due to a lack of legal backing for bankruptcy procedures. Although the CCC's decision was not mandatory, in practice the courts submitted to it. The entire legal

---

[83] Tom Samuelian (2000) provides a detailed analysis of legal obstacles to investments.

[84] In 1999-2000, about 35 SOEs were liquidated by Government decisions.

mechanism for processing bankruptcy cases effectively ground to a halt. Ongoing bankruptcy procedures for about 200 - 250 companies were interrupted.

After the Government's intervention, the CCC on August 16, 2000 rescinded its previous decision, and allowed courts to hear bankruptcy cases under the 1997 Bankruptcy Law. However, it requested the courts to apply the Bankruptcy Law only to the extent it did not contradict the Civil or Civil Procedure Codes. This did not resolve the legal problem. In the view of legal experts, any decision rendered in a bankruptcy case by a lower court, if appealed, would be overruled by the Cassation Court on the grounds that bankruptcy litigation has to be conducted according to the Civil Procedure Code, which does not contain bankruptcy provisions. Still, as of April 2001, more than 150 bankruptcy cases had been under court hearings but not a single court hearing on bankruptcy has been completed so far. The weak capacity of courts and some uncertainties in the existing procedures make the process very slow.

The ultimate and simple resolution of the problem relates to an amendment of the Civil Code, which has to say that bankruptcy is handled in accordance with "other legislation" rather than by the Civil Procedure Code. After such a "quick fix," amendments to the 1997 Bankruptcy Law have to be made. Specifically, they should clarify the criteria for creditors' petitions, harmonize deadlines and timetables for reorganization/liquidation of bankrupt companies, and introduce stronger guarantees against Government interventions. The legal amendments should be accompanied by further efforts to strengthen capacity of the judiciary to handle bankruptcy cases. This requires additional training of bankruptcy administrators, judges, bailiffs, and other judicial staff.

Annex 3.1. Enterprise Survey: Sample Characteristics

The business survey described in the first section of this chapter was administered in 22 CEE countries under the supervision of the World Bank Group and the EBRD by AC Nielsen in April 1999 to a sample of 125 firms, stratified by size, activity and ownership as described in the Table below. The survey was part of a broader international effort to create a standard survey instrument to evaluate national business conditions in a consistent and comparable methodology known as the World Business Environment Survey. General findings from the survey as they are applicable to the whole set of participating economies in transition are provided in the EBRD Transition Report (1999).

Table A3.1. Composition of Sample, Armenia Enterprise Survey

Size # full time		Activity		Location	
Small (<50):	80	Agriculture:	7	Capital city:	63
Medium (51-199):	30	Industry:	5	Other Large:	0
Large (>=200):	15	Commerce:	66	Small cities:	62
		Services:	17		
Total:	125	125		125	

Source: World Bank.

The most popular legal form for firms in the sample is privately-held corporations, which account for 38.4% of the sample. Sole proprietorships are also popular and account for 24% of the firms in the sample. 8% of firms were identified as firms listed on the stock exchange and 3% of the firms are co-operatives.

Table A3.2. Organizational Form of Firms, Armenia Enterprise Survey Sample

Organization	#of Firms	% Firms
Sole proprietorship	31	24.8
Partnership	7	5.6
Cooperative	4	3.2
Corporation, privately-held	48	38.4
Corporation listed on a stock exchange	9	7.2
SOE	25	20
Other form	1	0.8
Total	125	100

Source: World Bank.

The average firm age in the sample is 9 years. Larger firms tend to be more experienced, averaging 16 years in operation. 75% of small firms have been in operation for 5 years or less.

Ownership of firms is mainly domestic and private. 25% of firms reported having some state ownership. By sector, 31% of firms in manufacturing had some state ownership, as did 14% of firms in commerce. Very few firms in the agriculture and services sectors have state ownership. By size, state ownership is more common for medium-size firms—60% have some state ownership. Among small firms, none have any state ownership.

Only 2 firms (1.6%) of firms in the sample reported having any foreign ownership. Few Armenian firms have holdings or operations overseas – only 3 firms reported such foreign activities.

The firms in the sample have limited experience with export. Only 7.2% export any share of their sales, with an average export-sales ratio of 36 percent among these firms. Larger firms are more likely to export—20% of the large firms in the sample export as compared with 13.3% of medium size firms and only 2.5% of small firms. Industry and services are the export-oriented sectors with 17% and 12% of firms in these sectors exporting, respectively, as compared with 1.5% of firms in the commerce sector and 0% enterprises in agriculture. However, of the firms that do export, firms in the industrial sector average a 48% export/sales ratio, vs. 18.5% for services exporters.

Annex 3.2. First Movers: General Description of the Sample

Total number of companies: 27

Insider privatization 8
Outsider privatization 6
Start-ups 9
Major recipients of FDI 7
Business emerged as an expansion of traders into manufacturing 6

Export mainly to Russia, based on all kinds of old networks 11
Export diversification to non-CIS just started 6
Export to non-CIS well established 3 (o/w diamonds 2)

Main product is import substitution 9

Major support from subsidized credit line programs 11
Have access to suppliers' credit 5 (o/w diamonds 2)
Diaspora connections were critical for financing 6

High level political connections 5

Involved in food processing and related packaging 12
Light industry 2
High-tech (software, medicines, modern equipment) 5

Strong technical (engineering) background of the management/owners 7

Real restructuring – change in product mix 3

Strong competitive pressures 6 (wine, water, juices, cigarettes, tomato paste, construction materials), also diamonds

Institutions of export facilitation – 3 cases : local consulting company, specialized exporter, TACIS business trip

Export is hindered by transportation bottlenecks (Georgia) 2
Main constraint (perceived) -- unfair competition (including lobbying, unregistered import) – 7.

4.   WAY FORWARD: STRATEGY TO IMPROVE THE BUSINESS ENVIRONMENT AND FACILITATE ECONOMIC RESTRUCTURING

This Chapter first provides an outline for the overall Government growth strategy, and, second, spells out major elements of one of the pillars for such a strategy – removing administrative barriers for business activity.

This report argues that to address numerous growth challenges, the Government medium-term (3-5 years) strategy has to be based on the following three pillars:

- Maintaining a sustainable macroeconomic framework and liberal trade regime;

- Fundamental improvements in the quality of the business environment; and

- Active policy to facilitate economic restructuring and new private entry.

The report is advocating an export-based growth strategy, which given the size of Armenia's internal market, would not be surprising. Also, the analysis of the country's comparative advantages does suggest that Armenia has comparative advantages in skills. However, weak existing institutions and an unfriendly business environment currently block the transformation of comparative into competitive advantage, as seen from both trade and investment data. Overall, it seems justifiable to support a two-prong strategy: a) skill-based growth -- built around the nascent export-oriented clusters such as in software and diamond-polishing; and b) a broader, more general "push" for export, which would reflect existing skills and assets in sectors that have been doing relatively well over the last 4-5 years: food processing, tobacco and wines, some parts of garments, mining, etc.

By establishing a stable macroeconomic environment and liberal trade regime, the Government of Armenia introduced one critical pre-condition for future export-driven growth. The binding constraint now relates to structural and micro-level fundamentals, including quality of the business environment, managerial training, and infrastructure bottlenecks. Also, improvements in relations with Armenia's neighbors will significantly facilitate growth in external trade and the development of the country's transit potential.

Why is Removing Administrative Barriers for Business Providing the Immediate Priority for Growth Strategy?

Among various problems in the Armenia business environment, immediate priority should be to advance a deregulation agenda. This is a first critical step for the Government to regain the confidence of those investors who are already active in Armenia, and to start building a new business-friendly image of the country to accelerate new entry. In transition economies, as in other parts of the world (e.g. Latin America), the core of enterprise-level restructuring has been about a change in management culture (see, for instance, Kornai, 2000). For new managers to come from inside (i.e. an engineer turning into an entrepreneur) or outside (FDI), credible institutional reforms that create incentives and opportunities for restructuring are paramount.

Additional reasons why the Government should start removing administrative barriers include:

- the fact that the impact of deregulation on the incentive regime of private agents would be immediate and high;

- gradually emerging consensus in the government and business community that the deregulation agenda is a top priority;

- it is an institutionally light agenda, i.e. it does not, at least initially, require extensive institution building; thus many government interventions (including some of those presented below in this Chapter) could be prepared and adopted quickly; and

- progress in deregulation is tangible and easy to monitor through periodic business surveys.

At the same time, deregulation could be treated as a key entry point for advancing a broader reform effort in Armenia. Box 4.1 provides an example of how reforms in deregulation helped to accelerate across-the-board economic reforms in Mexico. At the same time, it should be noted that Mexico's deregulation czar was a temporary solution for rapid deregulations, which within a very few years evolved into a more standard OECD-style deregulatory strategy, based on the regulatory affairs office and specialized regulatory monitoring and analysis.

Box 4.1. Deregulation as Entry Point: Mexico's Deregulation Czar

In 1988, the president of Mexico appointed a "deregulation czar". Each month this official reported directly to the president and his economic council of ministers. Every business in Mexico, large or small, was promised equal access to the czar's office to complain about burdens associated with government rules and regulations. When the deregulation office received a complaint, it was obliged to find out why the rule existed, how it interacted with other regulations, and whether it should continue in effect. The office operated under a strict timetable: if it did not act to maintain, revise, or abolish the disputed rule within forty-five days, the rule was made void automatically.

The work of the deregulation czar over the first four years of his tenure is widely credited with greatly accelerating Mexico's reform program. It provided struggling private business-people with an effective, responsive champion at the highest level of government. The factors behind this success included:

- Unequivocal presidential support, signaling to both bureaucrats and citizens the need to comply with the czar's decisions.

- The fact that his decisions could be overruled only at the highest level of government.

- The setting of tough penalties for officials who failed to implement the rulings.

- The time limit, which ensured quick and visible results.

- The czar's staff, who were skilled in the economic consequences of regulations, in understanding complicated interactions within the regulatory field and their administrative requirements -- no single person can effectively carry out a government-wide program of deregulation.

Finally, it was critical that the czar won credibility with both officials and the public by giving a fair hearing to the powerless and the influential alike, and setting a consistent record of impartiality.

Source: World Development Report (1997), p. 73.

Other priority directions to improve the business environment. Removing administrative barriers is critical but just an element of the strategy to improve the business environment. Other priorities described elsewhere in the report include:

- Support financial deepening by advancing policies that would lead to reduction of lending risks and hence costs of borrowing; continue its policy of consolidating the banking system, by requiring banks to increase their capitalization.

- Improve the quality of infrastructure services, such as telecommunications, road, rail and air transportation, and urban water supply; strengthen regulatory capacity to support privately-owned operators in energy and infrastructure.

- Improve the transparency and technical quality of the privatization processes, with the objective of attracting strategic investors into the largest state-owned companies.

Business environment, new entry, and poverty reduction. International evidence suggests that in most cases economic growth, based on positive changes in the investment climate, is beneficial to the poor. There are several channels through which the poor would benefit when a country improves its business environment. First and most importantly, they benefit from better employment opportunities associated with the creation of new firms that respond to lower costs of market entry. Even those who are engaged in informal activities would benefit through a stronger demand from the formal sector. Additional benefits for the poor are associated with more competitive markets for goods and services, which would support prices for goods and wages in sectors (such as agriculture) that otherwise are affected by restricted competition.

Restructuring Strategy. In addition to improvements in the business environment, the report emphasizes the need for active government policies in support of private sector development, which would ensure that private sector agents are able to utilize potential gains associated with a better investments climate. The following two chapters provide a detailed justification why such an "interventionist" policy is needed, and what main instruments and components it may incorporate. Overall, such a restructuring strategy would include policies to facilitate:

- Increasing employment in small and medium enterprises, based on reducing costs of new entry;

- Restructuring assets in large enterprises which once served value chains that no longer function;

- Selection of one or two skill-based sectors in which to develop and exploit core competencies as engines for broader economy-wide growth; and design mechanisms for their spillover in the economy;

- A much consistent effort in attracting established exporters ("quota-jumpers") in low-skill goods such as textile[85]; building longer-term relations with such exporters in order to increase gradually a local share of total product value added.

- Expansion of business development services to support an expansion of companies which survived the transition and serve local value chains;

- Upgrading sectoral policies to maintain local competencies to produce needed services in an efficient manner in sectors such as agriculture, housing, utilities, transportation, etc.

---

[85] At the moment, the Government underutilizes existing opportunities in the textile and garment sector, related to Armenia's preferential access to European and US markets.

The core of the proposed restructuring strategy relates to support of the first movers and development clusters that emerge around these first movers. The importance of this focus could be clarified if it is compared to its major alternatives, which it seems are not appropriate for Armenia: (i) picking the winners; and (ii) extreme liberal response – do nothing. To avoid both such extremes, the report proposes a focus on spontaneously emerging positive trends, seeks to recognize these trends and accelerate them through specially designed public interventions.

Public Administration Reforms to Facilitate Improvements in the Business Environment

The Government increasingly recognizes the need for more focused efforts to improve the business environment. The remaining part of this chapter presents a package of policy initiatives needed to advance a deregulation agenda and ensure major improvements in the business environment[86]. The package to a large extent overlaps with the recent Government program, which has been developed with the assistance of the World Bank in the course of preparation of the Fourth Structural Adjustment Credit (SAC4). Implementation of the program has been initiated in 2000 but is still at a rather early stage.

As was discussed in Chapter 2, several independent evaluations of the Armenia business environment revealed that firms (both foreign and domestic) find the current regulatory environment, including taxation, highly restrictive to economic practices. It appears as if the adoption of the fundamental market principles has not been accompanied by the development of corresponding public institutions to support their practical implementation. As a result, intrusive government interventions and unfriendly practices are the source of the real sector problem by producing major distortions in incentives for enterprise managers and potential investors. Specifically, the following points are often made:

- Rules are not transparent and are not readily available to the public.

- The costs of learning rules and regulations are high for newly-created enterprises.

- Rules are applied differently by different public agents.

- Rules change often and businessmen find it difficult to keep track of them.

- Enterprises are visited by a host of government officials without clear and often overlapping mandates.

- Appeal procedures are weak and the court system is not effective in resolving disputes between private businesses and Government agencies.

Tax Administration

Armenia's inherited tax administration practices are not conducive to a market economy. Specifically, the tax administration did not operate according to the principle of self-assessment. Also, taxpayers have been assigned to specific tax officers who covered all functions, providing the opportunity for collusion between the two parties. The lack of self-assessment and weak internal control capacity that led to fairly obstructive control practices created an environment that favors corruption and harassment at high and low levels of tax administration.

---

[86] For a more detailed discussion of the existing administrative barriers for investments see the FIAS Report (2000).

For the last two years, the Government has been building its effort to reform the tax and custom administration with the support of the IMF, USAID and other donors. Recently, this work has been accelerated and linked with Government plans to simplify the tax system. More importantly, the Government has taken a broader approach to the reform. It shifted the focus from a purely fiscal objective of improving revenue performance to a more balanced combination of goals, which emphasizes both a need for reduction of compliance costs for taxpayers as well as attainment of higher collection targets.

The key objectives of these efforts include:

- Introduction of the functional organization of the district tax offices, which would reduce contacts between tax officials and taxpayers.

- Other reforms to reduce opportunities for corruption, which would include the development of internal audit/investigation functions in the Ministry of Revenue, transparent appeal procedures, and personnel and salary reforms for tax and customs administration staff.

- Introduction of a new transparent system of taxpayer audit and reduction in a number of audits that require inspectors' visits of businesses.

- Full integration in operations of tax and customs with a special focus on realignment and better compatibility of existing systems and practices in information management, internal control and investigation, salary and incentive strategies, regulatory development and enforcement, and criminal investigation.

- Gradual shift of responsibility for payroll tax collections from the Pension Fund to the Ministry of Revenue, which would reduce an overall number of interactions between businesses and government agencies.

- Strengthening enforcement of VAT on imports by completing the shift of its collection to the boarder – this would help to reduce current inequalities in the tax burden between importers and domestic producers.

- Improvements in administration of tax refund, including VAT refund for exporters.

- Setting up a system to support an efficient exchange of information between the banking system, the Treasury, the social insurance system, and the Ministry of Revenue.

- Introduction of mechanisms that encourage taxpayers' participation in the design, implementation and monitoring of tax reforms.

- Improvement in taxpayer services.

- Use of performance measures to track progress with reform implementation.

Customs Administration

As in tax administration, Armenia has also faced a two-fold challenge to develop a customs system that facilitates the trade flow, while helping generate revenues and prevent the flow of illegal goods. Advances have already been made, like the introduction of ASYCUDA, to the four district customs offices. Also, a successful pilot has been undertaken to introduce a classification system that speeds up the flow of goods. But problems remain, for instance, in the evaluation of goods, which is considered by businesses to be highly arbitrary. In the summer of 2000, the Ministry of Revenue, with donor support, undertook a customs diagnosis with the participation of importers and public officials. Based on the diagnostics, the following points are identified as priorities for a medium-term action plan.[87]

- Redesign the customs import and export procedures to facilitate movements of goods based on increased transparency, automation, consolidation of required documentation, improved classification procedures, switch to selectivity technique in cargo examination, etc.

- Improve customs capability for valuation of imported goods.

- Complete implementation of the ASYCUDA and create an integrated national information framework.

- Adjust customs regulations to make them fully consistent with the requirements of the recently adopted Customs Code and with WTO standards.

Improving Tax/Customs Services

Special attention should be paid to improving taxpayer services, which is a key to building taxpayers' confidence as well as to setting-up a scene for public-private dialogue in this major area of the reform program. Immediate priorities would include:

- Develop a Tax Code that brings together all relevant tax information, including procedural aspects. The code would also spell clearly the right and obligations of the taxpayers and the government.

- Expand provision of information to taxpayers free of charge.

- Improve quality and availability of advice given to taxpayers and stand by the advice provided. That is, if the taxpayer follows the advice given by the tax districts, it cannot be found in error later on for using it.

- Involve taxpayers in the evaluation of tax and customs operations through a systematic dialogue between public officials and the private sector and through periodic taxpayer surveys.

- Develop measures to track the reduction of interface between tax officials and taxpayers. This can be done with the development of an internal management information system, or based on external surveys.

Tax Policy: Simplification and Equal Treatment

Tax reforms of 1997-98 introduced a rather modern tax framework with a limited, by standards of an economy in transition, number of distortions. Still, there have been growing concerns that the existing tax system is too advanced relatively to the existing capacity of both tax administration (which struggles

---

[87] In April of 2001 the Government adopted Resolution No. 310 which outline a specific action plan to accelerate a comprehensive custom reform.

to enforce it in a non-arbitrary way) and taxpayers (who found costs of learning and compliance to be too high). In consultation with the donors, the Government has prepared and adopted in late 2000 a far-reaching proposal to reduce the existing level of nominal tax burden and simplify the tax system. In early 2001 tax rates for both personal and corporate income were reduced.

The new law has been adopted in the summer of 2000 that simplifies taxation of small businesses. The law seeks to address a particularly irksome problem in Armenia, which is the difficulty in obtaining invoices to justify business costs. Small businesses with a total turnover below a threshold are allowed to pay a new presumptive tax, which substitutes for both VAT and income tax obligations and is calculated as a percentage (7 percent) of total turnover. Taxpayers are also allowed to reduce further such tax liabilities if they have their business expenses properly documented.

Additional measures to simplify taxation, adopted in December of 2000, include: (i) streamlining of the provisions for carryover of losses; (ii) reduction in penalty rates for tax arrears; and (iii) introduction of consolidated taxation of 'related parties' aimed at the limitation of opportunities for tax evasion. A significant increase in the threshold for VAT registration and payment was also introduced in late 2000. The previous threshold at 3 million drams (less than US$6,000) in annual sales was too low and cumbersome for the revenue administration and the taxpayers, and it was increased to 10 million drams.

The Government also proposed several steps to further advance equity in tax treatment of various groups of taxpayers. This includes:

- Cuts in VAT exemptions (estimated as 2.5% of GDP a year).

- Collection of VAT for all goods at the time of import. Currently, importers of goods not subject to custom duties or excises do not pay VAT at the point of entry but when the final product is sold. This mechanism provides an opportunity for evasion and would be best eliminated.

- Consolidation of income and payroll taxes and reduction in the combined rate of wage taxation.

- Reduction in the threshold and frequency allowing individuals (shuttle traders) tax-free imports of goods.

- Simplification of the current documentation requirements: e.g. currently invoices valid for income tax purposes may not be valid for VAT and vice versa.

The measures above can help expand the tax base and thus in perspective provide for lowering the VAT rate, which presently is too high for the country's level of income. Lower rates for both VAT and payroll tax, accompanied by improvements in tax and customs administration, is considered to be a major element of the new incentive structure that would support a gradual reduction of informal operations in the economy.

Deregulation

Inspections and Audits. In Armenia, too many government agencies can and do visit enterprises for different but often overlapping objectives. This represents a heavy burden on enterprises. A new Law on Inspections, which was adopted in May 2000, is intended to limit discretionary audits of private business and also increase the accountability of auditors. While this law would help, drastic actions are needed to consolidate, downsize and rationalize government inspections, i.e. to reduce the number of both agencies and agents with inspection powers. Charter documents of various inspecting agencies, which in many cases are still operating under old Soviet regulations, have to be reviewed and amended to reflect new market principles (which imply a reduced level of government control), as well as new realities related to a lower per capita income level of the country. Government inspections have to monitor only core parameters of business activity, which make their auditing functions more affordable to the budget and less disruptive for the private sector.

Specifically, the Ministry of Revenue should not be charged with obligations outside its sphere of influence. Just the same, other agencies, such as the Prosecutor office, should be limited in their ability to perform tax-related audits and activities. Specifically, mandates of fire, sanitary, and trade inspections need review and amendment. Road inspection remains among the most visible signs of petty corruption and discretion.

Registration and licensing. The Government needs to implement other relevant measures in the area of public administration, with the objective of reducing the costs of interaction between the public and private sectors. Initially, the Government should concentrate its reform efforts in a number of core areas that, from a business perspective, represent the major obstacles to investors. These include:

- Amendments to the Law on Registration of Legal Entities to liberalize and simplify market entry;

- Upgrade the whole infrastructure of the registration process to ensure a transition to a centralized registration process and improve coordination between various participating agencies;

- Simplify registration rules and procedures that cover development of established enterprises (e.g. increase in charter capital, other amendments to a company charter, etc.);

- Simplify and make more transparent procedures for issuing construction and site development permits;

- Abolish the requirement for obtaining a company seal;

- Streamline licensing procedures to reduce a number of different agencies involved in the licensing process, reduce discretion of sectoral ministries in administering the licensing process, and reduce the scope of commercial activities that require licensing;

- Prepare a comprehensive description of company registration and licensing processes, available to the public;

- Develop a new Administrative Code, which would set up a broad regulatory framework regarding the relationship between Government agencies and private business, including a transparent framework for administering penalties and fines.

Cleaning the regulatory framework. As in other economies in transition, Armenia inherited a vast volume of non-market regulations, which makes the cleaning up of the existing regulatory framework a priority task. The GOA has started this process in late 1998. Based on the review conducted by the Ministry of Justice, the GOA invalidated about 500 decrees and decisions of the Armenian Government issued between 1990 and 1993. The GOA also approved a decree under which all the decrees adopted by the Council of Ministers of Soviet Armenia prior to August 23, 1990 would be invalid from March 1, 1999, except for a rather restricted list that had been reconfirmed by the GOA. This regulatory review and cleaning has to be continued.

Legal Framework and Enforcement

Over the last several years, Armenia has adopted a number of laws and regulations building the infrastructure for a market economy, including company laws, banking laws, bankruptcy law, land law, etc. The key accomplishment was the passage of the new Civil Code, which became effective in early 1999. The Government also adopted a Law on Intellectual Property in 1999 and joined several international conventions on intellectual property rights protection. What must follow in the area of legal framework is the adoption/amendment of several core commercial laws, which are complementary to the Civil Code, as well as institutional strengthening of the regulatory authorities responsible for administration and enforcement of those laws.

The Government priorities in the area of legal drafting include:

- Establishing a modern framework of company laws by making appropriate amendments to Law on Joint Stock Companies and developing a new Law on Limited Liabilities Companies, which would govern operations of companies that are not able to meet requirements of the Joint Stock Company Law;

- A new Concession Law to support an inflow of foreign direct investment (FDI), especially into the mining industry; and

- A new Land Code to enable, *inter alia*: a) State-Owned Enterprises (SOEs) and privatized companies to gain ownership of the land they occupy (not just permanent user rights); and b) development of land markets in both urban and rural areas.

The adoption of new laws has to be accompanied by steps to strengthen the institutional capacity of various implementation agencies, including the Ministries of Finance, Revenues, Privatization, and Industry and Trade, the Armenian Development Agency, and the Energy and Securities Commissions.

The Government has also developed a comprehensive program for reforming its judiciary, with particular focus on strengthening judicial governance, re-designing the court administration and case management system, rehabilitating court infrastructure, improving judicial training and enforcement of court decisions. The Ministry of Justice has to develop the capacity to monitor business practices and, in cases of legal uncertainty, issue recommendations to the Government on needed changes to streamline law enforcement. In the medium term, the Judicial Reform Project of the IDA will be the main instrument in assisting the Government to implement the program. In addition, to strengthen the effectiveness of the judiciary, the GOA, supported by bilateral and multilateral donors, initiated certain legislative and institutional measures to reform the legal education system, develop the legal profession, reform the prosecutor's office and establish alternative dispute resolution mechanisms.

With donors' assistance, the Government should also strengthen the capacity for enforcing bankruptcy legislation through providing training to judges and building a profession of independent liquidators. Another area for priority training relates to the capacity of the judicial system to interpret tax laws. Given the existing constraints, Armenia could consider the development of specialized tax chairs within the courts.

Strengthen Mechanism of Public-Private Consultations

As mentioned in Chapter 3, lack of communication between business and the Government has been a serious deficiency of the business environment in Armenia. At least part of the problem relates to the weakness of business organizations. Business lobbying in Armenia is focused at getting individual or group benefits but not at defending broader business interests. But the core difficulty relates to a lack of tradition of public-private consultations and weak accountability mechanisms. As a result, the Government does not have the capacity to monitor problems which are faced by the enterprise sector, and address them without considerable delays.

Box 4.2. High Level Business Council: Main Objectives and Basic Principles of Organization

The primary objective of the Council is to establish a venue for dialogue and joint work between the Government and the private sector, which would help identify, prioritize, and gradually remove major constraints for investment and business development. It would help to:

- Increase the efficiency of Government policy making through improved prioritization and evaluation, and through better reflection of preferences of private sector agents;

- Build trust between leading public and private sector players, based inter alia on a better understanding of the Government policy;

- Cut costs of doing business, including costs of entry, through reduction of major "administrative costs";

- Increase accountability of the Government through regular reporting on implementation of the agreed policies to the private sector.

In the Armenian environment, the Council could also play (probably at a later stage) an important role in mobilizing various private businessmen for participation in joint investment projects. The Council could become an instrument of "private-private" dialogue to support communication and cooperation between various private investors (e.g. local and from the Diaspora).

The personal composition of the Council is quite important. It should include senior officials from leading Ministries and businessmen with the "right" reputation (both local and from the Diaspora). It makes sense to have a larger representation of various business associations (collective bodies of the private sector) than just individual participation. While it is important to have several major investors with "big names" among the Council members, they should not be in the majority. Big investors often do not face the same problems as a regular small investor does. Also, big investors may not have sufficient time and incentives to be actively engaged in Council work.

The main volume of the Council work has to be conducted in specialized working groups, composed from the staff of respective ministries, interested business people, and representatives of civil society. The working groups would develop suggestions on modification of existing regulations and laws; comment on Government initiatives and suggestions; prepare reports on implementation of Government decisions.

Activities of the Council should be supported by a professional Secretariat, working on a full-time basis. Decisions of the Council and main implementation outcomes should be made public.

An important principle of the Council's work should be its flexibility and openness to change. If successful, the priority of Council work would evolve, driven by demands of its members and the investment community at large.

Source: Biddle and Milor (1999).

The Government of Armenia has recently prepared a number of steps to strengthen its capacity to support investors and exporters, especially through establishing a High Level Business Council as a primary venue for ongoing consultations with the business community (Box 4.2). As international experience suggests, well-established public-private consultative mechanisms could be quite efficient in both improving the business environment and resolving coordination problems.[88] They could trigger a chain reaction – virtuous circle of continuous reform of the business environment to improve logistic services and enhance the competitiveness of the private sector with resulting trickle down benefits for the entire economy. At the same time, World Bank projects have confirmed the difficulty of identifying, agreeing and implementing project components that cut horizontally across multiple, "stove pipe" government agencies. The experience requires not only a strong initial commitment from the top level government but also the creation of a transitional platform – e.g., special committee, task force, etc. – which is empowered to maintain continuous pressure for fundamental change and, importantly, which is also empowered to resolve inter-jurisdictional issues.

The GOA also plans to strengthen the capacity of the Armenian development Agency (ADA) to conduct efficient investment promotion, including delivery of full-range services to foreign investors. It would also clarify functions and responsibilities of the Ministry of Industry and Trade and the ADA to avoid overlap and competition. In compliance with WTO requirements, the GOA would set up and make fully operational the National Notification Center. A separate priority relates to the need to strengthen the public sector's capacity to provide information and advisory services to the private sector. An immediate priority is for the Government (in cooperation with the Business Chamber) to establish a depositary of relevant business legislation and regulations.

Reforming Civil Service: Role of Autonomous Agencies

A massive civil service reform in the transition environment is a challenging administrative task. As a rule, a government with limited administrative capacity can not do everything at once – otherwise, the comprehensive administrative reform just would not be necessary. Therefore, right sequencing of administrative reforms becomes an important policy issue. The challenge is to select a limited number of "administratively affordable" interventions ("entry points") to be focused on major bottlenecks in the system. This report argues that in Armenia the main priority at the moment relates to reforming those parts of the Government that have the most frequent interactions with the private sector, i.e. those which have a critical impact on the quality of the business environment.

In addition to a sample of targeted policy interventions, described earlier in this Chapter, the basic "institutional message" of this report relates to the importance of cross-cutting Autonomous *Agencies* at the initial stages of the reform process. The role of such agencies is to pilot new principles of public services with greater managerial flexibility, better pay, and greater accountability for results. The idea of an Autonomous Agency is based on the assumption of limited administrative capacity for reforms and the importance of fiscal constraints that preclude a full-scale introduction of new public administration principles across the board. Starting from a single agency, the Government would be able to test new principles and gradually expand them to the rest of the public sector. During the transition, the Autonomous Agency plays the role of local center of excellence.

Autonomous agencies with some strategic and implementation capacity have been routinely created by donors, including the World Bank, as PIUs. The challenge seems to relate to: a) establishing Autonomous Agencies in a way that would have a policy-making impact on the government; b) staff them by capable local experts, exposed to marketing and consulting expertise; and c) assure sustainability – continuity of the 'Autonomous Agency' life after an initial pilot project ends.

---

[88] See Biddle and Milor (1999) and Biddle at al. (2000) on international best practice in setting consultative mechanisms.

Other main requirements to such an Agency include:

- Existence of a well-defined mandate, for which the Agency may be held accountable, that reflects a top priority policy task;

- Close links between the Agency and other parts of the Government that provides for indirect impact on other public sector agencies and allows for gradual expansion of public administration reforms.

Another important requirement to the Autonomous Agency: it has to have a cross-cutting multi-sectoral mandate to maximize its interaction with the rest of the government. A good example of such a cross-cutting function is investment promotion: an efficient investment promotion agency deals on a daily basis with issues that overlap with responsibilities of almost all government agencies. It means that an FDI agency has two clients -- potential private investors and the government at large. Private investors have to be attracted and served, other government agencies have to be convinced to change their policies and be broadly cooperative.

The example of an FDI agency reveals a specific feature of cross-cutting mandates: they deal with tasks where, as a rule, there is no binding institutional constraint. A poor investment environment derives from hundreds of medium and small-size distortions, interaction of which makes costs of investments prohibitive. As a result, design and implementation of a number of institutional reforms itself requires considerable institutional capacity, which creates all the pre-requisites for a vicious circle.

From this perspective, the GOA's intention to establish a capable investment promotion agency on the basis of the Armenian Development Agency (ADA) is very important. When it is implemented, the question of interaction of the ADA with other branches of government would be among the central ones. Also, as it is argued in Chapter 6 below, in Armenia other perspective areas where establishing an Autonomous Agency would be appropriate relate to enterprise restructuring (Restructuring Agency) and business support (Business and Advisory Center).

International experience suggests that Autonomous Agencies could perform rather well even in a challenging environment of low competencies and high corruption.[89] Their "reform impact" on other agencies is achieved through at least three mechanisms:

- Mobility of capable personnel between the Autonomous Agency and other parts of the government;

- Design by the Autonomous Agency of policy initiatives to which the government has to react;

- Consolidation of constituencies for reform by developing broader consultative mechanisms and regular reporting on experience of the Autonomous Agency.

Through mobility of personnel, flow of policy proposals and voice of the constituencies for reform, the Autonomous Agency exerts pressure for change on the rest of the government and changes real-life government practices. But the government also exerts pressures on the Autonomous Agency

---

[89] In Armenia and several other FSU states, the Central Bank has de facto an Autonomous Agency status, setting it aside from the rest of public administration. However, by nature of its mandate any Central Bank has limited interactions with the rest of the Government, which prevents any significant reform spillover from the reformed Central Bank.

through accountability mechanisms. The Autonomous agency and the government transform each other by engaging in challenging tasks in which they have to cooperate. From this perspective, the entire public sector reform becomes a gradual, bottom-up process driven by business needs of the Autonomous Agency (ies).

Establishing an Autonomous organization that is private in form but public in purpose carries considerable risk. It can fail to fulfill the expectations of catalyzing the enterprise restructuring if any of the following occurs:

- The organization is captured by the government and becomes an instrument of rent-seeking and/or a channel for allocation of subsidies.

- The organization is run as a bureaucracy rather than a business establishment, headed by a social entrepreneur with exceptional problem-solving skills.

- The organization tries to accomplish too much and becomes overwhelmed with multiple tasks it has no capability of handling.

The first challenge could be addressed by making the organization autonomous from the government. The second group of risks underlines key importance of entrepreneurial and managerial skills of agency managers, who should combine business instincts with diplomatic tact and skills to handle inevitable tensions with the government and other stakeholders. The latter risk means that the agency should start modestly and low-key and expand in line with evolving capabilities.

5.   STAGNATION TRAP AND ENTRY POINTS TO BREAK IT

This chapter provides an analytical framework for more practical recommendations on restructuring policy presented in the following chapter. The chapter argues that even when compared to most other economies in transition, restructuring challenges in Armenia are much more difficult. In Armenian circumstances, the institutional vacuum deriving from discontinuity of the post-socialist transition resulted in a potential stagnation trap, which in turn requires rather non-traditional institutional solutions. Thus, the main question of this chapter is as follows: given the severity of simultaneous market and government failures, how to design and establish institutions capable of facilitating development of dynamic forward-looking economic agents?

The chapter presents a strategy of addressing these challenges on the basis of gradual and incremental interventions focused on small but tangible improvements. The core of the strategy relates to a country-specific design of entry points – private-public initiatives to facilitate incipient positive trends and encourage attaining restructuring objectives through many diverse bottom-up changes. The key to the identification of entry points is better utilization of existing resources - equipment, office space, managerial and labor skills – through specially design institutions.

5.1.   Stagnation Trap

Armenia presents a specific challenge of an income- and resource-poor landlocked economy characterized by high, although rapidly diminishing, stock of human capital. How does one promote economic growth in a situation of rudimentary institutions and income level both comparable to Sub-Saharan Africa yet human capital comparable to the US? In Armenia, massive brain drain and social instability are the two most salient features of the business environment. The growth paradox of Armenia – a tremendous promise of both high (but quickly diminishing) human capital and potentially high (but still not coming) foreign investment – is summarized in Table 5.1.

Coordination Problem and Stagnation Trap

Institutional capacity to support enterprise restructuring. Even if the business environment is reasonably friendly (which is not the case in Armenia), firms have to have minimum skills to benefit from it. Enterprise restructuring is a challenge for a post-socialist manager who needs new skills to deal with new markets, partners, and ways of doing business. Dramatic discontinuity of the post-socialist transition left a vacuum of intermediary organizations that typically facilitate entry, exit and restructuring of enterprises, and connecting firms to each other in mature information-rich market economies. Information-based constraints are especially severe in small, rather isolated economies such as Armenian that have featured thin internal markets for information, weak traditions of inter-firm cooperation, weak interest from outside investors, and therefore, overall high costs of entering new export markets. This alone provides justification for public interventions: public sector institutions may facilitate enterprise learning by providing management training, informational and advisory support, promoting advantages of local producers externally, and supporting local and international networking and partnerships.

Coordination problem. Another challenge for a sustainable growth strategy relates to the coordination problem[90]. Poor expectations keep investments low, but lack of investments confirms negative projections and expectations. The profitability of an individual investment is dependent on what happens elsewhere in the economy. This situation creates a sequencing problem for investors: if nobody

---

[90] Options theory of investments, which underlies irreversibility of investments and a possibility of deferring an investment decision indefinitely due to actual or perceived uncertainty, provides a modern treatment of the coordination problem (see Serven and Solimano, 1994).

goes first, nothing happens. Even though everybody may keep saying that fundamentals are right, all hold off on investments except of the most liquid kind. This is why <u>first movers</u> – firms actually making investments of any sorts (i.e. in human capital, managerial capability and fixed capital) in the risky environment -- are critical for changing expectations and triggering investments.

Table 5.1. Bermuda Triangle of Armenia

Points of the Triangle	Weaknesses	Strengths	Operational opportunities and threats
1. Unusually high educational level (in particular technical education)	Massive brain drain High rates of brain drain High expectations for living standards and employment possibilities	Emerging high value-added clusters of new economy Software cluster/IT industry in general: number of firms, output, exports, percentage of growth	Marshall Plan-type Secondments for managers should be introduced with caution. Could be a channel of brain drain.
2. Wealthy Diaspora and large amount of Donor funding	The Diaspora with its philanthropic grants delays search for creative solutions to revive the productive sector Private sector development has been of secondary concern for donors	Marketing, financial and technical linkages with the Diaspora could be a major source of growth In a small country a small number of investment projects can make a difference	Facilitation of linkages with the Diaspora as one of central themes for public sector interventions
3. High transportation, image-related and cultural costs for trade and investments from the West	Image of a country still at war Scarce routes to the outside world	Brains and investment-friendly business environment are the only long run competitive advantage	Waking up and catching up agenda: conveying a sense of urgency among the political and private sector elite that 'Brains is the only long-run competitive advantage but brains could be gone soon'

Even though coordination is central to initiating the investment flow, we know little about how to facilitate non-distortionary coordination, i.e. coordination with full costs which do not exceed their benefits. Occasionally, help comes from extraordinary (one time) opportunities: e.g. in Mexico, in the aftermath of the Free Trade Agreement (NAFTA), the large amount of flight capital returned to the country and cemented economic stability. Owners of the capital, it seems, were waiting for "a piece of good news" to start the stampede. The creative presentation of opportunities, associated with the NAFTA, has become a part of *the credible coordinating device* to send a message that it is safe to invest at home. When such a message gains credibility, it triggers a self-enhancing chain of events, and coordination becomes a done deal.

Another example of a coordinating device relates to activities of the first movers: a critical mass of first movers, making stable progress in implementation of their projects, may be sufficient to change perceptions about the quality of the investment climate. The latter example seems to be relevant to Armenia.

The unfriendly business environment, compounded by the coordination problem and knowledge-based constraints for restructuring, results in the following <u>stagnation trap</u>: the unfriendly business environment in the isolated economy generates negligible amounts of first movers, which in turn aggravates the coordination problem, resulting in even lower investments. In addition, low entrepreneurship in such an economy produces too little pressure to reform the business environment and therefore further supports stagnation.

In Armenia, such a stagnation trap could be rather stable because:

- By regional standards, the country has shown a strong (but unsustainable) economic recovery, which provides a latitude to delay painful reforms and a basis for complacency; however, recent growth, which was greatly supported by massive international assistance, by rather successful sectoral reforms (e.g. in energy) as well as by a depth of the earlier crisis was not accompanied by sufficient expansion in capabilities of Armenian firms;

- As usual in similar situations, the most able and vocal proponents of reforms tend to emigrate: they prefer 'exit' to 'voice';

- Donors' assistance acts as a balance-of-payment shock absorber, weakening demand for change[91]; also in Armenia, where nominal growth rates are rather high and the Government has an established reformist reputation, donors have been less suspicious and less pushy with respect to improvements in the investment climate;

- Private external investors are passive; because of the small internal market, Armenia attracts little investment interest; there is no independent watchdog to push for reforms; the Diaspora is concerned not to damage the Government's reputation and so far has been a source of limited reform pressure.

Effective vs. Notional Incentives

There is a lot of debate on what matters more to assure the government to push for reform and the managers to push for restructuring: incentives or capabilities. Similar to a familiar contrast between effective demand and notional demand, it seems important to distinguish notional and effective incentives. <u>Effective incentives</u>[92] – incentives that guide actual behavior, that account for available opportunities to act on notional incentives.

The manager or government official who faces the right incentives (hard budget constraints, credible threat of bankruptcy, right salary scale) but has no available options to act on them has no effective incentives at all. The challenge of development assistance in breaking a low-equilibrium trap is to assure synergy between improvements in incentives (e.g. through strengthening budget constraints and/or through better definition of property rights) and options-expanding training. Such a synergy would result in: (a) emergence of effective incentives for a larger number of economic agents; and (b) increased incidence of first movers, who would be capable of implementing real projects suggested by such incentives.

One can make a similar distinction between a notional and effective investment environment. A notional investment environment (which is reflected in laws and regulations) could be relatively good. However, the state may have little incentives and no capability to enforce this favorable legal framework, i.e. to transform a notional business environment into an effective business environment. To put it

---

[91] Collier, Paul (2000).

[92] Trade theory provides another example of a difference between nominal and effective incentives. It distinguishes between nominal and effective rates of protection. If import duties on inputs are higher than nominal protection of outputs, an effective protection rate would be negative.

another way, the business environment is permissive to investments. However, to transform it from merely permissive to friendly is the responsibility of the investor and the government.

In the situation of simultaneous market and government failures characteristic for transition economies, specially designed institutions, which would facilitate the formation of both new right incentives and new options to act on them, could be an entry point for a Government restructuring strategy. Institutions as diverse as micro-finance institutions, social investment funds, local economic development agencies, restructuring agencies proposed below could be institutional platforms for formation of effective incentives to learn and restructure. One of the functions of such an agency would be an enforcement of an investment-friendly business framework (initially – for a limited group of firms that are clients of the agency). Box 5.1 provides an example of how service organizations like technology parks could perform all these functions for their tenants.

Box 5.1. Moscow University Science Park

The Park was established in 1991, as a joint venture of the Moscow State University, Russian Ministry of Science and the private sector. More than 30 companies in software development, laser technology and biotechnology are currently its tenants.

Benefits for companies:
- Umbrella from state and mafia harassment (any inspector first deals with Park's administration);
- Clustering effect: access to human capital and R&D of the university and synergy between tenants (at least in two cases communication between seemingly unrelated tenants produced new commercial ideas);
- Access to modern telecommunications (the Park has a satellite teleport) and office infrastructure.

Business development services appear to be of lesser importance to Park's tenants. When they are provided, it is done mainly by private service providers rather than by Park's staff. This is consistent with the trends in international best practice. The park does not provide financing to the tenants.

Evolution of the Park:
The current structure of the Park is the result of three stages in its evolution:
- Russian start-ups came to the Park;
- These start-ups generated interest from foreign investors and formed joint ventures with them, which led to FDI into some tenant companies and also brought a considerable expansion of the Park's premises;
- Global companies came as both shareholders of the Park and co-sponsors of its further expansion. For instance, the third office facility of the Park is being constructed jointly with Samsung, while Intel plans to co-sponsor a contest for best commercial idea.

Factors of success:
- Strong leadership;
- Incremental growth, as opposed to a single grand project – start small, establish credibility and reputation and on that basis attract brand-name tenants and investors.

5.2.   Entry Points to Break the Stagnation Trap

The key to a successful strategy to break the stagnation trap appears to be in establishing the correct mix of top-down (macro-level) and bottom-up (enterprise-level) reform approaches. Policy or regulatory measures alone will not be sufficient to sustain the growth of the real sector, an emphasis on capacity building at the enterprise level through appropriate restructuring, training, and privatization will also be necessary. These enterprise-level reforms will help create and empower constituencies to support further policy, regulatory, and institutional changes.

This is a formidable agenda that in principle requires a coordinated effort of virtually all government agencies and donors. Yet there is tension between, on the one hand, the gains from an integrated comprehensive approach and, on the other, the benefits of an incremental, sequenced strategy that does not attempt to take on more than could realistically be achieved. Many reform efforts in the past have become hopelessly discredited and blurred in attempting to manage too broad an agenda. Once a realistic reform vision is agreed, implementation needs to emphasize phasing and sequencing – an area where we still have much to learn -- as one successfully completed task builds on the last one and presages the next one.

In stark contrast to Eastern-European economies, in Armenia, a first round of reforms produced fewer benefits for both the general public and the entrepreneurial class. Due to this legacy and given existing institutional constraints, to unlock the virtuous spiral of reforms it may be useful to put special emphasis on tangible (concrete, visible) initiatives – not as a substitute for a continuing policy and institutional reform, but as an "entry point" from which: (a) public trust could be somewhat regained; (b) expectations of the private sector improve; (c) systemic constraints for restructuring could be identified more specifically; and (d) from which less tangible reforms would follow as corollaries.

This emphasis on tangible initiatives carries a variety of practical benefits. First, it enables a focus on specifics of the business environment with greater attention to details of doing business; it makes it possible to get at the root of some of the systemic problems in the business environment, which may not be readily seen at the macro level. Second, concrete goals translate much more readily into benchmarks to measure progress in implementation and to signal when policy modifications are justifiable.

This section describes three entry points relevant to Armenia's environment:

a) managed work space, created on the premises of former industrial behemoth, to be used as an e.g. enterprise incubator or industrial park;

b) export processing zone; and

c) business center to promote business linkages and FDI.

(A) Managed Work Space

The managed work space is usually used to perform the following primary functions:

- <u>Recombination of assets</u>: a technique (formalized in an operation manual) to carve out viable assets and lease them to spin-off SMEs;

- <u>Facilitation of 'forced entrepreneurship'</u> by convincing and cajoling most capable incumbent managers to become managers/owners of spin-off SMEs;

- <u>Provision of a better business environment</u> (security protection, some protection from inspections) and business development services to spin-offs, which are tenants of the industrial park.

Recombination of assets through industrial parks has been successfully piloted in Moldova since 1996[93]. The success of the Moldovan Restructuring Agency, ARIA, in large part is associated with the

---

[93] See Chapter 6 for more detailed discussion on the ARIA.

fact that it has found an efficient solution to politically-charged issues of liquidation of largest local SOEs and their restructuring by working with existing capital and human resources (Box 5.2). This was a second best solution to the restructuring challenge, given the absence of strategic investors interested in these enterprises. Another strength of the ARIA relates to its unique position as an autonomous government agency with a strong and committed leadership and dedicated and skilled staff.

Box 5.2. Reviving a Large Enterprise of Former Military-Industrial Complex: Lessons from Moldovan ALFA

ALFA belongs to the group of large electronics enterprises of the former USSR. ALFA received no orders for military equipment since 1990-91, and in the early 90s, as a result of conversion, the production of TV-sets comprised the core business of the company. By 1994-1995, it became clear that ALFA was not able to survive in this highly competitive market – it lost its traditional markets (FSU, Romania) to imported TV-sets. The reorganization procedure was started in January 1998, after the reorganization plan had been proposed by the Moldovan Agency for Enterprise Assistance (ARIA), which suggested converting the company into the Industrial Park (IP). An external administrator was appointed, who has been running "ALFA" for 2.5 years by now.

Despite the financial crises of 1998, which was a serious blow to the business of IP residents, results of the reorganization are quite encouraging. By mid-2000, 85 enterprises were functioning in the Industrial Park "ALFA", of which 9 had foreign capital participation. 35% of the residents are owners of production assets – they are buying them from the IP through financial leasing arrangements. Total effective employment within the boundaries of the IP increased by almost fourfold, from 400 to 1,500 employees. Annual sales increased 17 times, and taxes paid by more than 10 times. However, IP "ALFA" still has huge untapped potential – about 60% of its assets are still idle.

"ALFA" restructuring was a very labor intensive exercise for ARIA. It took about 6 months of work of several consultants to develop the reorganization plan, 4 consultants were engaged for a year assisting with the plan implementation. ARIA assistance was focused on the following areas:
- Diagnostic analysis, asset evaluation and recommendations on their future use;
- Development of reorganization plan;
- Suggestions for debt minimization and rescheduling, and debt/equity conversion;
- Facilitation of negotiations with the creditors and signing of the Memorandum Agreement;
- Development of detailed Industrial Park regulations, rules for leasing and selling of assets, tariffs for utilities, use of infrastructure and other management company services;
- Assistance in reorganization plan implementation, including advisory services and training of management staff;
- Assistance to would be owner-managers of spin-offs, typically former ALFA middle managers, in business plan development, forecasts of cash-flow, in-country training and internships abroad;
- Assistance to IP management in negotiations with state authorities in respect to social assets divestiture, bureaucratic harassment, public relations, etc.;
- Facilitation of business contacts with foreign companies, potential partners or investors.

Source: World Bank (2001a). Armenia. PSD strategy, Discussion draft.

(B) Export Processing Zone

International experience suggests that a well-functioning, privately-developed and managed Export Processing Zone (EPZ) can be a powerful way to break through the wall of ignorance of a country's potential and kick-start a country's visibility in the global business arena. To achieve such objectives, the EPZ has to satisfy two groups of requirements.

First, the prospects for success are greatly enhanced if the EPZ is developed and operated by a private operator with the reputation and networks in the international marketplace capable of attracting export-oriented manufacturing tenants into a new and uncertain environment. Preliminary indications are that such an EPZ operator could indeed be attracted into Armenia but only if the operator is provided with a credible assurance that some key off-site infrastructure and institutional issues are addressed first.

Second, in order for an EPZ to be a successful platform for attracting export-oriented manufacturing investors, a variety of complementary trade facilitation services need to work effectively (business registration, transport, customs, immigration, etc.). While institutional reforms are underway in Armenian public agencies, it will take many years before their service standards meet international standards. In the interim, to ensure that trade facilitation for the EPZ works smoothly, the Armenian authorities may want to develop a set of precise performance benchmarks, which would be required from the country's customs, immigration and investment promotion agencies, and to establish clear mechanisms for holding these agencies accountable for a gradual improvement in performance. Meeting the benchmarks will require substantial efforts on the part of each of these agencies and thus may justify external support to underpin these efforts.

(C) Non-government Business Center to Promote Business Linkages and FDI

As discussed below in this chapter, success in FDI promotion depends significantly on upgrading local management practices. This creates a demand for institutions such as Information and Advisory Center (IAC) which would accelerate managerial upgrading of the Armenian private sector by providing systematic training, information, business advice and related services, and thus expand opportunities for more traditional investments (Box 5.3). An important part of the IAC portfolio would be brokering business linkages between Armenian companies and the outside world. The first priority is to support linkages with businesses controlled by the Diaspora Armenians, specifically to participate and promote various relevant sectoral initiatives currently sponsored by the Diaspora business groups (e.g. software development).

Box 5.3. Links Between Managerial Training and FDI Promotion

As part of two World Bank Projects in Moldova, about 100 Moldovan managers have completed 10-12 week secondments in similar enterprises in the Czech Republic, Hungary, Poland and Slovenia. As a result of this collaboration, an unexpectedly high number of entrepreneurs, who served as hosts in the program, came to Moldova to explore possibilities of doing business together with their new friends. There are already over 50 partnerships between Moldovan enterprises and firms from the above four countries. Twenty of these are joint ventures, which were expected to generate at least 1,000 new jobs before the end of 2000. The rest are export contracts, which will help integrate Moldovan enterprises into international markets, move the country away form barter trade, and diversify its traditional markets in the FSU.

Source: Kuznetsov and Astrakhan (2000).

In Armenia, the "knowledge transfer" function of such non-tangible FDI would be critical. It would help to establish new patterns of corporate behavior, including skills for penetrating new markets, dealing with large corporations, and establishing a new culture of inter-firm cooperation and coordinated collective actions[94].

---

[94] Blomström and Sjoholm (1998) provide statistical evidence of significant positive impact of FDI on local companies without foreign participation. In addition, as suggested by Caves (2000), quality of local management is a critical factor for augmenting the scale of FDI spillover in the local economy.

Main functions of the IAC could be summarized as follows:

- Provide expert advice to domestic and foreign companies with respect to business development (business plans, accounting, trade opportunities, information support, assistance with certification and promotion of quality standards, etc.), supporting development of business associations, promoting partnership arrangements with foreign companies.

- Administer various management training programs, including programs for public servants involved in business regulations; this would include rather advanced forms of training (on-the-job training in foreign companies; twinning arrangements; matching grant schemes for individual training).

- Policy advocacy: monitoring developments in the business environment, identifying regulatory problems and lobbying for a change. The IAC as a champion of reform and managerial upgrading: convincing the clients (both the Government and managerial corps) in the necessity of change.

5.3.   Institutional Design of Entry Points: Second-best Principle

The literature on institutional reform and enterprise restructuring has evolved in three stages. The first is the *market-failure* stage, in which the focus is on how a benevolent government can correct market failure. The second stage is the *government failure* stage. Here, the "capture" theory of government actions is an important example. The third stage, *institutional analysis,* recognizes the potential for both government and market failures but then goes one step further. It examines how various schemes produce different degrees of failure, comparing how each scheme fits, or fails to fit, a specific institutional environment[95].

There is a general second-best principle in institutional economics that has a parallel in price theory. Before the introduction of imperfect information and incomplete markets, we considered the problem using the first-best solution as the only benchmark. Later, with the development of the second-best theory, we broadened our perspectives. Similarly, when we first think about restructuring, we take reallocation of assets through strategic investor or via bankruptcy/liquidation as the only benchmarks. There is no doubt that as a normative recommendation, we need to strive for the best institutions. But institutional changes take time and when there are simultaneous market and government failures, second-best institutions (such as industrial parks) could be viable alternatives at least in the medium term.

It is worth noting that the proposed approach to the design of institutional solutions for restructuring (entry points) is very opportunistic and as such it does not require a full-scale public sector reform. Countries like Armenia have neither budgetary resources, capabilities, nor time to engage into a full-scale institutional reform. There is little hope that in the short term the government would be able to remedy most significant market failures (and vice versa). Given their resource and time constraints, this report proposes to economize on institution building by establishing institutional short-cuts – highly imperfect, risky, and idiosyncratic institutions assuring a functional fit between country conditions and reform challenges.

---

[95] R. Picciotto, E. Wiesner (eds.) (1998). *Evaluation and Development. The Institutional Dimension.* Burki, Shaid Javed and Guillermo E. Perry. (1998). *Beyond the Washington Consensus. Institutions Matter.* World Bank Latin America and Caribbean Studies.

Before drawing more specific recommendations for design of second-best restructuring institutions in the following chapter, let us discuss one more example of strategic restructuring: town-village enterprises in China.

Many have been puzzled by the remarkable success in China of enterprises owned and controlled by local governments (township-village enterprises, or TVEs). In the standard theory, it is hard to come up with good arguments to explain why TVEs have comparative advantages over private firms in terms of incentives. However, the puzzle can be solved if we make the realistic assumption that the rule of law and institutions that credibly constrain the state from expropriation are largely missing at the market where TVEs operate. In this institutional environment, private ownership suffers from the fear of state predation and thus is less efficient than it would be in an ideal institutional environment. But local government ownership, which integrates government and business activities, may achieve credible commitment for limiting state predation.[96] Hard budget constrains for local governments and the effective merger of government and business activities make the local government akin to a corporation, exerting pressure for performance of TVEs while providing on-demand assistance with procuring inputs and marketing of outputs (see Box 5.4).

Box 5.4. Why Lack of Transparency Could be Efficient? Trade-off Between Transparency and Efficiency in China.

In addition to TVEs, other evidence from China illustrates the importance of non-traditional instruments to build investors' confidence. In the absence of the rule of law, access to information gives the state at least hypothetical possibility to expropriate the wealth of its citizens. One way of achieving credible commitment to avoid expropriation is not to collect such information on individuals. It is well known that China's household bank saving are very high. Why do Chinese citizens have such confidence in state banks, given that the state in principle can confiscate a citizen's wealth? In part, because in China all private savings accounts are anonymous. In fact, China has a "Swiss" banking system. People can make deposits into banks under several fake names, and they do. By not asking for real names, the state credibly commits to not confiscating bank deposits from individuals. Of course, it can still confiscate the wealth of all depositors (say by inflation), but such a move would be very costly.

Notice that lack of transparency is essential here. News from China indicated that China is now considering a change in this practice for two reasons: to tax interest payments and to increase transparency. Transparency is desirable; it is an important part of the rule of law but must come with credible institutions to constrain the state. When the state is not constrained, the lack of transparency may require an alternative mechanism for making credible government commitment and strengthen an incentive regime.

Source: Based on Y. Qian (1998), pp. 196 – 198.

Export processing zones (EPZs), already mentioned in the previous section, provide another example of the second-best restructuring instrument. EPZs are often plainly ineffective and are rightly criticized for distorting incentives and inviting fraud and corruption. Yet, there are many ways to design EPZs. Traditional design creates a territorial *enclave* with an implicit objective to minimize its interactions with an unpredictable, unstable and corrupt domestic economy. Second-generation design of EPZs, successfully piloted in many African countries (for example, Mauritius and Madagascar[97]), creates a *pilot incentive regime* for any exporter in the country (irrespective of its territorial location) with an explicit objective to expand such a market-friendly incentive framework to the whole economy. This regime includes both substantially reduced tax and regulatory burden as well as light-touch non-distortionary assistance. Introduction of a new incentive regime becomes an entry point to establish:

---

[96] For details see Che and Qian (1995).
[97] Madagascar Private Sector Assessment, World Bank, 1996.

- *Critical mass of 'first movers'* -- firms successful in export markets -- which create powerful demonstration effects for other domestic firms to follow.

- *A precedent of policy reform* with particular emphasis on deregulation and tax reform. In the EPZ regime, firms exporting 100% of output are shielded from regulatory and tax burden. That creates a powerful demonstration effect of how the reformed tax and regulatory environment should be beneficial for an entire economy.

- *Constituency for reform,* consisting of first movers and others benefiting from the enhanced private dynamism that has pushed for both deepening of the reform and widening the initial reform efforts (i.e. to expand it beyond the limits of EPZ firms to other enterprises).

Critical mass of first movers, piloting a policy reform and establishment of consistency for reform – these are what a strategic restructuring model is all about. Change takes time. It may never take-off if institutions are too weak to make the country attractive for shakers and movers to come (or once they arrived, to establish local supply chains). Examples of demonstrated strategic restructuring: ARIA in Moldova, TVEs in China, and second-generation EPZs reveal a principle of economizing on institution-building by inducing change first among the first movers and subsequently diffusing the change to the rest of the economy by creating constituency for reform, policy and knowledge networks. These examples also suggest that one needs to be creative in the institutional design of entry point to push a restructuring process.

5.4.   Will FDI Break the Stagnation Trap? FDI as a Response to Domestic First Movers

For almost a decade, a potential inflow of FDI, particularly from the Diaspora, was thought to be a main tool to break up the stagnation trap. Apart from infrastructure (telecom, gas distribution) and processing of natural resources, very little FDI materialized. There is enough inflated enthusiasm and expectations for FDI in Armenia. For some government officials and managers of moribund Armenian industrial behemoths, an omnipotent strategic investor from the West tends to have exactly the same role as the Gosplan used to have in Soviet times: a hope of last resort materializing out of thin air to rescue the enterprise. This signals the central problem inherited from the Soviet era – the propensity to shift painful and effort-intensive restructuring and reform from oneself -- a manager or government official - to someone else, be it a strategic investor or central planner.

Yet in a sobering reality, FDI is highly concentrated: the top 10 recipient countries got 64% of FDI flows to developing countries in 1986-91 and 76% in 1997, while the bottom 50 recipients received 0% in 1990 and 0.8% in 1997. As economic policies converge and liberalize worldwide, FDI will be even more than in the past driven by competitive factors. Importantly, modern integrated production clusters may need few locations for organization of production and core services. This new reality, however, does not preclude entry of new countries into high-value added markets. Quite the contrary, recent successes of the software cluster in Bangalore (India)or Sialcot medical instruments cluster in Pakistan are good performance benchmarks for any country.

But given a fierce global competition for FDI, it is quite naïve to assume that leading multinationals can be talked into Armenia. The country first needs to demonstrate its readiness and show its capabilities to implement small mundane projects through strategic alliances with external partners.

From this perspective, FDI is not a salvation but rather a reaction of the outside world to improvements in the business environment and to the emergence of critical mass of first movers.[98]

FDI promotion in the CIS has its specifics. Traditionally, in the least developed countries, the challenges for FDI promotion derive from major constraints in the available labor skills, technical capabilities, and infrastructure capacity. These are not, however, the major constraints in the CIS countries. If anything, socialism left a reasonably developed supply base (human capital, technical and R&D capability, obsolete but functional fixed capital). The challenge is on the demand side – find a way to use these assets productively by inserting them into commercial value chains. Hence, focus on recombination of capabilities and investments in management skills as a stepping stone to more traditional forms of FDI.

Thus, one may think about FDI promotion as a three-stage process:

a)   <u>Clearing the way</u>: making a credible stride in improvement of the business environment. This includes an effort to build Government capacity to support private sector investment, monitor trends in the investment climate, and build political constituency for reforms.

b)   <u>FDI in intangible (managerial) assets</u>. While conventional FDI in fixed assets could greatly accelerate economic growth, it can rarely initiate it. Considerable changes in the local business environment and managerial culture may be needed before the country can graduate into the world of regular project finance. Therefore, one may argue that massive (public and private) investments in domestic managerial capabilities are necessary to prepare the country for FDI. The main objective is to create a larger group of managers within both the public and private sector who are capable of cooperating with foreign partners, including the capacity to search for such partners. But the resolution of the problem could be partially provided and funded by foreign investors themselves as soon as they are engaged in some forms of cooperation. This is an intermediate stage of FDI promotion – FDI present in the country through strategic alliances, buyer-supplier relationships and other light touch involvement, characterized primarily by investments in managerial and marketing capabilities of local partners.

c)   <u>FDI in tangible fixed assets</u>: traditional investments in fixed assets. This is the stage when investors make large irreversible commitments. Hence, both stable an investor-friendly business environment and qualified management are a prerequisite. Even at this stage, creative solutions might be required to assure an adequate business environment for global shakers and movers.

From this perspective, FDI respond to critical mass of first movers – domestic enterprises, mainly new entry, making investments to upgrade their capabilities, forming strategic alliances with foreign firms and in this way credibly demonstrating that the environment is ripe for global companies to arrive and take risks. In other words, FDI is just an element in the overall chain of private dynamism that includes local new entry, their consolidation into a viable cluster, successful functioning of the cluster to attract interest of first multinational investors, and spillover of FDI based on the demonstration effect of initial investments. The process is not automatic, and continuous improvements of the investment environment, driven by concerns of the private sector, define the core of Government policy to support this process. Yet such incremental improvements of the investment environment and competitiveness could be sufficiently robust and have been observed in countries as diverse as Mexico (see Box 5.5) or Israel.

---

[98] For instance, in Poland the noticeable inflow of FDI emerged only in 1996, in the sixth year of reforms (Pinto at al., 2000).

Box. 5.5. How did FDI Come About? Facilitating FDI-driven Growth in Aguas Calientes, Mexico

In the last decades, the state of Aguas Calientes, about 250 miles north of Mexico City, has experienced an extraordinary growth performance. The state is one of the smallest in the country with 851,000 inhabitants in an area covering only 0.3% of the national territory. Traditionally, local economy had relied primarily on agriculture, complemented with some production of wine and garments. This situation has changed radically since the early 80s, when Aguas Calientes has experienced high rates of growth in both manufacturing and exports. This growth has largely been fueled by FDI inflows, particularly from the Japanese automobile and U.S. electronics industries. How did this growth come about? The process could be described in several steps.

1. Self-evaluation of needs. In 1974, the new state governor decided to pursue a radically different development strategy, and shift emphasis from agriculture to manufacturing. His first action was to determine the main needs of local manufactures. This was done by asking the business owners in what were then the most advanced sectors, as well as representatives of trade unions. The results of the initial survey were not encouraging, for they realized that the state lacked important conditions to attract investment, particularly basic infrastructure. At the same time, it revealed significant market and institutional advantages such as low land and labor prices and existence of a considerable pool of labor with some manufacturing experience. More importantly, local business and labor leaders expressed their desire to support the state government's effort towards industrialization.

2. Improving the business environment for first movers -- an industrial park. In 1973, NAFIN, the federal industrial development bank, decided to support the development of medium cities all over the country as part of the National decentralization program. The state government of Aguas Calientes took advantage of the program by creating a trust for the Industrial Park and donated 200 ha, 40 of which were urbanized with the support of NAFIN. This assistance included the creation of physical infrastructure, provision of business development services, plus a very wide array of support mechanisms such as fiscal incentives and project evaluation assistance.

3. Firms invest, *private* industrial parks flourish, the image of the state changes. This effort to strengthen the necessary infrastructure and services soon brought new investments and a broadening of the local manufacturing base. In the late 70s, several large national firms in metal processing and automotive components opened production in the state. Since the first industrial park was so successful in attracting new companies, 3 more parks were built. Positive investment trends were accompanied by the creation of important networking institutions, such as business chambers, where businessmen gather to exchange views that facilitated problem-solving and dispute resolution. This also led to a change in the image of the state: Aguas Calientes was no longer perceived by the rest of the country as an agricultural state. With the critical mass of suppliers and buyers present, the state became attractive for firms searching for an adequate location of new plants.

4. Attracting a first multinational corporation. The first international investor in Aguas Calientes was Texas Instruments (TI), which started exploring options for a manufacturing plant in Mexico in 1979. The government worked intensively with TI to address various legitimate concerns of the investor. For instance, the waiver was obtained from the country president on the existing limitations on foreign ownership. Among other factors that proved to be attractive for TI were stability of the labor force and high participation of women in the labor force, particularly important for the electronics industry.

5. First multinational comes, others follow. Once TI decided to settle in Aguas Calientes, Xerox and Nissan soon followed. These three major multinational firms have all played an important development role by giving their employees access to a global knowledge networks and modern technologies.

6. Current challenge. Even though both government and firms have actively pursued vendor development programs, the amount of inputs provided by local firms to multinationals is still small. This is the current challenge.

Two institutional features were particularly noteworthy to support this progression: local development agency and public sector entrepreneur.

- *Catalyst of private-to-private and private-public coordination*

The Comision Estatal de Desarrollo Economico y Comercio Exterior (CEDECE) is possibly the most active institution promoting regional economic development in Aguas Calientes. CEDECE has acted as a catalyst and information broker for other agents: government and firms, federal and local, firms and universities. CEDECE's main objectives were attracting foreign investment and supporting local small and medium enterprises. The development of industrial park infrastructure was among the most important programs, it helped to start moving industry outside the capital city.

- *Public sector entrepreneur*

New collaborative actions were catalyzed by a small group of dedicated individuals -- champions of change, who created and then broadened a network of private and public actors involved in cooperative problem-solving. It was led by the General Director CEDECE Carlos Lozano, a dynamic individual with the ability to listen to the private sector and gets things done in most difficult circumstances. He represents an institution of public sector entrepreneurship, responsible (and accountable) for innovative solutions to improve a local investment environment and competitiveness.

Source: World Bank.

5.5. Public Sector Role: Bottom-Up Reform

The basic assumption of this chapter with respect to the role of the public sector in the restructuring process is that the best the public sector can do is to accelerate change already underway, yet it can hardly initiate it. In addition, any attempt to pick winners, however well-meaning, is self-defeating. Instead, the best thing public sector institutions can do to accelerate change is to facilitate sharing of experience between private sector participants, especially between advanced first movers and those who do their first steps in restructuring. People in the government and enterprises learn mostly from each other, not from donors or multinational organizations. Hence the view of development assistance as a catalyst of horizontal learning networks encompassing, inter alia, a rich uncle from the Diaspora, his prospering offspring venture in Armenia, its near-by struggling firm, and government officials trying to make sense of all this. Hence the priority of establishing new business linkages, especially with the world market.

Another major assumption relates to the diversity of restructuring outcomes that include robust restructuring, unsophisticated fragile restructuring, waiting trap, exit, etc. Restructuring programs have to contain mechanisms of information sharing on diversity of these outcomes and relevant economic strategies. To put it simply: in Armenia, examples of robust restructuring are still extremely rare, it is more a promise than a widespread fact of life. But it happens (through a rich uncle or otherwise), and this fact provides a powerful demonstration effect and gives the Government a powerful restructuring tool: use actual examples of restructuring as demonstration, try to expand it, replicate and generalize.

Bootstrapping Reform

One can visualize this approach as bootstrapping – the process of incremental bottom-up change in which a favorable balance of risks and returns encourages first steps from many diverse entry points, and each move increases chances to unlock the virtuous spiral of institutional reforms and private sector development.

The following characteristics of bootstrapping reform are noteworthy:

- **Focus on unexpected coalitions for reform**. Since the focus is on doable projects today, all the obstacles non-withstanding, implementing such projects requires creative action and may result in unexpected coalitions (see Box 5.5).

- **Integral view of reform and restructuring**. Because implementation of small PSD projects in a difficult business environment requires improvements of the business environment and public sector management (like setting a market for tractors in the Box 5.6) all three elements reinforce each other. This presents a significant challenge for an established way of delivery of development assistance, which tends to compartmentalize objectives of public sector reform, private sector development and sector-specific issues.

- **Focus on the process of reform rather than on its precise institutional outcome**. The prevailing view of reform starts from designing the blue print of change. To start moving, one presumably needs to know where to arrive. In the proposed approach, the institutional outcomes are decidedly open-ended and an attempt to draw a blueprint is considered an arrogant remnant of central planning. How could one predict a strange design of Foundation Chile? Yet precisely because of its hybrid qualities, it proved so effective. Since institutional details are open-ended by design, to detect problems and errors one should constantly monitor and benchmark the process of reform and restructuring.

- **Focus on second-best, hybrid and imperfect institutions**. This point is discussed in the next Chapter.

5.6.   Strategic Agenda for Accelerating Restructuring Processes

It is helpful to separate three large groups of economic agents in Armenia that are currently at quite different stages of the restructuring process. The Government strategy should reflect such heterogeneity of constituency for a policy dialogue and structure its policy agenda respectively.

- *'Waking up' agenda for those who are in the waiting trap,* economic agents having neither incentives nor capabilities to learn and restructure. 'Red directors' surviving from rents on the assets they now own are given as a typical example of this policy constituency. Such rents are now close to exhaustion. However, a new generation of policymakers in need of waking up has emerged.

- *Accelerating catching-up for struggling 'first movers'-* economic agents facing broadly correct incentives to learn and restructure, but lacking capabilities to act on such incentives. A focus of public agenda to accelerate catching-up is to facilitate demand for learning from both the enterprise sector and public officials[99] and make arrangements for meeting this demand. First movers in both the enterprise sector and the government and associations of first movers is a primary constituency for policy dialogue and policy reform. Crystallization of such a constituency, advancement of its skills and ability to get things done is a central focus of 'catching up' agenda.

---

[99] Young, bright and open-minded but inexperienced government officials are often struggling first movers on their own. They too need assistance in expanding knowledge on policy agenda for catch up. It also may well happen (as it happen in many semi-industrialized countries in similar circumstances) that lately some of these officials decide to leave the government for the private sector or business associations.

- *Diffusing experience of advanced 'first movers'-* successful firms that have both incentives and capabilities to catch-up. Such companies should not be a first priority for public assistance in restructuring. However, it is important for the Government to learn from their experience, to inform the public on their successes (demonstration cases), and facilitate backward linkages from them to the rest of the local economy.

Box 5.6. Bootstrapping Reform: Unexpected Alliances Push for Change

In the 70s, following bold macroeconomic reforms, Chile found itself with a liberal and stable macroeconomic climate yet with sluggish export growth. For a country with impressive mineral and natural resource wealth, agro-industry appeared to be a promising route to follow but institutional infrastructure (market information, etc.) was lacking. Agro-processing was dominated by huge enterprises, created by Allende, now privatized but still monopolists. Bottom-up facilitation of new agro-processing value chains became the task of National Development Bank, ProChile (export promotion agency) and Foundation Chile (an enterprise incubator). Foundation Chile, in particular, is now widely credited for ensuring a surge of Chilean exports in salmon, tomato paste, table grapes and other food products. In their effort to provide support to institutional infrastructure, these organizations became champions of a better investment environment. They drafted necessary laws and regulations and became platforms to consolidate coalition for reform.

Similar efforts are underway in Ukraine. Yuzhnoye (located in Dnipropetrovsk) was the world's largest ballistic missile producer. Yuzhnoye is also a major producer of agricultural tractors. But as domestic tractor demand declined, Yuzhnoye managers concluded that supporting the revival of agricultural production was the best way to revive tractor production. Consequently, they started making plans to establish an agricultural leasing company that would lease Yuzhnoye tractors to newly-established agricultural production units. Yuzhnoye managers (who are employees of a 100% state-owned enterprise) recognized that existing collective farm managers were intrinsically bad credit risks and even worse managers. But, as more and more land was being idled due to declining supplies of seed, fertilizer, diesel fuel, etc., an opportunity was emerging for new managers to lease this idle land, along with Yuzhnoye tractors. Yuzhnoye and the National Space Agency of Ukraine (which is the line ministry to which Yuzhnoye reports) understood that this scheme couldn't work without a viable system of agricultural credit and improved leasing laws. They were hoping to foster these rural finance reforms to strengthen an investment environment in partnership with the Government and the World Bank.

Organizations like the ARIA in Moldova or Foundation Chile could be instrumental in consolidation of alliances for reform. To be able to fight established rent-seeking coalitions, these alliances must be rather broad. Recall that in the Ukrainian case, a potentially strong and powerful ally for rural reform was the National Space Agency of Ukraine and Yuzhnoye -- not the sort of partners that you would typically think of in the context of agricultural reform. Foundation Chile itself was a result of an arranged marriage between ITT corporation (which put 50% of an initial endowment in exchange for retribution of its assets nationalized by Allende) and the government of Chile. The origin of such alliances is not transparent by definition: they are creative responses to an often unexpected window of opportunity.

Source: World Bank.

To put it slightly differently, a strategy to accelerate restructuring includes three components:

- *Wake up* government officials and enterprise sector managers caught in the waiting trap;

- *Accelerate catching up* for those with correct incentives but weak capabilities;

- *Deepen the catching-up* for those with both incentives and capabilities for restructuring.

One of the important elements of the waking up agenda includes managing expectations of economic agents about the future, based on a shared long-run vision or development agenda. International experience provides several examples of successful private-public dialogue, which helped to jump-start institutional reforms and turn-around expectations (El Salvador 2021, Malaysia 2020, shared vision in Rio de Janeiro, see Box 5.7). This experience is quite relevant to Armenia.

Box 5.7. Building Credibility with Tangible Results: Shared Vision Process in Rio de Janeiro

The city of Rio de Janeiro has been in gradual decline since the mid-seventies. In 1993, motivated by the successful vision-building process undertaken by the city of Barcelona (its rebirth culminating in the hosting of the Olympic Games in 1992 and continued dynamism), the mayor launched what has become the most inclusive vision-building process in Latin America.

A very sophisticated marketing operation underlay the entire process. The process initially was driven by a small "promotion group" (three dynamic individuals who have legitimacy within the community -- the Secretary of Urban Development appointed by the mayor as his representative, the President of the Federation of Industries, and the President of the Commerce Association of Rio de Janeiro). Next, a full-time Executive Director was appointed, an individual with tremendous communication skills, with five full-time staff assisted by a team of external consultants. This small Executive Committee had full-time responsibility for fostering the process and drafting the development Plan. The Executive Committee, in turn, reported to a somewhat larger Directive Council (24 recognized leaders of the City, including representatives of trade unions, academia, the private sector, media and government), who met on a monthly basis and acted as a de facto decision-making body. Finally, a City Council (a large assembly of 400 individuals representing the broad spectrum of society) met on a bi-annual basis and provided legitimacy to the entire process by examining proposals ex-ante, giving feedback and formally ratifying key decisions. In terms of financing, the mayor provided basic office facilities and roughly one-third of the project budget.

Importantly, two-thirds of funding was sought from private sector sponsors: a consortia of 40 firms was assembled with each contributing $1,000 on a monthly basis over an eighteen month period. Throughout this process, the mayor appears to have been able to shield the Plan's development from excessive political influence; in fact, at every possible opportunity, the mayor has emphasized that the plan "is not the mayor's plan but belongs to the City as a whole". The consensual process of drafting the City's strategic plan took 18 months from initiation to formal ratification.

The results have been impressive to date, with substantial impact even prior to ratification of the plan. It has been important in identifying critical investments for the City (infrastructure, educational, training, and other social development needs), as well as perspective business projects in industry and services. A number of major private-public initiatives in distant learning, tourism development, housing and infrastructure have been initiated and some already resulted in specific, sometimes sophisticated project finance deals. Perhaps most importantly, the consultative process of development of the plan has been instrumental in changing the expectations, from resignation to upward momentum. There is now a consensus that the City has turned the corner and is in a strong positive growth phase.

Source: Information from Claudio Frischtak, a key participant in the described process.

Entering the global market and participation in global competition requires a concerted and pragmatic effort by the private sector and the government. The job of the government is to create a good image of the country and provide a market-friendly business environment. The job of the private sector is to incur risks of breaking into new markets. Yet, neither private firms nor the government can do their jobs without communication and coordination with each other. Rather than blaming each other for poor performance, the growth policy agenda should be about private-public collaboration to jointly engineer 'win-win' situations. Increasing popularity of clustering – designing and implementation of private-public initiatives to take advantage of new global opportunities in specific sectors and/or locations – is explained by the ability of cluster processes to be strategic and pragmatic at the same time.

The cluster approach to development[100] suggests that industrial clusters (group of companies that share positive vertical and horizontal linkages) determine a country's competitiveness and development prospects. Synergies between firms within the cluster attract new firms and investments and create reinforcing growth dynamics. The approach views a collective action[101] - in both the private and public arenas - as a way to transform a country's comparative advantage into competitive advantages. The collective action is a cumulative process of change that can start from small incremental changes and be expanded through proper coordination.

The cluster approach empathizes the role of information and learning as well as coordinated collective actions as key development factors that are frequently missed. These factors are particularly important for small economies in transition, which are populated by "isolated" companies with weak traditions of inter-firm cooperation, and which have thin internal markets for information. In term of policy recommendations, a cluster approach to industrial restructuring underlines:

- A shift from subsidizing the recovery of large established enterprises to support spin-offs and start-ups;

- A shift from direct financial assistance to the provision of business development services;

- A shift from an emphasis on development of traditional physical infrastructure to facilitating corporate learning and information sharing;

- A shift from an exclusive focus on broad policy reforms to a more narrow concentration on specific initiatives to amend the business environment in specific sectors, to support new entry and replication of the first successes in enterprise restructuring (experience of "first movers").

Another element of the strategic agenda relates to realistic assessment and benchmarking of the country's endowments and institutions against relevant countries. One needs a strategic vision of both home country capabilities and global trends in order to position the country in market niches with relatively low entry barriers[102]. In Armenia, as in other CIS countries, there is a high sensitivity to the issue of benchmarking. Despite a recent loss of real incomes, many in Armenia still would be shocked and infuriated by a suggestion that it is countries like Mauritius and India they have a lot to learn from. 'Our educational level is on a par with France and Spain, thus these should be our performance benchmarks'. Learning from challenging examples is never harmful, as long as one is aware of how much time and costs it had taken advanced countries to establish institutions they have today.

This report argues that it is important to have pragmatic international benchmarks, which are affordable for Armenia to learn from and follow. We propose three such benchmarks: Israel, Bangalore clusters in India, and South Africa.

Israel has obvious similarities with Armenia: a powerful Diaspora as a source of assistance and investment, high educational level that supported explosion of high tech export over the last 20 years, location in the region with high political risks. At the same time, Israel has been a part of the global

---

[100] Porter (1990). *Competitive advantage of nations.* Piore and Sabel (1984). *Second Industrial Divide.*

[101] In a somewhat typical for cluster players move, Armenian software entrepreneurs announced in summer 2000, a plan to form a common management and marketing organization to expand distribution channels, reduce risks and increase export of outsourced software development.

[102] Software manufacturing, organic juices, fruits and vegetables, and made-to-order garments are different examples of such high value-added niches.

economy for decades. Thirty years ago, its financial infrastructure was rudimentary but human capital mobility with the outside world was already impressive. Hence, one needs another country benchmark, a country that was also excluded from such 'permanent conversations'.

Bangalore software cluster is instructive to Armenia for at least three reasons:

- It emerged, almost spontaneously, on the basis of government space and military programs;

- It is based almost entirely on subcontracting;

- Successful software companies were essential in establishing a new sector -- venture capital industry in India, which in turn facilitated further growth of software. But the causality is quite important here: growing companies helped establish a venture capital industry, not the other way around.

The third benchmark, combining the features of compelling vision and mundane actions, is South Africa. Much like the former socialist block, for many years it was isolated from the world both politically (apartheid) and economically (heavy import substitution). Social tensions still remain high (including high levels of unemployment and crime), yet human capital is still impressively high. Result? Massive brain drain on scale similar to Armenia. Yet, South Africa responded to this threat with unusual institutional creativity. Its cluster processes are one of the most sophisticated and action-oriented in the world[103].

All three benchmarks -- Israel, South Africa and Bangalore/India are important in their own right:

- Israel – to motivate Armenian stakeholders on what could be achieved by a country in a hostile environment but equipped with a vision of utilization of its human capital;

- Bangalore -- for design of 'next step' initiatives to expand a software cluster after the initial success;

- South Africa -- for insights on potential government/public policy.

---

[103] See for instance, World Bank (1997b). "South Africa: Industrial Competitiveness and Job Creation Project."

Table 6.2. Instruments to Promote Restructuring

Instruments	Target by population of firms	Objective	Assumptions and major risks	Lessons from successful examples in developing economies
Managed work space: business incubators, technology parks, asset management companies	Spin-offs of assets being liquidated Start-ups	To facilitate new business creation by: --'push' of existing assets; --'pull' of market demand; -- better logistics and business environment of the managed work space	Entrepreneurship needs nourishing and facilitation through specialized structures Soft budget constraints of industrial behemoths under restructuring is a major threat	Moldova (ARIA) Hungary (Videoton)
Case-by-case privatization	SOEs	Acceleration of restructuring of SOEs	Prohibitively high costs of retooling the plant in question compared to benefit to a foreign buyer. Consequently, low foreign interest in case-by-case privatization	Poland: Successful case-by-case privatization and FDI in general appear to be an investors' response to opportunities of the rapidly growing economy, not trigger of economic recovery itself.
Private-public seed funds	High-tech and high-value added start-ups and spin-offs	Provision of capital and managerial knowledge to new firms	Existence of local entrepreneurs with lucrative projects; Interest from the Diaspora	Israel, India, Brazil (Lalkaka, 1998) Public sector participation is useful to an extent that it leverages private sector resources. Public sector accelerates and facilitates response of the private sector, but does not create it.
Matching grant schemes	Any firm starting to export	Acceleration of entry into export activities	Additionality as a critical issue (whether the matching grant induces new activities or just subsidizes activities that would have occurred anyway).	India, Argentina, South Africa, Zambia
Information and advisory centers	Firms with high demand for business knowledge	Promotion of access to business information (on prices and business opportunities) and facilitation of local content creation	Demand-driven nature of the center (otherwise becomes a room with computers) and its sustainability once initial public subsidies are terminated	Chile: CepriNet Peru
Sector partnership funds to facilitate collective initiatives of enterprises	All firms	Formation of enterprise support infrastructure through formulation and implementation of collective initiatives	Capture of the fund by the established interests	South Africa

Box. 6.1. Accelerating Enterprise Learning through Matching Grant Schemes

First movers in doing new things (breaking into export markets, for instance) are critical for breaking a stagnation trap. But, since firms learn most productively from each others, the successes of first movers provide powerful examples to follow and thus have positive spill-overs. For that matter a public subsidy to first-movers is justifiable. How to deliver such a subsidy?

The relevant knowledge about export markets and on necessary upgrading of the firm is highly specific and could be provided only by specialized consultants and other independent service providers. A firm-level management governance scheme (applied in Mauritius, Zimbabwe, Zambia, India, Argentina, South Africa) proved to be a promising solution.

This scheme includes creation of a public fund to offset partially (usually on a 50/50 basis) certain fixed start-up costs of breaking into export markets. Grants are provided on a "first come, first served" basis – every firm that meets transparent eligibility criteria receives support and uses it to purchase needed services/advice through regular market channels. This is a simple, institutionally-light approach to support enterprise learning.

The fund is managed by a private management company, which operates under a time-bound contract with performance benchmarks. It performs several functions: markets the scheme to local firms, provides free up-front support in preparing firm's programs/applications, works as a global information broker (by providing relevant information to participants), and acts as an impartial administrator.

Such a fund should be considered as a temporary mechanism (usually 3-4 years): once exporting ceased to be an innovative activity and since there is no learning spill-over, there is no reason for continuation of public subsidization of learning.

Source: World Bank.

6.4.   New Entry Through Recombination of Assets

A post-soviet organization – an enterprise or government agency – can be characterized as a bundle of assets (human capital, buildings, equipment and other physical assets) often producing negative value added. This value can be conceived as a negative market value (e.g. a TV set producer with no market to sell the output) or a negative public value[108] -- value subtraction through provision of harmful government "services" (e.g. excessive inspections and other forms of rent-seeking). This is not to say that assets of these firms and public organizations are inherently unproductive. On the contrary, there is a diversity of valuable assets – engineers with entrepreneurial aspirations, highly-skilled blue collars workers longing for diligent disciplined work, public sector employees full of promising initiatives, general-purpose and fairly modern equipment imported during the last days of socialism, office and manufacturing facilities in the center of the city – all of which can be utilized productively.

However, those assets are hidden within larger organizational units – huge industrial enterprises and Soviet-style public sector organizations. These assets were introduced for a completely different "market", which is mostly gone by now. Comparing these inherited enterprises with their counterparts in the West, one can see many similarities, especially around the production function of enterprises.

---

[108] Notion of public value is a key conceptual construct of so-called 'new public management' school. See for instance, Moore (1997).

However, if a post-Soviet enterprise is analyzed as a part of the value chain[109], and then this value chain is compared with a value chain from a market economy, almost all similarities are gone. Post-Soviet organizations are inserted in highly inefficient value chains of equally problematic customers, suppliers and other stakeholders that allow little, if any, opportunities to produce value that could be realized at the local let alone export markets.

Successful market adjustment in the CIS thus entails double transformation:

- *Redefinition of organizational boundaries of enterprise/public organization* in order to free up hidden valuable assets to allow their productive use through start-ups, spin-offs, profit centers or other commercial entities with changed organizational boundaries;

- *Redefinition of value chains of suppliers and customers* to match newly-created assets with market opportunities.

Any model of enterprise restructuring (or public sector reform for that matter) should simultaneously address both such sides of the transformation process. To get restructuring going, it might not be sufficient to sell or give away assets of a former military plant to a private entrepreneur. Inserted into existing military-related value chains, the value of its assets is close to zero. To generate demand for assets one has to indicate how, when and with which resources the assets can be positioned into a profitable value chain. Positioning into a new value chain may require a *critical mass of changes* – often the whole management team should be retrained or replaced, new markets identified and fixed cost incurred (e.g. related to retraining and to establishment of new business links), costs reduced and labor downsized. Critical mass effect is about coaching a new managerial team capable of finding a new input/output mix and a related set of new partners.

Common success of restructuring through involvement of a strategic investor vs. a frequent failure to restructure through bankruptcy and liquidation illustrates this point. A strategic investor not only carves out valuable assets by engaging in extensive lay-offs and downsizing, it also provides critical mass of managerial and technological changes by matching these assets with new customers and suppliers, i.e. positioning the assets into viable value chains. Liquidation and bankruptcy, by contrast, end up giving away an industrial behemoth containing some hidden values in the expectation that somebody somehow will: (a) carve out valuable assets from the existing junk and reconcile claims of creditors and other stakeholders on the firms' assets; (b) create new companies by matching these assets with entrepreneurs, labor and other factors of production; and (c) insert these new companies into profitable value chains. It should not be surprising that, given overwhelming uncertainties of transition economies and skill limitations, these processes do not produce a high success rate.

These tasks are not only costly but they are inherently risky and require highly specific capabilities. In the USA, a country with highly-developed market institutions, a turn-around industry – companies that have professional expertise to take care of all three tasks outlined above – is increasingly becoming a domain of venture capital industry. Venture capitalists provide investments and professional expertise to induce *demand-driven recombination of assets*. It is demand-driven because it starts from identification of market opportunities and value chains into which the new 'right-sized' and 'carved-out' firm could be inserted. It is a recombination of assets because it puts the emphasis on carving out hidden existing valuable assets rather than on new massive investments. It is the domain of venture capital

---

[109] The value chain analysis suggests that it is useful to think of industrial development in terms of a sequence of interdependent activities linked together in a vertical chain ranging from raw material production at one end to the delivery of final goods and services to the consumer. These chains tend to be defined in terms of particular markets and products – garments, electronics, pharmaceuticals, etc.

because even in cases where extensive market infrastructure exists (bankruptcy institutions to reconcile claims on assets, investment banking to place assets into new hands, market research to position the assets in value chains, etc.), the turn-around business is highly risky: failures are common and unavoidable, but successful turn-around provides returns that are sufficient to offset losses from failures.

In Poland in the early 90s growth came mostly from de novo firms. At the same time, empirical evidence shows that many of these start-ups acquired equipment and other assets from state enterprises, pressed hard budget constraints and competition (Buckberg and Pinto, 1997). In other words, the initial growth was fueled not by physical investments in new assets but by market-driven recombination of existing assets.

Most of the post-Soviet enterprises can be classified into four groups along the "viability of assets -- potential rents" cross as illustrated in Table 6.3. The major lesson from enterprise restructuring in the FSU over the last 10 years is that the most likely restructuring strategy to materialize has considerable correlation with the position of companies in this taxonomy:

- Paradoxically, the best candidates for restructuring/turnaround are companies from the I quadrant ('shock absorbers') because a collective action problem of reconciling numerous claims on assets is not significant when rents from the assets are small.

- Once companies are "restructured" from the I into the III quadrant, it is much easier to find for them strategic investors from Non-FSU environments, who otherwise are reluctant to take a risk of large potential social liabilities.

- It is quite difficult to identify a case of the enterprises from the II quadrant (High rents - Low viability of assets) that have been privatized to a strategic owner from a non-FSU environment, nor are there many cases of companies from this quadrant that have been successfully restructured and moved to the IV quadrant. High rents make such companies extremely attractive to local interest groups, which as a rule are able to exclude outsiders' attempts for control.

Since demand from foreign strategic investors for enterprises with low asset value (quadrants I and II) is likely to be small, while access of outsiders to 'high rent – high value' enterprises is likely to be limited, these enterprises may need to be restructured locally. Locals have at their disposal two effective strategies – recombination of assets by local turnaround teams and liquidation. In standard liquidation, assets are auctioned away to whomever is willing to buy them at whatever price. Armenia's experience shows that often there are no buyers for assets even when they are free, idle and devoid of claims of labor, creditors and other stakeholders. The problem is that an effective owner of the assets still faces the same three tasks (i.e. downsize and carve-out valuable assets; match them with entrepreneurs/managers to form a new organizational entity; position this entity in a profitable value chain). These are complex tasks and relegating them entirely to the market has given the same results as when *assuming a can opener where one is required*. If capabilities and institutions to perform these tasks were readily available, market transition would not be required in the first place. Since these institutions are definitely weak, liquidation in the FSU is not very effective in reallocation of assets and creation of new jobs. No wonder that it remains politically unpopular.

Table 6.3. Armenia: Taxonomy of Enterprises and Asset Management Strategies

(I)	(II)
Rents -- low **Viability of assets** -- low	Rents -- high **Viability of assets** -- low
Shock absorber: **Enterprise as an institution of social protection**	*Cash cow:* Enterprise as a source of rents for stakeholders
Examples: Firms e.g. in military industrial complex; light industry	Examples: Enterprises with valuable real estate or equipment that can be exported, e.g. in machinery building and processing industry; jewelry; mining)
Asset management strategies: **Liquidation** **Liquidation through industrial parks**	Asset management strategies: **Liquidation** **Privatization**
(III)	**(IV)**
Rents -- low **Viability of assets** -- high	Rents -- high **Viability of assets** -- high
Emerging star: **Low barriers for recombination of assets to reveal value**	*Subject of disputes:* **Competing claims on the firm's assets**
Examples: software companies, food processing, flour-mills	Examples: Diamond companies, power companies, Armenian airlines, airport
Asset management strategies: **Continuous improvements by local owners. Advanced restructuring by strategic investors**	Asset management strategies: **Privatization via tenders**

Source: Kuznetsov and Astrakhan (2000).

A separate institutional structure – industrial park or asset management company – might be a second-best institutional solution to help the private sector: a) to sort out whatever assets are deployable; and b) facilitate reallocation of assets to newly-established entities (start-ups and spin-offs) led by new management teams. Ideally, such an asset management company would perform three functions[110]:

- Identify valuable assets of a liquidated firm (office and production space, some fixed assets) and match them with potential entrepreneurs;

- Develop capabilities by providing management training and consultancy services to assure 'critical mass of changes' that facilitate entry of new firms into viable value-added chains;

- Reduce costs of doing business: provide security, reduce regulatory costs of entry and doing business, i.e. shield start-ups and spin-offs from vagaries of predatory behavior of the outside world.

---

[110] There is extensive empirical literature on so-called 'convergence of enterprise support systems' (see Lalkaka (1998) for a relevant survey) which shows that institutional structures such as enterprise incubators, industrial, technology and science parks are successful to the extent they integrate various services provided by an enterprise support system of a particular country in a demand-driven package of services that includes access to and 'bundling' of assets; managerial training and consultancy; reduction of regulatory costs of entry and doing business, etc.

Note that the main source of value added under this approach comes from a packaging of various services. E.g. facilitation of access to assets, as such, may not suffice: Armenia already has a rather strong market for used equipment and real estate with a marginal impact on creation of start-ups and spin-offs. Similarly, setting up an advisory center as part of the industrial park could become more efficient compared to a more traditional independent advisory service because consultants would have in-depth knowledge of assets, inherited by the park, and have longer-term relations with park tenants.

If established, industrial parks or asset management companies in Armenia would work in the conditions of rudimentary institutional development of post-socialist economies. The challenge for them would be to make liquidation and promotion of entrepreneurship (destruction and creation) two sides of the same coin rather than two disconnected social processes. In the advanced market economies, both processes are well developed (robust) and independent so that we can tinker with one and not worry about how it could affect the another. But pushing bankruptcy/liquidation in an environment without effective entrepreneurship and managerial skills beyond the kiosk level proved to be both politically and economically unfeasible.

Let us summarize the discussion so far as a checklist of issues to be addressed in a viable model of enterprise restructuring applicable to Armenia where it has to satisfy two significant constraints: a) mass restructuring backed by foreign strategic investors is unrealistic, at least initially; while b) liquidation through a simple auctioning of assets is not supported by a sufficient demand and as such is perceived as too disruptive. Such a checklist comprises the following four major questions:

1.   How are **collective action problems** resolved? In other words, how are claims of creditors and other stakeholders reconciled? What assures the credibility of liquidation, bankruptcy or a restructuring plan agreed upon by creditors and other stakeholders?

2.   What are **effective incentives** for new entry and restructuring? Effective incentives is a package of:

- *Carrots* – assistance to expand firm's capabilities and opportunities through e.g. possible managerial training, access to business development services, and a limited time protection from creditors;

- *Sticks* – hard budget constraint, e.g. demonstrative liquidations to make the threat of liquidation credible.

3.   Which **institutional structures** facilitate reallocation of assets from incumbent management and existing enterprises to newly-created companies led by new management teams?

4.   How is **critical mass effect** achieved? How is a managerial team retrained or replaced? How are marketing capabilities acquired? How does the managerial change become self-sustainable, i.e. endures after restructuring assistance is withdrawn? What assures that the enterprise would position itself in a viable value chain?

The proposed model of strategic restructuring is clarified in Table 6.4 by contrasting it with two more traditional models: takeover by a strategic investor and liquidation/bankruptcy.

Table 6.4. Three Models of Enterprise Restructuring in Economies in Transition

	Strategic investor	Liquidation	Strategic restructuring
Guiding principle	Sell enterprise/assets to a strategic investor in the expectation that it would restructure the assets	Liquidate/close enterprise, sell assets through competitive bidding in the expectation that they would be bought by existing entities and new entrants	Facilitate 'strategic restructuring': -- carve-out profitable core of the firm and assure transfer of other assets to spin-offs and start-ups -- assure a 'critical mass' of changes: changes in management, customers, suppliers, and other stakeholders
Incentives for restructuring: sticks	Agent not willing to learn or restructure is fired	Business failure	Hard budget constraint is enforced during restructuring-cum-liquidation For incumbent managers: if the manager is reluctant to implement restructuring plan, she/he is removed
Incentives for restructuring: carrots	Opportunities for advancement Training opportunities	Rewards of market success	High intensity technical assistance is provided Breathing space – temporary protection from claims of creditors
Creation of opportunities/ capabilities for restructuring	Expatriate managers initiate restructuring/downsizing; over time, local capabilities are created	Learning from other firms Learning from consultants and other professional services firms	Restructuring plan is formulated and implemented by a restructuring agency Training and advisory support to managers and owners of spin-offs and start-ups
Positioning in profitable value chains -- critical mass effect	Insertion into global value chains of multinational companies	New entrants usually start from orientation to local markets, over time export orientation is paramount	Restructuring/liquidation plan identifies new potential markets and suppliers Assistance in making relevant contacts with customers and suppliers
Factors supporting a high-case scenario ('deep' restructuring)	Good quality assets assuring demand from strategic investors	Sufficient supply of entrepreneurs, favorable business environment for private economic activity	For core enterprises and for start-ups/ spin-offs – creation of a package of 'effective incentives', combining hard budget constraints with technical assistance
Risks that may trigger a low-case scenario	The enterprise could be closed as a possible competitor for the investor	No demand for assets: assets are liquidated but not utilized	Hard budget constraints are not enforced so that technical assistance delays rather than facilitates restructuring

Source: Kuznetsov and Astrakhan (2000).

6.5.   Formation of Restructuring Organization

A privately-run managed work space (business incubators, industrial parks, export processing zones) would not emerge by themselves. A non-government restructuring organization, autonomous from everyday political contingencies but supported by the government, has to be created to engineer a set-up of such entry points. In what follows, we discuss a life cycle of a generic restructuring agency assuming, for simplicity, that it is invariant to a specific task at hand.

Performance of a Restructuring Agency (RA), just like of any other organization, is a matter of incentives and capabilities. The RA is expected to perform three basic functions. First, it facilitates *demand* for restructuring by making managers and government officials to share understanding of both needs for restructuring and necessity to intensively involve external consultants. Second, the RA assures efficiency of the restructuring: it trains enterprise managers how to utilize external consultants. Foreign consultants are often of limited effectiveness to domestic enterprises because they speak a different professional language and come from a different social and professional environment. As a result, local consultants are needed to facilitate interactions: trained locals understand both what makes a Soviet engineer tick and how to engage this engineer in a dialogue with a Western colleague. Acquiring the ability to utilize knowledge is sometimes called 'learning to learn' and in this role RA project teams act *as coaches to management teams* of restructured enterprises. Finally, the third role of the Agency is a familiar role of market-driven consultancy – direct provision of managerial expertise. Moldova has accumulated successful experience of a Restructuring Agency (Box 6.2.)[111]

Box 6.2. Enterprise Restructuring Agency (ARIA) in Moldova

Agency for Restructuring and Enterprise Assistance (ARIA) was created in 1995 with the principal objective of accelerating adjustment of newly-privatized enterprises to market conditions. It was supported by two Private Sector Development loans of the World Bank. The ARIA has been engaged in supporting the private sector through a number of instruments, including training, business support services, policy advocacy, etc. ARIA's experience with establishing Industrial Parks, based on the premises of large non-viable SOEs, was the most impressive.

Assessment of the projects, based on the firm-level database, indicates a strong restructuring impact of the ARIA. In 1995, the firms that would eventually find their way to ARIA's doorstep were on average worse off than firms that would never be assisted by the ARIA, both in terms of productivity and profitability. By the end of 1999, despite worsening economic conditions in Moldova, ARIA-assisted firms were more productive than their unassisted counterparts, exported more in relative terms, and paid more in taxes per worker. ARIA's assistance is positively, significantly, and consistently correlated with real productivity growth, with growth in exports, and with sales growth.

The ARIA was successful because it had found an efficient solution to politically-charged issues of liquidation and restructuring by working with existing capital and human resources. The key to success is ARIA's ability to co-opt managers, or if they are not cooperating, to replace them. The ARIA does not have formal authority to dismiss SOEs' managers. However, its "reputation authority" is such that it is often, but not always, able to achieve desirable outcomes. The "reputation authority" derives from ARIA's unique position as an autonomous government agency with a strong and committed leadership and dedicated and skilled staff.

Source: World Bank (2001b).

To perform the Triple-C role (Champion of reforms, Coach to management teams in the enterprise *sector* and the government, and Consulting firm), the Agency should have a *hybrid organizational form*[112]. It would combine features of:

- market institution -- provision of services to clients on the basis of cost recovery;

- public sector entity -- provision of a public good such as improved managerial skills in the nascent private sector;

---

[111] See also Box 5.2 in the previous chapter.
[112] Oi (1994) shows that in early stages of TVE growth, local governments in China did play a similar triple-C role. As TVE became more experienced, this role became redundant. Yet there is an apparent trade-off between transparency and efficiency.

- non-governmental organization -- operated rather independently from the Government ('embedded autonomy') but being sensitive to concerns of both the government and the enterprise sector.

Market incentives of the RA would reflect its motivation towards cost-recovery and client satisfaction. Its administrative incentives are about pressure to perform in line with initial benchmarks that come from the RA's administrative sponsors – Government and donors. Non-governmental incentives would reflect the agency's orientation to 'voice' and promote strategic priorities of its beneficiaries and founders.

Respectively, to be able to restructure enterprises, the RA may need certain administrative clout to implement restructuring plans and enforce reasonably hard budget constraints for enterprises it assists. This administrative power partially comes from a scale of available assistance: if the enterprise management is not cooperative, there is a threat of withdrawal of assistance. In fact, termination of the assistance, when justifiable, is an important element of building the RA's credibility.

Also, to be effective, the Agency's operational practices are unlikely to be completely transparent. This is particularly true at the early stages of its life when there is limited experience to guide both the RA's staff and potential clients on the most efficient organizational arrangements. Lacking the means of administrative control, the manager of the Agency would have to convince its clients to take risks and agree to a restructuring plan mostly on the basis of trust and personal reputation. Being unable to replace the management of participating enterprises, it would need to select only those managers who would volunteer and demonstrate their ability to learn.

To train enterprise managers to appreciate external consultants and to work with them efficiently, the Agency must first learn to do it itself. Therefore, creating a team of local consultants capable of continuous learning, more specifically building a capacity for adopting Western management expertise to local peculiarities is the key characteristic of the Agency. See Box 6.3 on continuous learning in the Moldovan ARIA.

Box 6.3. Continuous Learning of Consultants and Staff: Lessons from the ARIA in Moldova

The ARIA has a structured approach to recruiting and developing local consultants and enhancing their interactions with clients. Every project team has been:
- formed as a blend of youthful energy with experience: the ARIA recruits both young ambitious graduates from local and foreign universities and experienced managers and specialists and combines them within the same teams;
- exposed to international best practices and on-the-job training;
- learning with the client and from the client: almost every consultant is getting the opportunity to participate in study tours with managers from participating companies; thus, they have a chance to establish good personal relationships with actual and potential clients and understand better their needs
- given incentives for career mobility: every consultant is expected to be ready to accept a managerial position in the enterprise sector for at least 2-3 years.

Source: World Bank (2001b).

The process of establishing a Restructuring Agency could be divided into four stages as described in the checklist in Box 6.4.

Box 6.4. Agency for Strategic Restructuring: A Checklist of Actions

1.   Embryonic period: formation of a group of champions
<u>Objective</u>: to form a group of champions, which would agree on how the agency could facilitate incentives and capabilities for restructuring
<u>Steps:</u>
- a business model of effective incentives;
- core leaders: manager of restructuring agency, donor team, government support;
-    formation of a legal entity.

2.   Infant period: pilot restructuring of 6-10 companies
<u>Objective</u>: to demonstrate feasibility and effectiveness of restructuring to broaden support and win credibility within the government and other enterprise stakeholders (creditors, owners, managers, labor).
<u>Steps:</u>
- a list of pilot enterprises ('best of the worst enterprises');
- sending managers to Eastern Europe;
- formation of a group of local consultants;
- formation of teams working on enterprises;
- development and refinement of criteria for entry and exit for enterprises;
- analysis of successes and drop-out cases.

3.   Growth period: rolling out the model of strategic enterprise restructuring
<u>Objective</u>: to roll-out the restructuring model and introduce cost recovery elements in service delivery.
<u>Steps:</u>
- rolling out the restructuring model to other firms;
- extension of restructuring assistance to facilitate deeper restructuring and export development;
- formation of capable project teams of local consultants;
- reducing public costs of restructuring assistance by introducing partial cost recovery in delivery of RA's services.

4.   Graduation period: shift to demand-driven provision of enterprise development services
<u>Objective</u>: to make restructuring services sustainable upon termination of a Donor-sponsored project.
<u>Steps:</u>
- options for liquidation/transformation of the Agency;
- options for modification of the mechanisms of public support to enterprise restructuring (e.g. shift to the provision of direct restructuring grants to clients rather than to the restructuring agency.

Source: Kuznetsov and Astrakhan (2000).

6.6.   How Donors Could Help to Accelerate the Restructuring Process?

        This report argues for a more active Government role in enterprise restructuring and support for new entry by establishing a limited number of non-government private-public organizations (Restructuring Agencies) that would become core providers of consolidated public assistance to the private sector with respect to restructuring, export promotion, acquiring new skills, and international networking. These organizations, if established, would require considerable support and at the same time could be a natural focus of technical assistance provided by donors. At the same time, donors would accelerate the restructuring process if they could initiate the process of setting up such institutions and encourage a strong Government ownership by channeling a considerable amount of funding to these agencies. Such assistance is needed only for a limited amount of time: the proposed agencies have to become either sustainable or have a clear time-bound mandate, asking for a closing of the agency after some transitional benchmarks are achieved. Also, given the current volumes of assistance available for

Armenia, support for establishing institutions, described in this report, could clearly be funded within the existing donors' budget envelop, through reallocations and re-prioritization.

As a first cut for Armenia, one may argue for establishing three such organizations[113]:

- Enterprise Restructuring Agency to follow the ARIA model: to address restructuring problems of largest existing companies;

- Advisory Center: to provide basic TA and training to traditional start-ups as well as support development of local business associations and other business organizations;

- Investment Promotion Agency: to facilitate Armenia's country promotion globally and support expansion of emerging clusters which already proved its international competitiveness.

The major gain associated with the proposed approach to public support for PSD (and as such for donor support) relates to the consolidation of both institutional support and delivery of various public services under one roof, which would help reduce costs of institutional segmentation. In other words, given overall weaknesses of traditional market institutions, restructuring agencies fill a part of the institutional gap by packaging the assistance and protecting their clients from the unfriendly business environment. There seems to be a global trend in this direction: different countries have piloted highly unusual, hybrid organizations, specialized in support of private sector development, that are combining to various degrees functions of traditional consulting companies, investment promotion agencies, NGOs, and investment banks. These organizations may take the form of the foundation (Chile), equity seed funds (Denmark, other countries in Western Europe), business advisory center (FYR Macedonia), restructuring agency (Moldova), etc. The organizations have been using a combination of rather traditional restructuring instruments. However, packaging of such services in response to specific local needs seems to generate a considerable incremental value added (Box 6.5).

While Armenia has recently become one of the leading recipients of donors' technical assistance in the region, the outcome of numerous TA programs dedicated to private sector development so far has been much less visible than one could expect, given the amount of money spent.

As in the rest of the FSU, the focus of donors' assistance was on "top-down" initiatives, aimed at getting fundamentals right. These were not sufficiently complemented by programs to support capacity building in the private sector and more generally by the "bottom-up" initiatives. In those cases when such programs have been launched, they were carried out in the form of short term training programs and seminars, development of specific business proposals by short-term international consultants, publication of different types of handbooks and manuals, and microfinancing.

---

[113] At the moment, only an investment promotion agency (ADA) has been established but it is still at the early stage of its development.

Box 6.5. Combining Functions for Private Sector Support: Macedonian Business Resource Center

The Macedonian Business Resource Center (MBRC) was set up in 1995 by Crimson Capital Corporation, a consulting and investment banking firm, to implement a program funded by the USAID. MBRC provides advice and technical assistance on major policy reform issues including corporate governance, privatization, and FDI promotion, and serves as a facilitator and clearing house for much of the private sector development in FYR Macedonia. This very function of MBRC as a "hub" for the development of the emerging private sector was critical for disassociating the Center from the conventional image of a donor-sponsored consulting firm, thus maximizing the success of the projects, promoting efficient communication and cooperation, and minimizing duplication of efforts, both within a given donor agency and between donor agencies and government agencies.

MBRC is organized as an association of local and foreign experts. Separate teams have responsibilities for different professional areas (such as trade and investment services, training, public outreach, etc.) as well as for different regions of the country.

The grant funding provided to the MBRC for the first 5 years was about $2 million per year (it is anticipated to decline to about $1 million per year in the next two years). During that period MBRC has been directly involved in implementation of restructuring plans of over 235 companies, and helped another 150 companies develop trade and investment programs. This process was accompanied by a generation of considerable inflow of foreign investments (both debt and equity). So far, MBRC has trained over 4,300 local managers, consultants and government officials, and saw its graduates taking senior positions in industry, government, and academia. A group of local consultants, mentored by the MBRC, has turned itself into a self-sustaining professional consulting firm.

Source: World Bank.

From the perspective of this report, main weakness of donor-funded programs in the area of PSD support could be summarized as follows:

- institutional fragmentation of donor assistance in a situation where local institutional weaknesses justify consolidation and packaging

- low intensity of programs: technical assistance is spread all over the economy and delivered in small increments to numerous actors, while it would be more efficient to concentrate efforts at a limited number of potential leaders (first movers) with the established track record by providing them a broader package of longer-term assistance, which would help to set up proper benchmarks for the private sector

- insufficient participation of local counterparts and weak incentives to support effective transfer of knowledge/skills to the recipient

- gap between substance of provided assistance and local needs; a low share of on-job training[114]

- weak incentives of providers of technical assistance (see Box 6.6)

- insufficient attention to developing local private business organizations as instruments of collective learning[115] and private-to-private cooperation as well as major proponents of further reforms.

---

[114] Radosevic (1997) argues that growth in CEE seems to be more linked to different forms of firm-based learning (on-the-job training and learning-by-doing) and less to the formal educational activities.
[115] Fairbanks and Lindsay (1997, pp. 75-78) underline a link between local capability for private cooperation and firm-level learning, innovations, and improved competitiveness.

Box 6.6. Why Restructuring Organizations Fail? Lessons of Russian Privatization Center

Lessons of the Russian Privatization Center (RPC), established in 1992 as an implementing agency for the World Bank Privatization Implementation Assistance Loan (PIAL), confirm that matching incentives and capabilities of a restructuring agency with available restructuring instruments is critical for success.

The RPC core staff consisted of highly paid foreign advisors who had neither local knowledge to discover local sources of private sector dynamism nor incentives to do that. Ironically, their incentive structure mimicked the incentives of centralized bureaucracy: the motivation was to receive donors' funding and allocate it to restructured enterprises as grants. Reports on what needs to be done on the enterprises under the Center's supervision was the main output of the RPC. In no way was remuneration of the center's staff linked to changes in the performance of restructured enterprises. Conspicuous lack of incentives as well as mismatch between capabilities and local needs explain a less than satisfactory outcome of the project.

Source: World Bank.

6.7.   Industrial Policies to Support New Entry: The Case of Software[116]

Given the successful expansion of software production in Armenia in the late 90s, which was an entirely spontaneous and market-driven process, it is logical for the Government to explore ways to support and accelerate such recent positive trends. Various features of the software sector (on both sides – its potential promises and current constraints) could make it an ideal pilot case for the Government strategy aimed at promotion of private sector driven skill-based growth. This is because the sector has: a) low entry costs; b) a number of private SMEs already exporting to the Western market; c) a rapidly growing Western market for its product/skills; and d) firms that already undertake collective initiatives, and two active IT associations have been established. All these features are substantial.

These features suggest that there is considerable potential for expansion and acceleration of the existing positive trends. They also suggest that there is a potential to produce a powerful demonstration effect of appropriate Government interventions, which are relatively short term, replicable to other sectors of the economy, and non-distortionary.   Public interventions also have to result in trends that are sustainable upon their withdrawal. The need to generate a tangible demonstration effect is particularly acute in Armenia, where the most talented individuals leave the country because they have lost faith in the ability of the economy to turn around.

Key elements of the Government strategy in the sector could include:

- Developing a sector master plan and moving on the policy reforms that it would suggest;

- Setting up institutions (incubators or other form of managed industrial space) for new software and e-business firms;

- Improving the communications infrastructure and reducing costs of Internet communications;

- Strengthening key supporting institutions, including protection of intellectual property rights, payment system, etc.;

- Promoting spillover of software development and demand for software products in related sectors such as publishing, engineering, and other skilled knowledge-based services;

---

[116] This section follows recommendations of World Bank (2001a). Armenia. PSD strategy, Discussion draft.

- Facilitating intra-sectoral links and private cooperation in the sector to accelerate business learning, reduce risks and costs of external expansion, and support stronger international linkages.

Some of these objectives will be addressed through an IT Business Incubator Project, which is a joint project of the Government and the World Bank. The primary goal of the project is to create a demonstration effect of high-value added employment of local human capital through investments in: a) developing marketable skills of local IT personnel; and b) expansion of export-driven companies in the IT sector. The project also intends to test new and non-traditional, for Armenia, forms of cooperation between the Government, donors, the Diaspora, and the local private sector in the area of private sector development. If successful, the main features of the project could be scaled up and replicated in other sectors.

Constraints on it sector growth, exports and FDI were described elsewhere in these report and relate to problems with the business environment, availability of marketing skills, and infrastructure bottlenecks. How would the IT Incubator alleviate the constraints? The project intends to have the following components:

- *Managed work space* with a satellite dish to house SME companies – to alleviate business environment and infrastructure constraints;

- *Business development facility* to provide marketing, managerial and other business linkages with Western demand for software;

- *Skill development fund* to alleviate skill constraint by creating a joint university-industry process of continuous education, starting from apprenticeship of students in local export-driven companies and joint industry-university skill enhancement programs.

The IT incubator will have two branches: a) a branch in the US (e.g. Silicon Valley) to develop a pipeline of contracts for Armenian firms; and b) 'managed work space' in Yerevan. The first will assure demand for local skills, the second will assure just-in-time supply of project teams.

The primary objective of the project is to accelerate the emergence and expansion of first movers in the IT sector. The project will also serve as a springboard for market for business development services and could become a coordination device to accelerate investments to the sector, funded by donors, the Diaspora and the private sector. To achieve this objective, the project will be based on the following principles:

- It will focus on first movers, firms that are doing or trying to do things differently; it will supplement, rather than replace, the private restructuring effort.

- It will provide rather modest and temporary amounts of public support.

- It will assist firms in a non-distortionary way; support will be open to all agents willing to learn and restructure.

- Its assistance will be demand-driven with most subsidies concentrated on better access to business development services and skill upgrading.

7. SECTORAL POLICIES TO FACILITATE GROWTH

This chapter contains a set of key sectoral recommendations for five individual sectors. These sectoral interventions are rather important from for the overall strategy developed in the report. They would support expensing opportunities for business linkages (in transport and telecom), reduce critical constraints for skill-based development (in telecom), support new labor-intensive entry (in food distribution and housing), and could have a major short-term positive impact on macroeconomic and fiscal sustainability of the country (energy).

7.1. Energy

The Armenian power sector represents one of the major local industries, producing about 5,800 GWhs of electricity a year, with annual sales of about $155 million (8% of GDP) and with total employment of 30,000, or 14 % of total industrial employment. The imports of energy inputs (gas, nuclear fuel) amounted to 8% of GDP and to 20% of total imports in 1999 and therefore made a major contribution to the deficit of current balance (Table 7.1). The Armenian energy sector also includes considerable capacity in district heating and gas distribution. However, this capacity is currently underutilized and affected by heavy under-maintenance over the last 10 years.

Table 7.1. GDP, Energy Imports, Energy Consumption per Unit of GDP

	1996	1997	1998	1999	2000 (forecast)
GDP, USD million	1,599.3	1,639.1	1,899	1,893.1	
Total imports, USD million	855.8	892.3	902.4	801.7	
Imported energy inputs, USD million	181.7	202.1	197.6	159.1	
as % of total imports	21%	23%	22%	20%	
as % of GDP	11%	12%	10%	8%	
Energy (only electricity) consumption per unit of GDP, $	0.07	0.08	0.08	0.08	
Energy (electricity) consumption (sales), million AMD	43,703	62,247	72,886	79,324	84,677
o/w: consumption paid for	35,409	47,804	56,024	69,767	74,515

Source: Staff estimates.

Considerable progress has been made in reforming the power sector since 1995. Electricity supply has become much more reliable and is available on a 24 hour-a-day basis around the country (compared to several hours a day in 1993). Financial rehabilitation of the sector has been advanced through improved payment discipline, better budgeting, and increased electricity tariffs. As a result, the size of quasi-fiscal deficit in the sector has declined from about 5% of GDP in 1997-98 to about 0.4% of GDP in 1999. Also, an Energy Law has been adopted, and an independent Energy Regulation Commission established. The sector went through a major reorganization and consolidation of existing state enterprises to set up a structure that better suits forthcoming privatization objectives. Privatization of electricity distribution companies, scheduled for early 2001, is expected to provide an inflow of private capital through involvement of an internationally reputable strategic investor.

As a result of these efforts, in the short term Armenia does not face considerable energy-related constraints for economic growth. The power supply is rather reliable, and there is large excess capacity in the system. However, the current situation is not sustainable in the medium term. Major investments will be needed rather soon to replace existing generation capacity and modernize both transmission and distribution.

At the moment, Armenia has excess capacity in power generation and is a (small) net exporter of electricity. Total net export of electricity amounted to 4.6% of its generation in 1999 and is currently limited to Georgia[117]. In the short term, there is considerable potential for export expansion due to power capacity shortages in Turkey, Azerbaijan and Georgia.

The excess annual average generating capacity of Armenia is conservatively estimated at 1,000 MW. That will allow exports of 7,000 MWh a year worth over US$190 million (at an average unit value of 2.8 cents per KWh), which amounts to about 80% of the total Armenian merchandise export in 1999.

Armenia's power export has a high import content (natural gas and nuclear fuel currently imported from Russia). The import content of the above additional power generation would stand at US$100 million a year. If the unit values of gas decrease in the case of the substitution of Russian gas by Azerbaijani, it would save at least US$25 million[118] a year. This number will go down further if the efficiency of generation increases due to better use of capacity.

Overall, it is estimated that the increased electricity exports and lower generation costs could result in an increase of net export of about US$120 million, which would help to close up to a quarter of the existing deficit of the current account and would greatly improve Armenia's debt profile.

However, to realize this potential major improvements in the regional, political and economic environment are needed: at the moment, borders with both Azerbaijan and Turkey remain closed, while potential exports to Georgia are limited by its low purchasing power and weak payment discipline.

Growth of electricity export would be a major factor to boost efficiency of the energy system as well as a source for its further financial recovery. Without export, due to weakness of internal demand (especially lack of night-time demand) and peculiarities of the cost structure in generation (high share of fixed costs), the Armenian power system remains quite inefficient and inflexible. There is a potential for "low-equilibrium trap" in the sector: low internal demand requires to raise tariffs to cover costs, while higher tariffs may delay recovery of internal demand, in both household and commercial sectors[119]. Total electricity consumption by commercial users amounts to less than 40% of the total, while the rest is consumed by households and budget organizations (Table 7.2). The average tariff amounted to 4c per kwt in 2000, which is the highest tariff in the South Caucasus (while the Turkish price is higher).

Table 7.2. Electricity Demand by Consumer Groups in Armenia

	1996	1997	1998	1999	2000 (forecast)
End Consumption, GWhs	3,427	3,474	3,596	3,628	3,737
O/w: households	33%	36%	40%	35%	
Industry	36%	37%	35%	37%	
Budgetary & quasi-budgetary org-s	31%	27%	25%	28%	
Demand growth rate, %:		1.4%	3.5%	0.9%	3%
o/w: households		11.6%	16%	-12%	N/a
Industry		4.7%	-4%	6%	N/a
Budgetary & quasi-budgetary org-s		-13%	-3%	14%	N/a

Source: Staff estimates.

---

[117] Armenia also trades in electricity with Iran on a swap basis.

[118] At the 1999 levels of Russian gas imports for power generation, cheaper gas imports from Azerbaijan would result in annual savings of US$11 million.

[119] The average growth of domestic electricity consumption in 1997-2000 was about 2% a year, while the average GDP growth exceeded 4%.

The current comparative advantages of Armenia in the sector derive from two sources: (i) low cost generation by hydro plants (22% of total generation); and (ii) nuclear plant generation (additional 35% of generation in 1999-2000, Table 7.3), fuel for which is provided from Russia and financed through inter-governmental credits at rather preferential terms. The latter may not be sustainable in the long-run due to a scheduled shutdown of the Nuclear Power Plant in year 2004[120] and also because of increasingly less subsidized financing of the Plant's inputs. Political rapprochement with Turkey, which is the most attractive market for Armenia's power, would allow Armenia to convert these low-cost fuels in high value added electricity for export, making use of already existing transmission infrastructure and not relying on construction of new oil and gas pipelines. However, as Armenia has no significant low-cost fuel resources of its own, electricity exports would not be competitive when existing plants are replaced by a new capacity.

Table 7.3. Share of Nuclear Generation in Armenia

	1996	1997	1998	1999	2000
Total generation	5,759	5,504	5,734	5,316	5,563
o/w: nuclear generation, GWhs	2,102	1,423	1,417	1,890	1,837
Nuclear generation, % of total	36%	26%	25%	36%	33%

Source: Armenian Ministry of Energy.

While current electricity tariffs are close to cost-recovery, they don't include sufficient margins to cover long-term investment needs. As a result, the sector is able to finance only a minor share of future investments from internally-generated cash flows, and it has limited borrowing power. Total investment requirements in the sector for the next 15 years (both generation and distribution) are estimated to amount to about $1.4 billion (70% of the annual GDP)[121]. These investments are needed to provide a replacement for the Nuclear Plant and other aging and inefficient capacity, and also provide an upgrade in the distribution system. Without finding a source to finance required investments, Armenia would face a capacity shortage in about 4-5 years, which may become a major economy-wide constraint for growth recovery.

Given the existing fiscal constraints in the public sector, such investments have to be funded either by the private sector or international donors. A considerable additional reform effort will be necessary in order to mobilize these investments from the private sector. Main directions of the reform include:

- Setting up an appropriate power market structure that would support the 2-3 year transition to a competitive electricity market;

- Strengthening capacity and independence of the market regulator;

- Introduction of the legal and regulatory framework that would support a predominantly privately-owned energy sector; operations of private companies in both generation and distribution;

- Adopting a strategy for attracting private investments for electricity generation.

---

[120] According to recent reports, the Government of Armenia has been negotiating with the European Union an extension of the deadline for the shutdown of the Nuclear Power Plant to 2008 or later.
[121] Based on the Report by the Armenian Energy Commission and estimates of the EBRD.

In addition to attracting new private investments, another priority for Armenia's energy strategy relates to the introduction of an aggressive energy saving program, thus allowing the existing capacity to be freed for export, and later reducing needs in new investments. One of the primary sources for energy savings derives from moving households away from current electrical heating towards gas-based or other more cost-effective heating systems. Recent reforms in the energy sector brought a considerable decline in energy consumption in the late 90s, especially in the household sector, where many families were forced to cut consumption in line with their current incomes. Total primary energy consumption decreased by about 9% in 1996-99[122], while GDP increased by almost 15%. Still, there are considerable reserves for further improving energy use.

Within the appropriate policy framework, the power sector could contribute to economy-wide growth through the following main channels:

- Increased export in the short to medium term (conditional on the political settlement in the region);

- Increased efficiency and reduced consumption of imported energy inputs per a unit of GDP, which would contribute to improvements in the current account;

- Improved financial performance, which would reduce pressures on the budget by increasing net tax contribution of the sector.

In contrast to an established reform track record in the power sector, reforms in district heating have not started yet. District heating systems remained publicly owned, poorly managed and in a regular need of considerable (relative to the current size of the sector) quasi-fiscal losses (about 0.7% of GDP in 1999).

Before the transition, district heating systems used to serve 35% of households, including 70% of urban households. This share has now declined to less than 15% of the population due to lack of maintenance and unresolved issues of financing. The current institutional and technological structure of the sector prevents any serious increase in collections from final users of heat, while the budget can not afford larger heating subsidies. The collection in the sector was about the 17 percent during the two previous winter, while the tariffs are set by Energy Commission, and cover the current costs of heating.

Even at the existing, rather reduced level, heating subsidies can not be justified and should be fully removed. All alternative sources of energy in Armenia (including electricity, gas, kerosene, wood, and coal) are not subsidized[123], while only a small portion of the population who mostly live in large cities benefits from the heavily-subsidized district heating. There is no evidence that recipients of heating subsidies have a larger concentration of poor households, thus heating subsidies do not have any meaningful poverty alleviation impact. Just the opposite, heavy concentration of heating subsidies contributes to further differentiation in household quality of life.

The Government of Armenia has decided to prepare in 2000-01 an Urban Heating Strategy, supported by the World Bank and other donor agencies. The heating strategy is supposed to assess alternative options for heat supply, their affordability and will define an institutional framework for various scenarios of sector development. Based on feasibility studies, the strategy would identify both the regulatory and policy framework and a possible market structure to facilitate transition to commercial and

---

[122] As estimated by the Yerevan Center for Energy Strategy.

[123] Liquid fuels such as heavy oil and gasoline remain substantially more expensive in Armenia than in other CIS countries. This is primarily due to higher transportation costs but also relate to limited competition in fuel import.

private provision of heating services in a competitive manner. It is expected that implementation of the strategy would make less expensive heating options available for households, including poor, and free up a portion of household incomes (that is currently used for heating) for other consumption or saving.

Armenia's gas sector was state owned till the creation of the ArmRusGasArd joint venture with Russian Gasprom (45% equity) and ITERA (10% of equity) in the autumn of 1998. Gas transmission assets worth $148.5 million were sold to Russian counterparts through the gas-for-equity swap (against a total volume of 2,121 million cubic meters of gas to be delivered in 1998-2001). Currently, the ArmRusGasArd sells gas to four major consumer groups: population, industry, power generation companies and heat supplying organizations. While the population is a good payer for gas, other types of consumers have accumulated about $45 million in debts in less than two years. In view of current and future investment requirements of the gas distribution network, the joint venture will need to improve its commercial and financial performance in the domestic market.

7.2.   Agriculture

Over the last 10 years, the agricultural sector has been playing an increasingly important role in the Armenian economy. Currently, it accounts (together with food processing) for roughly 35% of Armenia's GDP and is one of the very few sectors to achieve pre-reform output levels. Economic blockade, so detrimental to industry and trade, has played a certain positive role for Armenian agricultural production, protecting local producers from potentially more cost-effective competitors in the neighboring countries (Azerbaijan, Georgia, Turkey). Since Armenia is still a large net importer of food (over 30% of food consumption is imported), additional import substitution could serve as a major source of further growth in both food processing and agriculture as competitiveness in food processing increases. However, lifting the blockade will definitely put Armenian producers in a much more competitive situation.

Recent Trends

Policy environment. The Government of Armenia has been pursuing a liberal agricultural policy since the early 90s. Most subsidies were abolished, while agricultural and food prices were liberalized very early in transition. International trade has been liberalized as well, and the country has adopted a liberal import policy on agriculture with duties of zero or 10 percent. The major remaining support measures to local agricultural producers include VAT and land tax exemptions, subsidies for irrigation water and seed loans. In 2000, government support to the sector was modest – about 1.6% without tax exemptions.

Armenian agriculture was swiftly privatized in 1991-1992, when 1/3 of all agricultural land and 70% of arable land was transferred to family farms and the Soviet-style collectives were disbanded. There is a regulatory and institutional framework which allows for using land as collateral. The former state monopolies for input supply and marketing of agricultural produce were privatised, experienced a dramatic decline of their activity, which has turned them into marginal operators. Although currently the dominant source of supply for all farm inputs are private individuals, the private sector has not yet been able to fill the vacuum left by the state distributors. As in other sectors, emergence of new private businesses in agricultural distribution was slow. This, combined with weaknesses in market infrastructure, represent a major factor that hinders development of markets for farm products and delays recovery in agricultural prices.

Output trends. Despite a dramatic decline in GDP in the early 90s, the gross agricultural product has not declined since 1990 (see Table 7.4). This is in contrast to the situation observed in most transition economies, where the decline in agricultural product roughly paralleled the decline in GDP. With slight ups and downs, the agricultural product in Armenia gradually grew in the process of privatization. The gains were mainly due to the growth in crop production, which by 1996 had increased steadily to 148% of the 1990. At the same time, livestock production suffered an initial decline, but essentially stabilized between 1993 and 1996.

Table 7.4. GDP and Agricultural Product

	1990	1994	1995	1996	1997	1998	1999
GDP Growth, percent	-	5.4	6.9	5.9	3.3	7.3	3.3
Agriculture Product, percent of total GDP, at current prices	15.8	43.5	40.7	34.8	29.4	30.8	26.2
Agriculture Product, percent of total GDP, at 1996 prices	13.7	37.0	36.1	34.8	32.2	33.8	33.2
Agriculture Product, percent of 1990	100	86.9	90.4	92.2	88.0	99.4	100.7
Agriculture Product Growth, percent	-	3.1	4.0	2.0	-4.5	12.9	1.3

Sources: Armenia Economic Trends and NSS.

Significant increase in the share of agriculture in GDP (from 16% in 1990 to 44% in 1994) stresses the vital importance of agriculture in the first years of independence. Table 7.4 shows a strong correlation between recent growth rates in agriculture product and GDP, thus illustrating that the fluctuations in economic performance of the late 90s to a certain extent were determined by the instability in agricultural output.

Structural changes in output. There had been significant changes in the structure of agricultural products in the last decade. In 1990, the share of livestock production in the sector exceeded the share of planting (57.5% against 42.5%). Livestock output declined by 38% between 1990 and 1993 in response to a severe demand shock of the early 90s. By 1996, the structure of the sector had reversed: the share of livestock amounted to 42.4%. Since then, there has been an accelerated recovery in livestock production, and it is expected that the trend would continue in the medium term.

Traditionally, Armenia has been a net importer of food and agricultural products, with main import products being livestock and cereals. In 1990, the country produced only about 25% of its grain, 35% of its dairy and 65% of its meat product requirements[124]. At the same time, Armenia produced quality fruit and vegetables exported in significant quantities in the form of fresh and processed produce, as well as wine and brandy within the Soviet Union. In 1990, food and agriculture products export from Armenia amounted to 10% of total exports and 16% of agricultural output. Since independence, because of changes in relative production and transportation prices, Armenia's position as an importer of grains and exporter of fruits and vegetables has declined. Sectoral restructuring was focused on expansion of grain production for domestic consumption, which largely replaced feed crops (due to a drop in the livestock herd, Table 7.5).

Agricultural Trade. Although transport blockade guarantees certain protection from import, it also increases transaction costs for exports. While food export increased somewhat after 1996, it still remained below 1% of GDP in 1999 (Table 7.6). While in 1996 the share of food exports comprised 4.5 % of total exports, in 1997 it increased to 12.1% and amounted to 9.8% in 2000. Agricultural export was seriously hit by the Russia crisis in 1998, which led to a 45% decline in sales of Armenian cognac, a major export commodity, in CIS countries. Russian recovery in late 1999 and 2000 led to a larger food export in 2000.

---

[124] Khachatryan (2000).

Table 7.5. Patterns in Cropping Areas and Livestock Herd, 1990-1997

	1990		1997			1990	1997
	Thousand ha	Percent	Thousand ha	Percent		Thousand heads	Percent of 1990
Cereals	138.2	32	198.8	59	Cattle	640.0	465.8	72.8
Potatoes	22.4	5	32.9	10	Cows	250.9	256.2	102.1
Vegetables, Fruits,	22.8	5	23.3	7	Pigs	310.9	56.9	18.3
Technical Crops	1.9	0	0.4	0	Sheep, goats	1,186.3	521.1	43.9
Feed Crops	251.3	58	79.6	24				
Total Cropped	437.1	100	335.0	100				

Source: NSS.

Table 7.6. Agricultural and Food Trade (million US dollar)

	1993	1994	1995	1996	1997	1998	1999	2000
Agricultural & Food Exports	10.7	13.6	13.8	12.9	28.1	18.2	16.4	25.8
As % of Total Merchandise Export	6.9	6.3	5.1	4.5	12.1	8.3	7.3	9.8
Agricultural & Food Imports	87.7	154.7	225.5	291.6	274.5	294.2	197.3	193.5
As % of Total Import	34.5	39.3	33.5	34.1	30.8	32.6	26.7	24.5
Agricultural & Food Export-Import Gap	77.0	141.1	211.7	278.7	246.4	276.0	181.0	167.7

Source: Khachatryan (2000).

The share of agricultural and food imports in 1996-1998 period was maintained on a relatively stable level and amounted to about a third of total imports. Total imports declined significantly in 1999-2000, reflecting in part a reduction in humanitarian supply of food.

Medium-term export prospects in the sector greatly depend upon prospects for restructuring in the food industry. As was shown in the previous chapters, the Armenian food processing sector used to play an important role in the economy before transition, but it has been exposed to a number of external shocks in the early 90s. The core of the sector is represented by about 150 large and medium size enterprises, which produce canned fruits and vegetables, dairy and meat products, mixed feed, flour and bread, alcohol, soft drinks, and cigarettes. Many of these enterprises were set up to supply most of their output to the rest of the FSU and currently they are too large relatively to the size of the Armenia market. Privatization of food processing started in 1995 and has yet to be completed. Privatization in the sub-sector had witnessed common problems such as lack of proper management expertise, inadequate incentives, and narrow domestic market. Failing to recover traditional markets, many of these enterprises currently operate at 5-20 percent of their capacity.

However, when compared to other major industries in Armenia, food processing represents the most successful example of restructuring. As shown in Chapters 2 and 3, at the moment this is the most productive sector in manufacturing. Also, food processing shows the highest incidence of first movers, including rather dynamic new entry. Several examples of successful industrial restructuring (in production of tobacco, dairy products, wine, beer, brandy, etc.) confirm that existing barriers for industrial recovery could be overcome and provide a vivid illustration of how this could be achieved. Such restructuring also proved to be quite beneficial for agricultural development through boosting demand and providing advance payments to farmers.

As recent experience suggests, these restructuring projects in agro-processing have low incremental capital-output ratios (1.0-1.5), and high gross margins (often in the order of 50-60%). Incremental capital needs per new job are $10,000-20,000. As such, they are a relatively efficient source of incremental jobs that do not require high skills, with wages well above the current agricultural yearly income, and thus they represent an important slice of future low cost job generation.

Price Trends. Another feature of Armenian agriculture had been the unfavorable changes in relative prices. Average annual growth of agricultural prices in 1996-1999 was much slower than increases in industrial and consumer prices (Table 7.7). In fact, agricultural prices remained depressed since mid-1998, reflecting both weaknesses of demand and weak market power of farmers compared to wholesales and food processors. The disproportionate price development indicates that recent growth in agriculture was mostly beneficial to consumers and food industry. Despite an almost 12% growth in output in 1995-1999, real incomes from farming declined by 40.3 % (when deflated with CPI).

Table 7.7. Agricultural, Industrial, and Consumer Price Changes, Annual Indices

	1994	1995	1996	1997	1998	1999	Average Annual Growth 1996-1999, percent
Consumer Price Index	5,062	276	119	114	109	101	10.3
Industrial Price Index	4,814	375	122	119	113	102	14.0
Agricultural Price Index	N/A	227	101	117.4	104.4	86.6	1.8

Source: NSS and staff estimates.

Land Use and Ownership. Agriculture in Armenia is greatly influenced by topography. Agricultural land makes up only 1.3 million ha (43% of the territory). With about 0.4 ha of agricultural land per inhabitant, the agricultural resource base of the country is among the lowest in Europe. Table 7.8 presents the ownership structure of agricultural land in Armenia as of January 1, 1997. Although two-thirds of agricultural land remains state-owned, most available land is used by family farms through a combination of private ownership and leasing. In addition to 321,000 family farms, the agricultural sector includes about 100 larger state farms that control 2% of agricultural land, mainly pastures. The private sector produces 98.5% of agricultural product, while in 1990 it accounted for only 35% of output.

Table 7.8. Structure of Land Ownership in Agriculture (as of 01/01/1997)

	Total, thousand ha	Private Ownership		State Ownership	
		Thousand ha	Percent	Thousand ha	Percent
All agricultural land	1,391.4	466.6	33.5	924.8	66.5
Arable land	494.3	345.4	69.9	148.9	30.1
Perennials	63.8	59.9	93.9	3.9	6.1
Meadows	138.9	61.3	44.1	77.6	55.9
Pastures and other	694.4	-	-	694.4	100.0

Source: NSS.

The average size of a private farm is 2 ha. In addition to their small size, farms are fragmented with an average of four to five parcels per farm. However, 15% of farmers additionally cultivate leased land[125]. Farms with leased land are substantially larger, averaging 3.2 ha. Leasing so far is the only real mechanism for increasing the size of holdings. The common lease term is 1-3 years. The land lease market in Armenia is strictly one-way: the private farmer leases land from the state. Two-way leasing

---

[125] World Bank (1999a). "Armenia's Private Agriculture: 1998 Survey of Family Farms".

among individuals has not yet developed. Despite the existence of pre-defined cadastral coefficient of indexation, the village councils have been given considerable discretion in regulating access to state land and deciding on terms of its lease. There are few requirements, such as minimum lease price (not less than the land tax of the same land plot) and maturity of lease (not more than 10 years). The system of land leasing is extremely decentralized and rather non-transparent, which potentially leaves room for abuse and uneven treatment by the village councils. While sales of private land are not restricted, there is little actual trade in rural land. Demand for land remained depressed due to low rural incomes and general uncertainties regarding economic prospects of the sector.

Availability of Irrigation. Armenian agriculture is heavily dependent on irrigation. Rainfall mainly takes place off the vegetation period, making regulation and management of surface water flow a strict necessity. About 32.9% of the total 483,500 ha of arable land is currently irrigated, of which 66.1% by gravity, and the rest by pumping stations. More than 70% of aggregated production of horticulture comes from irrigated plots. About a third of the overall annual water flow of 7.2 billion m^3 is used for irrigation purposes. The surveys suggest a rather high incremental value added from irrigation (which varies between 9 and 18 Dram per of m^3 of water), while average cost of supply is 8 Dram per 1 m^3.

At the moment the irrigation system operates below its full capacity. Compared to its peak in the late 80s, total irrigated area declined by about 11.2% in 2000. This is because the system, originally developed to be heavily dependent on pumping, proved to be rather costly after initial price distortions were removed. Operation of several parts of the irrigation network was interrupted in the first part of the 90s due to insufficient funding for maintenance. In 2000, total water usage averaged 7,500 m^3 per ha.

Despite some progress in financial rehabilitation of the sector since 1996, the system remains heavily dependent on subsidies. The average cost recovery in tariffs amounted to 41% in 2000, while the collection level is only 60%. In 1998, only 45% of farmers paid their water bill in full[126]. In addition, while the Government introduced some differentiation in irrigation tariffs in 1988, cross-subsidization is still an existing factor. Total budget subsidies to irrigation amounted to 0.46% of GDP in 2000.

Use of Machinery. According to a World Bank survey[127], very few farmers actually own farm machinery (9% own tractors and 8% own trucks). All other types of farm machinery were reported by 3%-5% of respondents. Overall, less than 15% of families own any kind of machinery. Yet, actual access to machinery is much less problematic: 40%-60% of farmers use various pieces of equipment owned by others. Nearly two-thirds of respondents rent mechanical field services from private individuals. Rental markets for machinery and machine services apparently exist in rural Armenia, and this reduces the need for traditional ownership.

Major Constraints to Growth and Policy Priorities

In sum, taking into consideration the increased role of agriculture in the Armenian economy, as well as the fact that the agricultural sector serves as a safety net for a large share of both rural and urban population, the policy priorities for the sector include:

---

[126] World Bank (1999a).
[127] World Bank (1999a).

- Deepening markets for food and agricultural products;

- Strengthening land market policies, continuing land privatization, improving transparency of leasing arrangements;

- Improving cost recovery in irrigation, gradually eliminating water tariffs cross-subsidization and improving payment discipline;

- Re-focusing agricultural research and extension to the needs of small farmers;

- Reducing barriers for expansion of agricultural credit.

Removing barriers for more competitive domestic food markets. The current combination of low agricultural prices and high food prices in main Armenia cities indicates serious problems in agricultural procurement and distribution, more specifically barriers for new entry and high costs of doing business in food trade, especially at the wholesale level. Developing currently depressed markets for processed food products is a key for generating demand and higher prices for farmers. Although transport blockade guarantees certain protection from imports, it also increases transaction costs for exports. The Government strategy to address these bottlenecks (in addition to across-the-board improvements in the business environment) should facilitate development of market infrastructure, provide farmers with better access to market information, and encourage farmers' cooperatives in the areas of input supply and output sales.

Building capacity for marketing and export promotion in agro-processing. If the agro-processing sector is to continue to grow, support in marketing is crucial. While restructuring in food processing has been relatively successful, the sector has been facing major marketing constraints. At the same time, accumulated experience with FDI in food processing suggests that foreign investors indeed can and have accelerated exports in this sector. However, in most cases, the marketing linkage and marketing expertise provided by foreign investors is more important than the actual investment made (which so far rarely exceeds $500,000).

This experience confirms that the key to resolve marketing bottlenecks is not investment in traditional rural infrastructure but rather to pursue a much wider training program in marketing analysis and facilitate product-by-product enterprise linkages with foreign firms. But the Government has yet to agree to such a re-prioritization[128].

Rural Finance and Investment. Underdeveloped rural finance is perceived as a significant constraint to development of efficient commercial farms. Commercial banks have neither interest, nor appropriate skills to deal with the agricultural sector. They have avoided serving individual farmers, citing high risks and transactions costs. Credit resources flowing to agriculture seem to be well below the levels which current creditworthiness of the sector would justify. Expansion of agricultural credit from 8% of total credit in 1998 to 15% in 2000 mostly came from donor-funded credit lines.

As the survey data suggest, in 1997, borrowing from commercial banks was negligible: less than 1% of farmers reported that they had an outstanding bank loan. While in total 10% of farmers had outstanding debt in excess of US$350, the main source of this funding was relatives and friends.

---

[128] For instance, under the World Bank financed Agricultural Reform Support Project, the Government has been reluctant to fund marketing training.

Underdeveloped Land Market. While the family farm provides a dynamic basis for the agricultural economy, it has the disadvantage of being too small to benefit from economies of scale. Facilitation of land market development and farm consolidation will be of primary importance for achieving a more efficient production. While the present legal framework for the functioning of the land market is considered appropriate, the priority for the Government is to strengthen land titling and registration. In this regard, the GOA started the Title Registration Project, supported by the World Bank in 1999, whose main objective is to secure property rights and generalize the practice of pledging immovable collateral, particularly agricultural land, for commercial borrowing.

Another direction to promote farm consolidation relates to a continuation of the land privatization program. To facilitate demand for privatized land, the Government should introduce more flexible valuation mechanisms to keep initial land valuation in line with market prices. There is also a need to develop more transparent mechanisms for leasing land, which would ensure equal and fair access to such leases. In the medium term, when the land demand becomes stronger, the Government should consider the possibility of establishing centralized land banks available for lease by those who for any reason do not want to lease land locally.

Sustainability of Irrigation. Adequate attention to irrigation sector maintenance is a key for timely and satisfactory delivery of water to farmers and to preserve long term sustainability of the irrigation infrastructure. This requires further improvements in cost recovery and tariff differentiation through increased water tariffs and strengthening payment discipline. Public investments in the sector will be targeted to cost reduction in the system through expanding gravity-supplied water, reduced electricity consumption, and better accounting for water use.

Agricultural Extension. Since most of Armenia's small farmers are either overly specialized former collective farm workers or non-agricultural workers that have turned to subsistence farming, it is these new individual farmers who need to be the focus of Armenia's reformed agricultural extension, education and research institutions. For that purpose, the Armenian Extension Service was created in 1994 with the support of donors. Under this initiative, the focus of agricultural research has been almost entirely switched to the needs of small farmers, and extension is currently being decentralized and managed locally through regional Agricultural Support Centers. Considerable efforts have been applied to transform agricultural extension institutions, but the degree of cost recovery of their services is still poorly defined. The Government has to decide which services need to be charged for, promote privatization of such services, and then continue to finance extension services that are truly public goods.

7.3. Transport

Transport is an important factor in Armenia's economy due to Armenia's relatively isolated location, which adds to the cost of internal production as well as both imports and exports. Constraints to growth relating to the transport sector stem from three causes:

- Closed borders with Azerbaijan and Turkey restrict the movement of goods, and limit shippers' routing options. Measures that would improve transport in the event that borders are reopened is the subject of post-conflict studies now in preparation.

- There are physical constraints due to inadequate infrastructure that impose constraints for producers, exporters and importers.

- The are non-physical barriers to the efficient use of transport services that add to the cost of transport.

The first of these constraints will not be addressed here since it was discussed in Chapter 3.

Physical Constraints

The physical constraints in the transport sector include:

- Railways: The country's railway infrastructure is old and out of date. Rail transport has been slow and unreliable. The recently approved Transport Project includes US$15.2 million for the renovation of portions of the road bed, electrical system, communications system, and overhaul of locomotives and wagons for the line between Yerevan and the Georgian border, along with the restructuring of the railway company. Service has already improved somewhat recently. However, massive improvements will be needed in future years to replace old bridges and other basic physical works, as well as replacement locomotives and wagons as the present equipment already exceeds the normal useful life span. Thus, while the Transport Project will provide a temporary respite for rail traffic to Georgia and the Black Sea, additional support will be necessary in the not too distant future. Also, poor cooperation with the railway system in Georgia is a related transport constraint beyond the control of the Armenia authorities.

- Roads: The Highway Project and its successor, the Transport Project, have kept Armenia's main roads in operating condition. This has not helped the roads on the Georgian side of the border, some of which have become virtually impassable as the Georgians have only a limited interest in improving this portion of their road network. Also, financing from Armenia's own budget for road maintenance has been extremely limited, and raises doubts about the country's ability to keep the roads in operating condition without outside assistance.

- Air Transport: Air services suffer from inadequate physical infrastructure, as the runway and landing lights are old and need major upgrading, and the air terminal lacks modern conveniences expected by international business travelers and tourists.

Non-Physical Constraints

Non-physical constraints lead to high costs for transport services as well as inability to make prompt and timely deliveries. Overall transport costs are high in Armenia compared to other European countries, which places Armenia's exports at a competitive disadvantage. The Transport Sector Review (1997) by the World Bank made a series of recommendations to reduce these costs, including commercialization and/or privatization of most transport modes, financial restructuring to reduce excess staff and capacity, deregulation of markets, participation in International Conventions, improved customs procedures, enactment of appropriate insurance legislation to support the creation of transport insurance, promotion of the creation of freight forwarding companies, and careful analysis of all proposed transport investments to assure their economic validity. While some progress has been made since 1997 to liberalize markets and in some of the other areas recommended in the Transport Sector Review, much remains to be done. In particular, it concerns Armenia's entering international transport conventions, privatization of Armenian Airlines, better access to markets in Georgia and Iran for Armenian trucking companies.

7.4.   Telecommunications Sector[129]

In Armenia, a well developed and efficient telecommunications infrastructure is essential for both economic growth and institutional reforms. In addition to fostering competitiveness, the sector can lead the way in de-monopolizing and privatizing infrastructure services, attracting foreign investment, and developing local capital markets. The modern information infrastructure could also facilitate reforms in governance, public sector financial management, and the delivery of social services. Another very important factor that further stresses the urgency of sustainable long-term reform strategy for the Armenian telecommunications sector is the role that is being recently prescribed to the dynamic software industry by both Armenian government and donors as one of the most promising drivers of overall economic growth. Thus, addressing problems in telecommunications represents a core priority for the overall skill-based development strategy, advocated in this report.

Armenian Ministry of Transport and Communications (MOTC) is a principal policy-maker and regulator for the industry. In addition, several associations, such as the Armenian Internet Users' Group (promoting Internet development) and the Union of Armenian Consumers (lobbying against tariff increases) have been very active in shaping the telecommunications sector. A new Telecom Law came on stream in 1998/1999, but the regulatory environment still calls for major improvements. Legislation clearly determining relations between the state and natural monopolists, as well as a consistent anti-monopolistic policy, are still lacking. The Government is currently involved in an effort to review the law with a view to soon issuing a new, modern sector law that will allow Armenia to face the challenges of the information revolution. The new Law will set the framework for independent regulatory authority in the sector[130], as well as refine procedural rules and enforcement mechanisms. It should provide, *inter alia,* for the introduction of a non-discriminatory interconnection regime, equitable universal access policy, tariff re-balancing and regulation, as well as modern procedures for allocation of frequencies, numbering and rights of way.

Bottlenecks for Sector Development

The single most important bottleneck of the Armenian telecommunications sector development is the stringent position of Armentel – local telecom monopoly owned by Greek Hellenic Telecommunications Organization (OTE). Armentel completely dominates the market and is the only provider of local, long distance and international services, with a 15 year exclusivity which expires in 2013. The resulting private monopoly is maintaining inadequately high prices for certain services, low quality, low levels of investment, and in general is hampering the otherwise potentially explosive growth in the sector.

After the break up of the USSR, Armenia has inherited a relatively extensive, but low quality and inefficient fixed telephony network. Despite the fact that Armenia had the highest fixed line teledensity as compared to Georgia and Azerbaijan, non-commercially driven network design resulted in misallocation of lines and hence low call volumes. Low revenues per line due to the politically driven low local tariffs, which are cross-subsidized by high international tariffs, led to chronic underinvestment in the sector. As a result, equipment was outdated, network quality poor and digitalization stood well below other countries of similar income.

---

[129] This section is based on the findings of the Regional Study on Telecommunications in the Caucasus. World Bank. (2000).

[130] Preparations to set up independent regulator are being made with EBRD assistance.

As opposed to neighboring Georgia and Azerbaijan, Armenia prioritized privatization and its proceeds, failing to liberalize the sector. The Government has been advocating the view that at this stage of telecommunications development, basic fixed-line services in Armenia should remain a natural monopoly. As a result, emerged private monopoly on fixed and mobile services is hindering sector expansion. Despite the Government's fears of sending the wrong signal to future foreign investors, preserving a 15-year monopoly in one of the fastest growing sectors in the world, risks cutting Armenia off the information revolution, and should be re-negotiated.

At the time of privatization, OTE assumed Armentel's debts of US$43 million in supplier credits and made commitments to improve quality and to invest more than US$200 million in the sector within five years. However, currently the Government is concerned by Armentel's apparent lack of ability to expand service and improve quality, and is claiming that so far the company had been invested much less than was agreed.

As of 2000, Armenia still has the highest fixed line teledensity (number of main telephone lines per 100 inhabitants) in the region – 18. However, in the last five years, the fixed line park in Armenia grew at only half the rate of that in Azerbaijan or Georgia. Since 1994, the waiting list has doubled resulting in the highest waiting lists relative to population size. Despite the efforts to modernize the networks, the digitalization rate in late 1998 remained low in Armenia (11%), e.g. when compared to Azerbaijan's 20.9%. The impact of different policies is most striking in the area of mobile communications. Whereas Azerbaijan and Georgia, which have a liberal market access in the sector, have experienced exponential growth over the past three years resulting in approximately 3.5% and 1.8% mobile penetration, in Armenia less than 0.2% of the population has access to mobile phones (see Tables 7.9 and 7.10).

Table 7.9. Comparative Telecom Sector Statistics for Armenia, Azerbaijan, and Georgia

	Armenia	Azerbaijan	Georgia
Fixed lines			
Main telephone lines (k), 2000	700	873	860
Main telephone lines per 100 inhabitants, 2000	18.42	11.05	15.92
Public telephones per 1000 inhabitants, 1998	0.08	0.26	0.07
Digital (%), 1998	11.7	20.9	n/a
Faults per 100 main lines per years, 1998	20	75	n/a
Telecommunications investment per main line, 1998	29	20	n/a
Mobile telephony/Paging			
Mobile subscribers (k), 2000	7	280	97
Mobile subscribers per 100 inhabitants, 2000	0.19	3.54	1.80
Internet			
Internet users (k), 1998	4	0.9	5
Internet users per 10,000 inhabitants, 1998	11.31	1.24	9.18

Source: Regional Study on Telecommunications in the Caucasus. World Bank (2000).

Armentel operates a small GSM network constrained to Yerevan plus an ERMES paging network financed by a Siemens supplier credit, which counts for only about 500 users. Monopoly is obviously stagnating growth, with high tariffs (before 1999 Armenia was one of the few remaining countries in which users are required to pay for both outgoing and incoming calls) and limited investments, which do not allow for expansion of the network and its coverage, and hamper the introduction of innovative services. Even a relatively standard service such as international roaming, which most GSM operators in the world are offering to their clients, was not available in Armenia till 2001, depriving the company from a potentially important source of revenues from travelers.

Table 7.10. Comparative Network Sizes and Cellular Tariffs for GSM Operators in South Caucasus

Country	Operator	Subscribers	Monthly fee	Local calls
Armenia	Armentel	7,200	$18	$0.15/min
Azerbaijan	Bakcell	50,000	$10	$0.15/min.
	Azercell	230,000	$10	$0.25/min.
Georgia	Magticom	75,000	$5	$0.15/min.
	Geocell	20,000	$6.50	$0.15/min.

Source: Regional Study on Telecommunications in the Caucasus. World Bank (2000).

Interestingly, the only market segment that does not fall clearly under Armentel's monopoly – the data communications sector - is experiencing some, although very limited, competition and, as a result, tariffs for Internet and data services in Armenia are relatively competitive. Costs of Armenian "all you can eat" packages are among the lowest in the region, proving once again that competition can indeed benefit consumers (e.g. Armenia's internet rates amount to US$50 per month for unlimited access as compared with US$75-150 in Georgia and Azerbaijan).

Today in Armenia there are all together about 10 ISPs, including non-commercial ones. The largest ISPs are Armenian Information Company (Arminco), an Armenian-Russian joint venture, with around 2,000 customers, including virtually all foreign embassies and organizations; and Infocom, which was chosen by the MOTC as the national commercial data carrier.

However, despite the high competitiveness of the domestic market for data communications all operators wishing to transmit data abroad still have to rent their international link from Armentel. While there is no longer capacity constraint for connecting Armenia with the outside world, but tariff remain too high. Even after the recent reduction in tariff by 40%, the 128 kilobits/sec connection cost US$5,000 in late 2000, which was 20 times higher than similar tariffs in the USA. High tariffs continue to keep Internet tariffs beyond the reach of the vast majority of the population.

Apart from slowing down growth, Armentel's 15-year monopoly is a visible obstacle for Armenia joining the World Trade Organization (WTO). There are a number of policies Armenia will need to prepare and implement, such as enacting the relevant legislation, establishment of an independent regulator, adoption of a transparent interconnection regime and a clear universal access policy in order to be capable to meet the WTO accession criteria.

Armentel's dominant status quo is obviously a major restriction to market access for alternative investors. Some evidence suggests that there might be interest from other regional players to enter the market, which, although small, has potential for growth. For example, the major Turkish cellular operator, Turkcell, has investments both in Georgia and Azerbaijan, and would undoubtedly be interested in participating in Armenia too, if the market for cellular services were to be opened up to competition.

In sum, Armenia should streamline efforts to review and update the telecommunications law to allow the country to face the challenges of the information revolution. With the current 15 year restriction on market entry, there is little hope that the country could take advantage of the emerging technologies and business models of the information revolution. Therefore, all efforts should be focused on finding a solution to revisit the exclusivity period balancing the costs and benefits of all possible solutions. One of the possible solutions to resolve the current deadlock could arise from re-negotiating the existing agreement with Armentel that maybe based on the exchange of the reduced monopoly term for preferential longer-term credits from donors (EBRD) and future revenues from sales of licenses to new operators.

7.5.   Housing and Utilities[131]

From the growth perspective, the housing sector is traditionally considered as one of the major potential sources of economic recovery and expansion. In Armenia, the performance of the sector has been discouraging so far. Even by FSU standards, Armenia features quite a low volume of newly-constructed housing, despite major reconstruction efforts in the Earthquake Zone. On average for 1993-1997, annual new housing construction amounted to about 4,000 units. Per 1,000 inhabitants, the number of new dwellings is about 5 times lower than the average in mid-income countries and 3 times lower than the level prevailing in Eastern Europe before transition[132]. Even after almost a 20% increase in housing production in 1998, total investments in housing, as estimated, have been below 2.5% of GDP.[133]

Currently, demand for housing services in Armenia remains depressed through the combined effects of negative population dynamics, low real incomes, high relative prices of tradable goods, sector policy distortions (Box 7.1), and institutional weaknesses. Potential investors face serious price disincentives, associated with both low housing prices and low levels of cost recovery (non-payment of community and maintenance charges is over 80%), high construction costs, and weaknesses in enforcement of property rights. An immediate constraint relates to poor maintenance of the existing stock and its inefficient use due to lack of significant incentives to adequately maintain this asset, lack of financing for repair and maintenance.

Box 7.1. Main Policy Distortions and Institutional Weaknesses in the Housing Sector

- Low level of tariffs in maintenance and utilities that do not cover costs and weak collections.
- Lack of competitive market for housing maintenance.
- Weak capacity of condominiums to organize efficient management of the stock.
- Lack of market for urban land.
- Weak protection of ownership rights for house owners that discourages renting out vacant units.
- Weak capacity of local governments to manage residual public housing.
- Distorted structure of public expenditure in the sector: excessive focus on new construction compared to housing rehabilitation.
- Continued public dominance of the public sector in urban land ownership, new construction, and housing maintenance.

However, in the short term, low volumes of investments in housing should not be of serious concern for policymakers. Once the current market failures are addressed, and population incomes recover, investments in both new housing and rehabilitation will recover gradually. As international experience suggests, comprehensive policy reforms in housing could have a broader impact on the overall Armenia economic recovery. This beneficial macroeconomic impact would be felt through three main channels: (i) attracting additional investments in both new construction and rehabilitation of housing; (ii)

---

[131] This section is based on Duebel, A. and L. Freinkman (1999). *"Basic Principles and Short- and Mid-term Strategies for National Housing Policy"*, The World Bank.

[132] As reported by the CIS Goskomstat, in 1995-97, in per capita terms new housing construction in Armenia has been considered smaller than in countries with similar income level such as Moldova and Kyrgyz Republic.

[133] For comparison, Russian investment in housing amounted to about 3.5% of GDP in 1996. Housing production in Russia amounted to 3.2 units per 1000 inhabitants compared to 1.3 units in Armenia.

redirecting resources currently accumulated in the sector for other investment purposes and thus supporting overall expansion in investments[134]; and (iii) making the economic situation more socially sustainable through better use of existing housing as well as through better targeting of public funds to support the most needy.

Because of well-known problems with housing provision for victims of the 1988 Earthquake as well as for refugees, there is a strong public perception in Armenia of housing shortages. Moreover, the housing situation is rather a politically sensitive and complex area, with considerable implicit government liabilities. As a result, it will take the Government a significant political will to achieve the main reform objectives and ensure that this outcome is sustainable. Broad public consultations may be needed as a part of the revised Government strategy in housing.

However, relative to its current income and urbanization level, the Armenia housing stock appears sufficiently large. It is estimated that the existing housing stock provides an average of about 13 sq. m per capita, more than 50% above the average of countries with a comparable GDP level. There are, however, sizeable interregional and quality mismatches between demand and supply, and weak market mechanisms are not capable of clearing them.

The real core of the problem derives from distorted price signals and the poorly defined public sector role in the housing sector, which together contribute to support grossly inflated public expectations about future housing supply and budget subsidies to households to cover housing and utility costs.

Legal and Regulatory Framework

Overall, Armenia has an adequate basic legal framework for successful development of housing markets. The main bottlenecks relate to some missing supporting regulations and to insufficient implementation and enforcement capacity. The latter, in part, is not housing specific but derives from overall weakness of law enforcement institutions.

Over the last few years, various reforms have been introduced, including privatization of most of the housing stock, introduction of condominiums, adoption of condominium and mortgage legislation, adoption of the Civil Code, strengthening regulation and financial discipline in the energy sector, etc. The swift give-away mass privatization program[135] was implemented in the early 90s. However, these drastic changes without a clearly-defined reform strategy in the sector resulted in numerous distortions that hamper market developments at the moment. In particular, while only a small proportion of the urban housing stock remains unprivatized (about 10%), the vast majority is still expected by their dwellers to be maintained by maintenance companies, owned by local governments and their own employees, which remained basically unreformed.

Reforms in the Existing Urban Housing Stock

In Armenia, as in most countries in transition, better allocation and use of the existing stock has a higher priority than intensification of construction efforts. Accordingly, the authorities need to make a shift in their strategy from mobilization of public finance for new public housing construction to rehabilitation and maintenance of existing housing -- primarily through removal of policy and institutional bottlenecks to allow private owners to organize their own financing and maintenance. In

---

[134] It allows "housing-wealthy" households to realize their wealth and use proceeds according to their own preferences.
[135] In 1998, total share of private dwellings was 90%, while 40-45% of apartments were registered in condominiums.

other words, the problem of Government's housing policy relates not as much to insufficient amount of budget financing (US$10-15 million a year) but to the fact that Government's strategy is seriously mis-focused.

The urban housing stock in Armenia is by all standards seriously under-maintained. This is largely because of extremely low levels of maintenance fees, which in addition have quite a low collection rate (10-15%). Increase in cost recovery will require substantial effort to improve payment collections, reduce arrears, and control utility tariffs through efficient regulation and corporate governance. In contrast to urban utilities, housing maintenance has a competitive nature, which would ensure that an increase in maintenance payments would result in adequate supply response and improvements in quality of service.

Armenia is currently lagging other FSU and CEE countries in creating a private market in housing maintenance services. While condominium associations are legally free to choose any service provider, few new private providers have emerged so far. The reasons for this failure should be attributed to both institutional and economic barriers for new entry: there is no regulatory framework for contractual arrangements in maintenance, and low nominal tariffs do not give enough incentives for entrepreneurs. To change the situation, clearly major political initiatives are needed. A program of small loans/grants for housing rehabilitation could be one of the potential instruments to facilitate development of the private market in maintenance.

More generally, progress with housing reforms requires an expansion in private participation in housing and the clarification of the respective roles of the public and private sectors. At the moment, the government role is over-expanded. The goal should be minimal public ownership of housing, with financing confined to a social safety net function. Avoiding direct involvement in housing construction, delivery of maintenance services, and collection of utility payments, the government should support developing markets for specific goods and services.

Also, the Government has to extend the regulatory framework to facilitate private participation in the utilities sector (including leasing and concession arrangements), provide room for non-traditional new private entry (e.g. operators of small block boilers), and accelerate the transition to new forms of contracting between utilities and consumers. Currently, the utility companies are monopolies with unclear corporate governance, and financing regimes. Restructuring these companies will improve their governance, increase their efficiency, and rationalize investment financing.

In the long term, effective management of the housing stock will require developing a diversified structure of housing owners capable to raise capital for investment, formulate and implement investment plans, and recover capital and operation costs from tenants or individual homeowners.

Another policy priority area relates to a stronger coordination between housing and social policies. In contrast to several other FSU states, where progress with introduction of modern poverty benefits has been rather slow, there is much less demand for setting up a separate (complementary) housing-focused system of social assistance in Armenia. Currently, Armenia may not need housing allowances as they are known from Russia but instead it would be better off if it provides for further strengthening of the existing means-tested poverty benefits, which should be allocated with explicit reference to housing costs as a component of poverty line.

To make government housing assistance more efficient, the central government should rather re-assume responsibility in supervising local housing allocation by making sure that local waiting lists are established and used consistently with the social assistance strategy pursued by the central government. As a matter of priority, the Government also has to change the nature of housing assistance from free allocation of publicly-constructed housing units to an equitable and transparent allocation of cash subsidies and investment grants. The latter would be much more affordable for the budget and would support better use of the existing stock and deepening of housing markets.

APPENDIX
ARMENIA GROWTH PROSPECTS:
LESSONS FROM THE GROWTH THEORY[136]

A renewal of interest in economic growth theory in the mid-1980's was sparked by the development of a new wave of growth models to explain the wide divergence in growth rates across countries. In addition to the factor inputs, associated with neoclassical growth theory, researchers incorporated a number of additional variables, including those on policy and environment. As more data became available, empirical studies have increasingly focused on the role of policy and institutional factors as determinants of growth such as monetary and fiscal distortions and institutional indicators such as the rule of law, property rights, the extent of corruption and existence of a sound/stable legal and regulatory system.

The empirical evidence could be summarized as the following:

- Initial conditions are important to growth. In particular, once other factors are accounted for, there is a convergence of income as poorer countries tend to grow faster than richer ones.

- Good policies are beneficial for growth. This includes macroeconomic stability, nonrestrictive/open trade policies, and effective control over government consumption.

- Strong institutions are also supportive of growth. Specifically efficient legal, judicial, and political institutions, captured by variables such as political stability and incidence of corruption and red-tape, are good for growth. There is growing evidence of the link between more-developed financial markets and institutions and growth.

- Unfavorable location and climate can hinder growth. Population growth tends to hold back growth.

Given the specificity of the transition process, analysis of growth in transition economies tend to pay less attention to traditional growth determinants such as investment and population growth and focus on factors that support improvements in utilization of existing resources. Main lessons for growth dynamics from 10 years in transition could be described as follows:

- Stabilization is a necessary but not sufficient condition for recovery in output. Countries that manage to bring inflation down below 50/40 percent per annum generally experience growth within 2-3 years.

- More reforms (including in areas of liberalization and structural reforms) are associated with better growth performance. There is also a positive correlation between growth and better legal and regulatory institutions. Reforms appear to have an initial cost (output initially falls). But lagged values of reform appear to be associated positively with growth.

- Initial conditions such as high degree of industrialization and other country specific factors such as wars or regional tensions, distance from rich markets, and political and economic history may have some impact. However, on balance, initial conditions appear to have less explanatory power than policy variables,

---

[136] The Appendix is based on the background paper prepared by Une Lee (2000).

- While investment is a major engine of growth in the long run, it appears to be less important for the initial recovery to growth. What this may be indicating is that reallocation of existing resources is more important than new investment early in the recovery process. However, there is a limit to resource reallocation. Over time growth will depend more on investment in physical and human capital.

- External assistance may support growth as it helps ease cost of transition, but its positive impact may happen only if certain policy conditions are met. Otherwise, foreign aid may be inefficient and even harmful.

Lessons for Armenia

Analysis of the growth literature suggests that the following factors could become the primary determinants of both recent and future (medium term) growth trends in Armenia.

As was argued in the report, Armenia needs to develop the institutions that support a market-friendly business environment and level playing field. This includes mechanisms to enforce laws, resolve arbitrate disputes, protect property rights, and reduce transaction costs.

The financial system in Armenia also remains weak. The level of financial intermediation is not consistent with the country's needs and does not reflect the high degree of macroeconomic stability and overall strict banking regulations. The banking system is small and is currently unable to mobilize any noticeable part of the existing private savings (estimated up to US$ 200 million in cash).

Armenia is a geographically landlocked country within a region suffering from instability. The research has shown that a country's landlocked position may reduce its growth through its effect on transport costs among other channels. For example one study showed that growth for a landlocked economy could be reduced by as much as 0.9 percent per year (Gallup and Sachs, 1998) compared to coastal economies. Given its locational disadvantages, Armenia is to compensate through other factors in order to achieve its targeted growth rates.

In Armenia, the overall investment and supply response has also been much weaker than what may be expected from reviewing Armenia's macroeconomic progress. Investment rates in Armenia are low relative to other transition economies (less than 15 percent compared to an average of 20 percent). The empirical evidence, however, points to progress on reforms as a better indicator of growth than investment early in the transition process. In the medium to long term, recovery of investment levels will become much more important. As Armenia moves along its reform path the explanatory power of the "transitional" factors is likely to become less important and the classic determinants of growth -- e.g. initial income, investment, human capital indicators and population growth -- will have greater weight.[137]

In Armenia, as in many transition countries, educational attainment as well as education level of the labor force tends to be high by international standards. In Armenia, however, both the quality of education and the enrollment rates, have suffered due to collapses in public finance and population incomes. If left unchecked, these developments could undermine the country's future economic growth.

Low initial income, low or falling population growth rates and high educational attainment all indicate a relatively high potential for per capita growth rate for transition economies. The investment

---

[137] Fischer, Stanley, Ratna Sahay, and Carlos A. Vegh. "Economies in Transition: The Beginnings of Growth." *Economic Reform and Growth*, May 1996, Vol. 86 No. 2, pp 229-33.

rate, however, may be the only variable capable of any variation, thus being the key to how rapid the growth will be in the long term.

How Fast Can Armenia Grow?

As indicated above, there is growing consensus that the long term GDP growth will be a function of a combination of traditional determinants including (conditional) convergence (catching up), investment in physical and human capital, and a number of policy issues including reform effort. An exercise to see Armenia's growth potential is to use standard cross-country growth models as a predictor of Armenia's long term growth rate. This is done below using four different growth models, which provide insight into the main patterns of growth observed for a wide range of countries.

Table A1 applies two Levine and Renelt's (1992)[138] basic growth equations and looks at the effect of varying investment rates and human capital ratios on per capita growth rates in Armenia while holding all other variables constant. Table A2 looks at the effect of varying government consumption rates and human capital ratios on per capita growth rates using models, described by Levine and Renelt (1992) and Barro (1991)[139]. Finally Table A3 is based on the World Bank growth projection model (GIST model). Here the effects of varying both the lagged per capita growth rate and the country's reform index (CPIA index) are shown. The CPIA index has been developed by the World Bank and represents an average of two dozen indicators, measuring policy progress in a specific policy area. The CPIA ranks countries between 1 (worst) to 6 (best) and it is closely correlated with other policy ratings, such as developed by the International Country Risk Guide (ICRG), Institutional Investor and Euro money.

International experience suggests that Armenia's long run growth potential ranges between 3 percent to 4 percent per annum based on its current parameters (1998 levels), as shown in the Tables. This interval maybe treated as benchmark growth rates that are achievable if basic policies are right (but not exceptionally good) and the external environment is moderately favorable. However, by varying some key parameters, the predicted growth rates are as high as 6 percent to below 3 percent.

Investment appears to have the greatest impact on growth rates with a five percentage point increase in investment rates increasing growth rates by about a percentage point. The deterioration in human capital ratios observed in Armenia has negative implications for it growth, with rates declining by as much as a quarter percentage point. The decline in government consumption rates, as observed between 1993 and 1998, on the other hand, has a positive effect on growth. The 7 percentage point decline in government consumption rates during this period could increase rates by as much as three-quarter percentage points.

Table A3 shows the effect a positive change in the CPIA. An increase in the CPIA index by 0.9 increases the growth rate by one and a half percentage points. The combined message from this exercise is quite simple: for Armenia to be able to maintain growth rates above 5 percent a year, an additional major policy reform package has to be implemented. Armenia's reform ratings have to reach levels of leading reformers among economies in transition. Investments have to growth substantially. However, as cross-country evidence suggests, with a much stronger reform history, it would be much easier to ensure a stronger investment response. From this perspective, the CPIA index maybe interpreted as an indicator of the investment climate of the country.

---

[138] Levine, Ross and Renelt, David. "A Sensitivity Analysis of Cross-Country Growth Regressions." *American Economic Review*, September 1992, 82(4), pp. 942-63.
[139] Barro, Robert J. "Economic Growth in a Cross-Section of Countries," *Quarterly Journal of Economics*, 96, May 1991, pp. 407-443.

Armenia's current growth rate (about 5% on average) is significantly higher than that predicted by the models given its current parameters. Armenia is recovering from the large transitional output declines suffered in the early 1990's. The growth rates since 1994 reflect its recovery from its severe collapse in output and may be unsustainable given its current reform and investment parameters. The empirical evidence indicates that for Armenia to maintain these kinds of growth rates over the long run, it must to continue to make improvements on a number of policy fronts.

Even small improvements in the growth rate can have compelling effects over the long run. Given real per capita income of $2,360 (PPP terms) in 1996 for Armenia, a one percentage increase in per capita growth rates from 3 percent to 4 percent would reduce the number of years it would take to reach the 1996 real OECD average per capita income of $18,602 by 18 years (from 71 years to 53 years). However, achieving long run growth rates of 6 percent per annum cuts by half the time needed to reach the current OECD average income (from 71 years to 35 years).

Table A1. Armenia's Potential Per Capita Growth, Percent

	Levine & Renelt 1 with Human Capital Ratios from 1993	Levine & Renelt 1 with Human Capital Ratios from 1996	Levine & Renelt 2 with Human Capital Ratios from 1993	Levine & Renelt 2 with Human Capital Ratios from 1996
Investment Rate = 10 percent (1993 level)	2.45	2.29	2.59	2.46
Investment Rate = 15 percent (1998 levels)	3.33	3.17	3.47	3.34
Investment Rate = 20 percent	4.20	4.04	4.34	4.21
Investment Rate = 30 percent	5.95	5.79	6.09	5.96

Base year for projections is 1993.
Source: Staff estimates.

Table A2. Armenia's Potential Per Capita Growth, Percent

	Levine & Renelt 2 with Human Capital Ratios from 1993	Levine & Renelt 2 with Human Capital Ratios from 1996	Barro with Human Capital Ratios from 1993	Barro with Human Capital Ratios from 1996
Government Consumption to GDP= 10 percent	3.23	3.10	4.19	3.94
Government Consumption to GDP= 13 percent (1998 level)	3.04	2.91	3.83	3.58
Government Consumption to GDP= 20 percent (1993 level)	2.59	2.46	3.00	2.75

Base year for projections is 1993.
Source: Staff estimates.

Table A3. Armenia's Per Capita Growth, Percent, GIST Model

	CPIA = 3.60 (1998 level)	CPIA = 4.00	CPIA = 4.50
Lagged GDP Growth Rate = 5.7 percent (1994-98)	3.1	4.0	5.7
Lagged GDP Growth Rate = 3 percent			
Lagged GDP Growth Rate = 0 percent (neutral effect)	1.1	2.0	3.1

Base year for projections is 1997.
Source: Staff estimates.

APPENDIX ANNEX:

GROWTH REGRESSION EQUATIONS

Levine and Renelt 1

Growth Rate of real per capita GDP= -0.83 - 0.35 * Initial per capita GDP + 17.49 * Investment Share of GDP - 0.38 * Population Growth Rate + 3.17 * Secondary School Enrollment Rate.

Levine and Renelt 2

Growth Rate of real per capita GDP= 2.01 - 0.69 * Initial per capita GDP + 9.31 * Investment Share of GDP + 0.08 * Population Growth Rate + 1.21 * Secondary School Enrollment Rate + 1.79 * Primary School Enrollment Rate - 6.37 * Government Share of GDP - 0.25 * Socialist Economy Dummy.

Source: Levine and Renelt (1992).

Barro

Growth Rate of real per capita GDP= 0.0302 - 0.0075 * Initial per capita GDP + 0.0305 * Secondary School Enrollment Rate + 0.0250 * Primary School Enrollment Rate - 0.119 * Government Share of GDP.

Source: Barro (1991).

GIST Model

Growth Rate of real per capita GDP= 0.029 - 0.023 * Initial per capita GDP + 0.353 * Lagged per capita GDP growth rate + 0.023 * Primary School Enrollment Rate + 0.015 * Telephones per capita + 0.022 * CPIA Index.

Source: World Bank.

REFERENCES

Alacacer, Juan. 2000. "The Role of Human Capital in FDI." *Transition.* May-July.

Amirkhanian, Alen G. 1997. "The Armenian Diaspora and their Contribution to the Socio-Economic Development in Armenia in the Soviet and Post-Soviet Periods." Background paper prepared for the World Bank. (March 1). Washington, D.C.

Aoki, Masahiko, Kevin Murdock and Okuno-Fujiwara Masahiro M. 1995. *Beyond the East Asian Miracle: Introducing the Market Enhancing View.* Center for Economic Policy Research, Stanford University. Stanford, CA.

Barro, Robert J. 1991. "Economic Growth in a Cross-Section of Countries," *Quarterly Journal of Economics*, (May) 96: 407-443.

_____. 1996. "Determinants of Economic Growth: A Cross-Country Empirical Study." NBER Working Paper Series 5698 (August).

Berkowitz, Daniel and David N. De Jong. 1999. "Accounting for Growth in Post-Soviet Russia." Mimeo. June.

Biddle, Jesse and Vedat Milor. 1999. "Consultative Mechanisms and Economic Governance in Malaysia." World Bank Private Sector Occasional Paper No. 38 (September). Washington, D.C.

Biddle, Jesse, Vedat Milor, Juan Manuel Ortega Riquelme, and Andrew Stone. 2000. "Consultative Mechanisms in Mexico." World Bank Private Sector Occasional Paper No. 39 (March). Washington, D.C.

Blomström, Magnus and Fredrik Sjoholm. 1998. "Technology Transfer and Spillovers: Does Local Participation With Multinationals Matter?" National Bureau of Economic Research (November). Working Paper Series (U.S.); No. 6816:1-15. Cambridge, MA.

Bremmer, Ian. 1996. "The Political Economy of Banal Authoritarianism: The Case of Armenia." Paper prepared for the World Bank. Mimeo.

Buckberg, Elaine and Brian Pinto. 1997. "How Russia is Becoming a Market Economy. A Policy Maker's Checklist." Mimeo, IFC. Washington, D.C.

Burki, Shaid Javed and Guillermo E. Perry. 1998. "Beyond the Washington Consensus. Institutions Matter." World Bank Latin America and Caribbean Studies. Washington, D.C.

Burney, Nadeem A. 1996. "Exports and Economic Growth: Evidence from Cross-country Analysis," *Applied Economic Letters* 3: 369-373.

Caves, Richard E. 2000. "Spillovers from Multinationals in Developing Countries: The Mechanisms at Work." The William Davidson Institute at the University of Michigan, WDI Working Paper No. 247.

CEPR (Center for Economic Policy Research). *New Trade Theories: A Look at the Empirical Evidence.* 1994. CEPR Conference Report. London.

Che, J. and Qian, Yinqyi. 1995. "Institutional Environment, Community Government and Corporate Governance: Understanding China's Township-Village Enterprises." Department of Economics, Stanford University, Mimeo. Stanford, CA.

Claessens, Stijn, Asli Demirgüç-Kunt, and Harry Huizinga. 1998. "How Does Foreign Entry Affect the Domestic Banking Market?" World Bank Policy Research Working Paper 1918 (Revised). Washington, D.C.

Collier, Paul. 2000. *Consensus-Building, Knowledge, and Conditionality.* Annual World Bank Conference on Development Economics (April 18-20). Washington, D.C.

Commander, Simon, Hamid R. Davoodi, and Une J. Lee. 1997. "The Causes of Government and the Consequences for Growth and Well-Being." World Bank Policy Research Working Paper 1785 (June). Washington, D.C.

De Melo, Martha, Cevdet Denizer, and Alan Gelb. 1996. "From Plan to Market: Patterns of Transition." World Bank Policy Research Working Paper 1564 (January). Washington, D.C.

Denizer, Cevdet. 1997. "Stabilization, Adjustment and Growth Prospects in Transition Economies." World Bank Policy Research Working Paper 1855 (November). Washington, D.C.

Desai, Raj M. and Itzhak Goldberg. 2000. "The Vicious Circles of Control: Regional Governments and Insiders in Privatized Russian Enterprises." World Bank Policy Research Working Paper 2287 (February). Washington, D.C.

Djankov, Simeon and Peter Murrell. 2000. *The Determinants of Enterprise Restructuring in Transition: An Assessment of Evidence.* The World Bank. Washington, D.C.

Duebel, Achim and Lev Freinkman. 1999. "Basic Principles and Short- and Mid-term Strategies for National Housing Policy." Mimeo. Washington, D.C.

EBRD Transition Report. 2000. "Employment, Skills and Transition". London.

_____. 1999. "Ten Years of Transition". London.

Ernst, Maurice. 1997. "Dimensions of Polish Transition: The Ingredients of Success." *Post-Soviet Geography and Economics.* Vol. 38, No. 1.

Evans, Peter. 1996. "Government Action, Social Capital and Development: Reviewing the Evidence on Synergy." *World Development*, 24 (6): 1119-1132.

Fairbanks, Michael and Stace Lindsay. 1997. *Plowing the Sea. Nurturing the Hidden Sources of Growth in the Developing World.* Harvard Business School Press. Cambridge, MA.

Fischer, Stanley, Ratna Sahay, and Carlos A. Vegh. 1996. "Economies in Transition: The Beginnings of Growth." *American Economic Review, Papers and Proceedings (US)*; 86, No. 2:229-33, May.

FIAS (Foreign Investment Advisory Service). 2000. "Armenia: Administrative Barriers to Investment." Washington, D.C.

Gallup, John Luke and Jeffrey Sachs. 1998 *Geography and Economic Growth*. Annual Bank Conference on Development Economics (April). The World Bank.

Granovetter, Mark. 1985. "Economic Action and Social Structure: The Problem of Embedeness." *American Journal of* Sociology (November) 91: 481-510.

Grigorian, Karen. 1996. "The Assessment of Export Potential of Several Armenian Industries." World Bank Resident Mission, Yerevan.

Gu, Shulin. 1996. The Emergence of New Technology Enterprises in China: A Study of Endogenous Capability Building via Restructuring". *Journal of Development Studies* 32(4): 475-505 (April).

Havrylyshyn, Oleh, Ivailo Izvorski, and Ron van Rooden. 1998. "Recovery and Growth in Transition Economies 1990-97: A stylized Regression Analysis." IMF Working Paper WP/98/141 (September). International Monetary Fund. Washington, D.C.

Havrylyshyn, Oleh and Donald McGettigan. 1999. "Privatization in Transition Countries: A Sampling of the Literature." IMF Working Paper WP/99/6. Washington, D.C.

Havrylyshyn, Oleh and Thomas Wolf. 1999. "Growth in Transition Countries 1990-98: The Main Lessons." IMF Conference "A Decade in Transition" (February). International Monetary Fund. Washington, D.C.

Hirshman, Albert O. 1970. *Exit, Voice, and Loyalty*. Harvard University Press. Cambridge, MA.

Hoff, Karla. 2000. *Beyond Rosenstein-Rodan. The Modern Theory of Underdevelopment Traps*. ABCD Conference on Development Economics (April). World Bank. Washington, D.C.

Humphrey, John and Hubert Schmidt. 1995. *Principles for Promoting Clusters and Networks of SMEs*. Institute of Development Studies. University of Sussex. Brighton, UK.

_____. 1996. *Trust and* Economic *Development*. Institute of Development Studies. University of Sussex. Brighton, UK.

Hurwitz, Elliott. 1996. "Prospects for Armenia Export. Case Studies of 20 enterprises." September. Mimeo. Washington, D.C.

IRIS (Center for Institutional Reform and the Informal Sector). 1997. "Mass Privatization of Enterprises in the Republic of Armenia: An Early Assessment" (November). Mimeo. Yerevan

IRIS Caucasus Center. 1999. *Investigation of Factors Inhibiting Foreign Direct Investment in Armenia*. Yerevan.

Knack, Stephen and Philip Keefer. 1995. "Institutions and Economic Performance: Cross-Country Tests Using Alternative Institutional Measures." *Economics and Politics* (November) 7 (3):207-227.

Kontorovich, Vladimir. 1999. "Has New Business Creation in Russia Come to Halt?" *Journal of Business Venturing*. Vol. 14, No. 5/6.

Kornai, János. 2000. *Ten Years After "The Road to a Free Economy"*. The World Bank (April). Washington, D.C.

Kuznetsov, Yevgeny N. 1998. "Public Policies in the World of Uncertainty and Change: Facilitating Social Learning", Background Paper for World Development Report. Mimeo.

Kuznetsov, Yevgeny and Irina Astrakhan. 2000. "Effective Initiatives for Enterprise Restructuring." (November). Mimeo. Washington, D.C.

Lalkaka, Rustam. 1998. "Convergence of Enterprise Support Systems. Emerging Approach at Asia's Technology Parks and Incubators." Mimeo. New York, NY.

_____. 1996. *Technology Business Incubators: Critical Determinants of Success*. The New York Academy of Sciences. NY.

Lerman, Zvi, Mark Lundell, Astghik Mirzakhanian, Paruir Asatrian, and Ashot Kakosian. 1999. "Armenia's Private Agriculture: 1998 Survey of Family Farms." ECSSD Environmentally and Socially Sustainable Development Working Paper 17 (September 1). The World Bank. Washington, D.C.

Levine, Ross. 1997. "Financial Development and Economic Growth: Views and Agenda." *Journal of Economic Literature* (June) Vol. XXXV: 688-726.

_____. 1999. "Law, Finance, and Economic Growth." *Journal of Financial Intermediation*. 8(1-2): 8-35.

Levine, Ross and David Renelt. 1992. "A Sensitivity Analysis of Cross-Country Growth Regressions." *American Economic Review* (September) 82(4): 942-63.

Levy, Brian. 1998. "Credible Regulatory Policy: Options and Evaluation", in R. Picciotto, E. Wiesner (eds.) Evaluation and Development. The Institutional Dimension. Transaction Publishers, for the World Bank. Washington, D.C.

_____. 1997. "Resolving Information and Coordination Problems: A Market-Enhancing Approach." (April 21). Mimeo. Washington, D.C.

_____. 1994. "Technical and Marketing Support Systems for Successful Small and Medium-Size Enterprises in Four Countries." World Bank Policy Research Working Paper 1400. Washington, D.C.

Maraboli, Leo. 2000. Armenia – Review of Draft Report prepared by IMC-MS. "Copper and Molybdenum Information Memorandum". World Bank. Mimeo. (May). Washington, D.C.

McKinsey Global Institute. 1999. *Unlocking Economic Growth in Russia*. October. Moscow.

Mitra, Pradeep K. and Marcelo Selowsky. 2000. "Transition After a Decade: Lessons and an Agenda for Policy." World Bank (November). Washington, D.C.

Moore, Mark H. 1997. *Creating Public Value: Strategic Management in Government*. Harvard University Press. Cambridge, MA.

Nadvi, Khalid. 1997. *The Cutting Edge: Collective Efficiency and International Competitiveness in Pakistan*. IDS Discussion Paper 360. University of Sussex. Brighton, UK.

Najarian, Nancy. 1997. "The State of Armenian Small and Medium-Sized Enterprises" Mimeo. (September).

Oi, Jean C. 1994. "Cadre Networks, Information Diffusion, and market Production in Coastal China." Harvard University (October). Cambridge, MA.

Piore, Michael J. and Charles F. Sabel. 1984. *Second Industrial Divide: Possibilities for Prosperity.* Basic Books. NY.

Picciotto, R. and E. Wiesner (eds.) 1998. *Evaluation and Development. The Institutional Dimension.* Transaction Publishers. Washington, D.C.

Pinto, Brian, Vladimir Drebentsov and Alexander Morozov. 2000. "Give Growth and Macroeconomic Stability in Russia a Chance." World Bank Policy Research Working Paper 2324 (April). Washington, D.C.

Poghossian, Alexander A. and Vahram S. Stepanyan. 1999. "Armenia Financial Sector Expansion." Mimeo. Yerevan.

Polyakov, Evgeny. 2001. "Changing Trade Patterns after Conflict Resolution in the South Caucasus." World Bank Policy Research Working Paper No. 2593 (April). Washington, D.C.

Porter, Michael E. 1990. *Competitive* Advantage *of Nations.* Free Press. NY.

Qian, Yinqyi. 1998. Comments on "Credible Regulatory Policy: Options and Evaluation", in *Evaluation and Development. The Institutional Dimension.* Transaction Publishers. Washington, D.C.

Radosevic, Slavo. 1997. "Post-Socialist Transformation of Countries in CEE and Knowledge-Based Economy: The Evidence and Main Analytical Issues." University of Sussex, (October). Mimeo.

Rodrik, Dani. 2000. *Development Strategies for the Next Century.* Annual Bank Conference on Development Economics (April 18-20). Washington, D.C.

_____. 1993. "Do Low-income Countries Have a High-Wage Option?" in CEPR *New Trade Theories: A Look at the Empirical Evidence* (May). London.

Sabel, Charles. 1995. "Bootstrapping Reform: Rebuilding Firms, the Welfare State, and Unions." *Politics and Society* (March) 23 (1): 5-48.

Sachs, Jeffery D. and Andrew Warner. 1995. "Economic Reform and the Process of Global Integration." Brookings Papers on Economic Activity. Washington, D.C.

Samuelian, Tom. 2000. "Legal, Legislative, and Public Policy Related Barriers to Development of the Information Technologies Sector in Armenia." Mimeo. Yerevan.

Selowsky, Marcelo and Ricardo Martin. 1997. "Policy Performance and Output Growth in the Transition Economies." *American Economic Review, Papers and Proceedings (US)* (May) 87 (2): 349-53. Washington, D.C.

Serven, Luis and Andres Solimano. (Eds.) 1994. *Private Investments in the Aftermath of Liberalisation.* The World Bank. Washington, DC.

_____. 1993. *Striving for* Growth *after Adjustment. The Role of Capital Formation.* The World Bank. Washington, DC.

Schmitz, Hubert. 1995. "Collective Efficiency: Growth Path for Small-Scale Industry." *Journal of Development Studies* (April) 31 (4): 529-566.

Shaid, Javed Burki and Guillermo E. Perry. 1998. *Beyond the Washington Consensus. Institutions Matter.* World Bank Latin America and Caribbean Studies. Washington, DC.

Sharafian, Armeneh. 1997. "World Bank Enterprise Survey of 60 Enterprises: A Summary Report" Mimeo. (February).

Sharafian, Armeneh. 1999. "Report on World Bank Enterprise Survey of 200 Private Enterprises." Mimeo.

Stark, David. 1994. "Recombinant Property In East European Capitalism." Paper presented at the Joint Conference of the World Bank and the Central European University Privatization Project (December 15-16). Washington, D.C.

_____. 1996. "Heterarchy: Asset Ambiguity, Organizational Innovation, and the Postsocialist Firm." Working paper. Department of Sociology, Cornell University. Ithaca, NY.

Tendler, Judith. 1997. *Good Government in the Tropics.* John Hopkins University Press. Baltimore.

Weidenbaum, Murray L. and Samuel Hughes. 1995. *The Bamboo Network. How expatriate Chinese entrepreneurs are creating a new economic superpower in Asia.* Martin Kessler Books. NY.

World Bank. 2001a. "Armenia. PSD Strategy." Discussion draft.

_____. 2001b. "Redeploying Moldovan Assets: Creating New Enterprises from Old." (June 29). Washington, D.C.

_____. 2000a. "Armenia: Targeted Financial Sector Review. Extending the Role of the Financial Sector: Challenges and Policy Options" (May). Washington, D.C.

_____. 2000b. "Armenia Institutional and Governance Review." Washington, D.C.

_____. 2000c. "Reforming Public Institutions and Strengthening Governance. A World Bank Strategy." Washington, D.C.

_____. 1999a. "Armenia's Private Agriculture: 1998 Survey of Family Farms." Washington, D.C.

_____. 1999b. "Improving Social Assistance in Armenia." Report No. 19385-AM. Washington, D.C.

_____. 1998-1999. *World Development Report: Knowledge in Development.* Oxford University Press. Washington, D.C.